The COMPLETE IDIOT'S Guide to Canadian History

- The simple way to learn about your country
- All the facts and dates-from before Confederation to present day
- Easy format makes history come to life

Ann Douglas

An Alpha Books/Prentice Hall Canada Copublication

Prentice Hall Canada Inc., Scarborough, Ontario

Canadian Cataloguing in Publication Data

Douglas, Ann, 1963-
The complete idiot's guide to Canadian history

ISBN 0-13-779126-7

1. Canada - History. I. Title.

FC164.D68 1997 971 C97-931741-X

Scarborough, Ontario
A Division of Simon & Schuster/A Viacom Company

Prentice-Hall, Inc., Upper Saddle River, New Jersey
Prentice-Hall International (UK) Limited, London
Prentice-Hall of Australia, Pty. Limited, Sydney
Prentice-Hall Hispanoamericana, S.A., Mexico City
Prentice-Hall of India Private Limited, New Delhi
Prentice-Hall of Japan, Inc., Tokyo
Simon & Schuster Southeast Asia Private Limited, Singapore
Editora Prentice-Hall do Brasil, Ltda., Rio de Janeiro

ISBN 0-13-779126-7

Managing Editor: Robert Harris
Acquisitions Editor: Jill Lambert
Editor: Susan Broadhurst
Editorial Assistant: Joan Whitman
Production Coordinator: Julie Preston
Art Direction: Mary Opper
Cover Design: Kyle Gell Art and Design
Interior Illustration: Judd Winick
Cover Photograph: Ken Straiton/First Light
Page Layout: Gail Ferreira Ng-A-Kien

1 2 3 4 5 RRD 01 00 99 98 97

Printed and bound in the United States of America.

Visit the Prentice Hall Canada Web site! Send us your comments, browse our catalogues, and more.
www.phcanada.com

Contents

Introduction

A long time ago, some disgruntled history student started a rather nasty rumour: namely, that Canadian history is boring. I thought I'd start this book by tackling this myth head on. I can't tell you how many people asked me how I could stand to write an entire book on Canadian history. These dear friends and relatives clearly had visions of me falling asleep at my keyboard after being lulled to sleep by yet another constitutional crisis!

While I must confess that I did doze off once or twice during the research process, it had more to do with the long hours I was putting in rather than the material I was writing about. You see, I developed this bad habit of going off on tangents, reading pages and pages of fascinating material on some obscure aspect of Canadian history. In order to meet my deadlines (and publishing deadlines are pretty relentless!) I had to burn the candle at both ends on more than one occasion.

The truth of the matter is that I had a darned good time researching and writing this book. Part of it was because I got to work with such terrific editors. (Thank you Jill Lambert, Karen Alliston, and Susan Broadhurst!) The other part was that I got to delve so deeply into a subject that has always been near and dear to my heart: Canada's history. I actually had such a terrific time writing this book that I almost would have done it for free. Almost.

That said, let me tell you a bit about the book. As you can see, it's divided into six sections, each of which deals with a particular period of Canadian history.

Part 1 discusses Canada's first people, the explorers who followed in their footsteps, and the country's first entrepreneurs—the fur traders.

Part 2 describes the century between the Conquest and the American Civil War. (If you think that Canada is experiencing its fair share of conflicts these days, wait till you see what went on during this particular period of Canadian history!)

Part 3 focuses on the era of nation-building, when a fellow named John A. Macdonald and his starry-eyed friends dreamed about creating a nation from sea to sea.

Part 4 talks about how Canada grew from a colony into a nation during the years leading up to World War I.

Part 5 examines World War I, World War II and the years in between, including the Great Depression.

Part 6 examines the years after World War II, when the country experienced such far-reaching economic, political, and social change that it seemed ready to come apart at the seams.

You'll also find a few other bits and pieces at the back of the book. Appendix A lists the country's prime ministers in order of appearance (a helpful aid given the number of episodes of Parliamentary musical chairs that we've seen since Confederation!). Appendix B lists the 10 provinces and indicates when each one entered Confederation. And Appendix C provides you with a list of recommended readings, should you develop a newfound passion for Canadian history and decide to do some further reading on your own.

Like any Complete Idiot's Guide, *The Complete Idiot's Guide to Canadian History* also contains some other important elements designed to make for a more enjoyable—and more informative—read. Be sure to watch for the following features as they appear in the text:

Stats

This is where you'll find the key numbers concerning a particular era: population stats, economic growth figures, the number of war casualties, and so on.

Voice from the Past

This is where you'll find memorable quotes from historically significant figures and documents, some of which is pretty juicy stuff!

Real Life

This is where you'll get to meet key figures from Canada's past and present.

I hope you'll enjoy reading this book as much as I've enjoyed writing it, and that you'll be convinced once and for all that Canadian history is anything but boring.

Acknowledgments

In addition to the terrific team at Prentice Hall, there are a few folks who warrant more than a little grovelling on my part. Thank you to Lorna Bolton and Barb Payne, whose last-minute research efforts helped me to meet a rather challenging deadline; to Bobbi Graham and Jim Gastle, for their unwavering cheering from the sidelines; and to my super-supportive husband Neil Douglas, for assuming responsibility for three kids and every imaginable household task so I could devote myself to the writing of this book.

Ann Douglas
August 1997

Part 1
In the Beginning...

By the time European explorers first set foot on Canadian soil, the country had already been in the hands of aboriginal peoples for many thousands of years. But once they arrived, the Europeans certainly made their presence known. They combed the continent, looking for furs, and ended up plunging it into a series of conflicts that lasted right up until the time of the Conquest.

Pssst.... Anyone who dares to say that Canadian history is boring (and frankly, we don't tolerate such blasphemy around here!) is sadly mistaken. As the first section of this book demonstrates, Canadian history is filled with grandiose schemes, wayward adventurers, and more than a few unscrupulous politicians. And that's just for starters....

Chapter 1

Who Discovered Whom? (50,000 B.C. to A.D. 1500)

In this chapter

- Where Canada's first people came from
- How they got to North America
- The native groups present at the time of first European contact

If the European explorers were expecting to encounter a land of untouched wilderness when they reached the Americas, they were certainly in for a shock. By the time they set foot on Canadian soil, the aboriginal peoples they encountered already had many thousands of years of history behind them.

While the native peoples of Canada clearly had a head start on the Europeans, they were also immigrants. They just happened to arrive a little earlier than Lief the Lucky and his fellow explorers (a few tens of thousands of years earlier!).

The Strait Goods

There's a strong resemblance between the native peoples of North America and the people of northeast Asia—and for good reason. Scientists

Word for the Day

Beringia is the name used to describe the land bridge that is believed to have joined North America and northeast Asia at the Bering Strait many thousands of years ago. Beringia is thought to have disappeared when the major continental ice sheets and other glaciers melted, causing the water level in the Bering Strait to rise.

believe that Alaska and Siberia were linked by a land bridge (called Beringia) some 10,000 to 45,000 years ago, and that people used this 88-kilometre outcropping of land and ice to cross the Bering Strait and make their way into the previously uninhabited continent of North America.

This migration from northeast Asia to North America is believed to have occurred at a time when ice sheets three kilometres thick covered the Rocky Mountains and the area around Hudson Bay. When these ice sheets melted, the land bridge became submerged by rising water levels, and North America's first immigrants found themselves stranded in the New World, whether they liked it or not.

Hunt or Be Hunted

North America's first peoples were hunters of large animals. They used spears tipped with stone points to kill woolly mammoths that were the size of elephants, and relied on the meat for food and the animal skins for shelter and clothing. It was anything but a glamorous existence: hunters in search of woolly mammoths were constantly in danger of being hunted down by giant panthers and sabre-toothed tigers.

Between 5000 and 8000 years ago, the North American climate began to warm up and large species of animals began to die off. Smaller animals and foods, such as nuts, berries, roots, and fish, began to take the place of these large animals in the diets of the continent's first peoples.

Native Society

When the first Europeans stepped foot in Canada 500 years ago, they found themselves in a country completely lacking in any national form

Word for the Day

Native is the term used by most historians and anthropologists to describe the aboriginal peoples of the Western Hemisphere. They are also referred to as First Nations people. The term "Indian"—first used by Christopher Columbus on October 12, 1492, to describe what he mistakenly thought were the people of India!—is no longer used to describe members of Canada's native community. (Thought for the day: How did a fellow as navigationally challenged as Columbus manage to make his way into the history books?)

Stats

There were probably no more than 220,000 to 300,000 natives in Canada when the Europeans first arrived in North America 500 years ago. Historians estimate that there were over 50 different groups of First Nations people representing at least 12 separate language families. In fact, 24 different languages were spoken by natives in B.C. alone.

of political organization. Natives paid allegiance to their families, bands, villages, tribes, and/or confederacies, but not to any recognizable "nation."

The reason for this lack of national political organization is obvious. The nomadic nature of many of the native groups and the massive size of Canada limited the amount of contact between groups—even between those that shared the same language and customs.

As a result of this isolation, natives living in different parts of Canada led dramatically different lives. Some groups grew their own food and enjoyed relative plenty, while others were forced to rely on hunting and fishing to survive.

Here's a quick look at who was living where at the time of first European contact, and what their lives were like.

Pacific Coast

Natives along the Pacific Coast in British Columbia lived in houses made of cedar. They lived off the sea, primarily relying on salmon and whale meat for food. They led relatively sedentary lives, as there was little need to migrate in search of food. Because they were able to stay in one location for a number of years, they enjoyed a higher degree of tribal and social organization than was possible for more nomadic tribes.

B.C. Interior

Sandwiched between the coast and the plains, natives in the B.C. interior lived in dome-shaped houses that were half-buried in the ground. They relied on a variety of plants, animals, and fish for food.

Plains

Natives living on the northern plains (in southern Alberta, Saskatchewan, and Manitoba) relied almost entirely on the buffalo for their survival. They ate buffalo meat and constructed teepees out of buffalo skin. Dried and smoked buffalo meat were consumed during the winter months when fresh food was less easy to find.

Subarctic Forest

Natives in the subarctic forest (the northern parts of British Columbia, Alberta, Saskatchewan, and Manitoba, and the southern parts of the Canadian Arctic) lived in bands ranging in size from a few families to several hundred people. They hunted game, fished, and gathered plants and berries. Because they were a nomadic group, their possessions had to be portable. Their wigwams were constructed from birch-bark rolls, woven rush mats, and skins, and were designed for an ease of assembly that would put present-day modular homes to shame! They relied on toboggans, snowshoes, and birch-bark canoes for transportation.

Woodlands

Natives in the woodlands (the northern parts of Ontario and Quebec) travelled in small bands, hunting moose, caribou, and small animals and camping in locations where fish were plentiful. Their nomadic existence and the size of the territory they wandered prevented them from developing the types of political organizations that less nomadic groups created.

Stats

Natives in the lowlands lived in multiple-family units (longhouses) that were capable of housing as many as 20 to 30 families.

Stats

Native families rarely had more than three or four children, something that anthropologists attribute to the fact that native women nursed their babies for the first two to three years of life. Native women tended to perform tasks that were compatible with their childcare responsibilities, such as farming or gathering nuts and berries.

Lowlands

Natives living in the lowlands (southern Ontario and Quebec) were blessed with fertile soil and a mild climate. They grew crops such as corn, beans, squash, pumpkin, sunflower, and tobacco. In the absence of metal tools, they relied on stone axes, pointed sticks, hoes made with blades of shell, and fire to clear their land. Every 15 years or so, they moved their villages in search of fresh soil. Despite these challenges, natives in the lowlands were able to grow more food than they actually needed, and used their crop surplus to trade with other groups for such goods as birchbark canoes and furs. Their relatively abundant lifestyle also left them enough time to enjoy the finer things in life, like sports! In fact, it was this group of natives who invented lacrosse, the sister sport to our beloved national game of hockey.

Arctic

The first people to live in the Canadian Arctic lived in skin tents and were constantly on the move, looking for food. It is believed that they didn't actually make their way into the Arctic until approximately 4000 years ago, when the glaciers began to retreat.

About 2000 years ago, the Arctic was inhabited by a group of people called the Dorset. They hunted seal and other animals and used animal blubber to fuel stone lamps to heat their igloos (snowhouses). Within 1000 years, the climate began to warm up, changing the distribution of sea ice and the migratory patterns of animals. The Dorset were unable to adapt and died out.

The Dorset were replaced by the Thule, a group of whale hunters. The Thule used whale oil for heat and light, whale meat for food, and whale bones for making tools and weapons. They were known for being great builders; some of their houses and animal traps still exist. Over time, the Thule divided into several different groups inhabiting different areas of the Arctic. Today, these groups are collectively known as the Inuit.

The Least You Need to Know

- ➤ Natives came to Canada by crossing a land bridge that joined North America and Asia some 10,000 to 45,000 years ago.
- ➤ There was no country-wide native political organization in place at the time of first European contact, mainly due to the vastness of Canada, the nomadic lifestyles of many native groups, and the fact that each native group had its own language and culture.
- ➤ Natives living in different parts of the country lived dramatically different types of lives. Some were hunters and gatherers, while others were farmers.

Chapter 2

The Great—and Not-So-Great—Explorers (1000 to 1600)

In this chapter

- The Vikings
- The European explorers
- The quest for the Northwest Passage
- Samuel de Champlain and the establishment of New France

You had to be a gutsy sort to embark on a career as an explorer: someone who was willing to head off to places unknown, all for a shot at fame and fortune.

And what a crapshoot it was! While the history books tend to focus on the successes and near-successes, there must have been hundreds of outright failures who never made it past the first mid-ocean gale.

Still, the urge to explore was powerful enough to make the early explorers set out despite the hair-raising odds. Some were motivated by greed: the desire to acquire countless riches in the Americas or to find the much-coveted passage to the Far East. For others, it was a desire to find out what lay beyond the horizon that led them to forsake the comforts of home.

But if life was difficult for the European explorers who crossed the seas in the 15th and 16th centuries, imagine what it must have been like for Canada's first tourists: the Vikings.

The Vikings

When the Viking Bjarni sailed west from Iceland in 986, he earned the distinction of being the first European to discover the coast of North America.

A few years later, he was followed by Lief the Lucky (son of the notorious murderer Eric the Red), who sailed west from Greenland in 1000. In addition to sighting two pieces of land—probably Baffin Island and Labrador—Lief landed in what is believed to have been either present-day Newfoundland or New England.

Using the gift for naming places that had served his father well (Eric named the ice-covered northern island that he discovered in 982 "Greenland" in an effort to lure prospective immigrants to the island), Lief set about naming these three pieces of land. He named the barren land of flat rock and glaciers in present-day Baffin Island "Helluland" (Flagstone Land), the heavily forested area of present-day Labrador "Markland" (Forestland), and the lush pastures of Newfoundland or New England "Vinland" (Wineland).

Lief established settlements along the coast and traded with the native peoples in the area, whom he called "Skraelings." Relations between the Vikings and the Skraelings were friendly—until the natives realized that these "visitors" were planning to stay for good. Within 15 years, whether due to conflicts with the Skraelings or the distance from their homeland, the Vikings abandoned North America. Today, all that remains of their early settlements is the archeological remains at L'Anse aux Meadows, discovered in the early 1960s.

The European Explorers

You have to give the early European explorers credit: when they set out to discover the New World, they didn't have the benefit of high-tech navigational or communications equipment, or any other modern conveniences. The moment they left Europe behind, they were on their own. Even if they managed to battle the elements and make their way safely to the New World—and frankly, not everyone did—they found themselves faced with the challenge of surviving in a harsh and unpredictable environment.

What led these explorers to leave the comforts of home in search of the unknown? For some it was sheer curiosity, the desire to chart unknown parts of the world. For others, it was the promise of fame or the lure of unknown riches. Still others were motivated by nationalistic fervour or religious zeal.

Although the Vikings had made initial visits to North America nearly 500 years earlier and the Portuguese had recently set up fishing operations in the cod-rich waters off present-day Newfoundland, it wasn't until the 15th century that the conditions were right for a large-scale exploration of the New World. Recent improvements to marine technology (the invention of the magnetic compass, the astrolabe, and better sails) had made travelling by sea a less risky undertaking. Europe had entered a period of relative stability, and many countries had managed to accumulate enough capital to finance costly overseas adventures. What's more, the growing affluence of the upper classes created an ever-increasing market for the luxury products of the Far East, and therefore an increased motivation to find an alternative to the established land-based routes to India and China.

While the transcontinental caravan route from Peking to Constantinople had been in existence for a number of years, it was anything but efficient. Importers could expect to spend up to three years travelling to gather riches from the Far East, only to have their goods pillaged by the many bandits who preyed on these early entrepreneurs. When the port city of Constantinople ultimately fell into the hands of the Ottoman armies in the 15th century, the caravan route disappeared altogether, and would-be merchants were forced to find alternatives to land-based travel to the Far East.

The Spanish and the Portuguese were the first to seek a route by sea. Throughout the 15th century, they tried to find a route around Africa that would take them to India and China. In 1492, Columbus made his first of four voyages to the Americas, landing on an island in the Caribbean, which he immediately claimed for Spain. In 1497, Vasco da Gama sailed around the Cape of Good Horn at the southern tip of Africa, and headed on to India. He made his return voyage in 1498.

John Cabot

While Spanish and Portuguese explorers were charting other parts of the world, an Italian explorer named Giovanni Caboto was busy trying to convince Venetian merchants of the benefits of funding his own voyage. Like the other explorers, he was anxious to find a route to the Far East.

Once it became evident that the Venetian merchants weren't interested in funding him, Caboto headed to Bristol, England, to seek support there. This enterprising fellow—whom the British called John Cabot—not only arranged to have his costs underwritten by the merchants of Bristol, but also convinced King Henry VII of England to grant him a trade monopoly and freedom from import taxes. (Clearly, tax avoidance is neither a North American nor a 20th century phenomenon!)

Cabot and 18 men left Bristol on May 2, 1497, on a 40-metre ship, the *Matthew*. They followed the route used by transatlantic fishermen, landing on Canadian soil 52 days later. Cabot planted the British flag and immediately named the area "New Found Land." (Historians now believe he might have been on Cape Breton Island, but what the heck.) Then he headed north along the coast, looking for settlements.

A short time later, helped along by westerly winds that made the return crossing a lot speedier, Cabot and his men returned to Bristol in just 15 days. He immediately spread the word about the great schools of cod that he had observed off Newfoundland. An accomplished salesman with the gift of the gab, he told the merchants and the King that the cod he encountered were abundant enough to slow down the progress of his ship. Cabot's enthusiasm sparked the beginning of what would become centuries of British fishing off of Newfoundland's Grand Banks.

Unfortunately, the story doesn't end happily for Cabot. Although he set out with five ships the following year, once again searching for a route to the riches of the Far East, he was never heard from again.

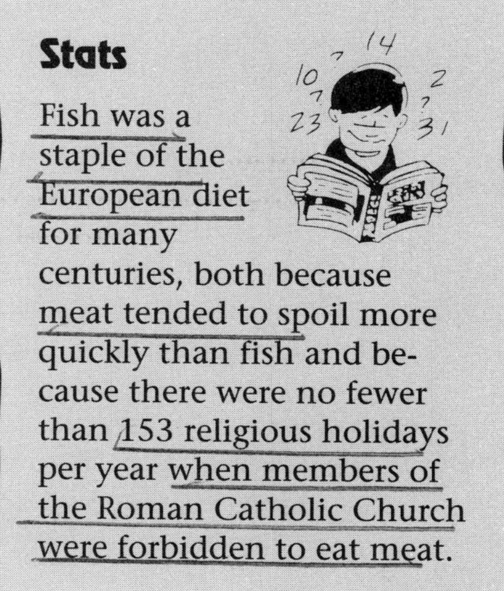

Stats

Fish was a staple of the European diet for many centuries, both because meat tended to spoil more quickly than fish and because there were no fewer than 153 religious holidays per year when members of the Roman Catholic Church were forbidden to eat meat.

Jacques Cartier

England wasn't the only country interested in finding riches in the New World or the Northwest Passage. King Francis I of France was also determined to seize emerging opportunities abroad.

In 1534, Francis I commissioned Jacques Cartier "to discover certain islands and countries where it is said that he should find great quantities of gold and other valuable things."

Twenty days after leaving France, Cartier spotted Canadian soil and began to travel up the Gulf of St. Lawrence. When he reached the Gaspé Peninsula, he encountered a group of Iroquois who were hunting in the area. Some of the Iroquois paddled out to greet him, and offered him furs in exchange for knives and hatchets. Although Cartier wasn't particularly interested in obtaining furs—beaver fur hats had yet to come into vogue in Europe—he recognized the advantage of forming alliances with these native people. Cartier invited two of the sons of Iroquois Chief Donnacona onboard his ship and took them back to France with him.

Francis I was so impressed by what Cartier had accomplished

Real Life

Donnacona was the Iroquois chief at Stadacona (present-day Quebec City) whom Jacques Cartier encountered while exploring the St. Lawrence region. Donnacona was kidnapped by Cartier and his men and taken to France, where he was enlisted to help convince King Francis I of the merits of financing another voyage to the New World. Donnacona had everything to gain by cooperating. In fact, he was so eager to convince the King to finance his trip home that he told incredible stories about the wonders that awaited France in the so-called "Kingdom of the Saguenay." Donnacona's tales of vast quantities of gold, jewels, spices, and oranges convinced the King to underwrite Cartier's next trip in 1541. Unfortunately, Donnacona died of scurvy in France before he got the chance to return to his people.

during his first voyage that he agreed to underwrite a second trip the following year. Cartier spent the first few weeks of this subsequent trip searching the northern shore of the Gulf of St. Lawrence to make sure that no passage existed. Then, in late summer, he reached the native village of Stadacona (present-day Quebec City), where he returned the two young Iroquois to their father.

The natives in Stadacona told Cartier about a village further up river, at Hochelaga. Donnacona tried to discourage Cartier from going beyond Stadacona, clearly feeling that the members of the Iroquois village at Hochelaga would cut into his trading opportunities with this group of Europeans. Cartier decided to travel to Hochelaga despite Donnacona's protestations, but soon returned to Stadacona to prepare for winter.

If Cartier and his men were expecting the Canadian winter to be anything like what they'd experienced at home, they were in for the shock of their lives. The winter at Stadacona was harsh, with 15 cm of solid ice coating the inside walls of their shelters. One hundred of Cartier's men fell ill with scurvy, a gruesome disease that left them with bleeding gums, swelling in their arms and legs, and high fevers; 25 died. Even more would have died if the Iroquois hadn't shown the European visitors how to make a healing infusion out of white cedar bark.

Not surprisingly, by spring, Cartier and his men were ready to return home. Before they set sail for France, however, they invited their Iroquois hosts to a feast. Then, in what has to be one of the most appalling breaches of etiquette in all of Canadian history, they kidnapped Chief Donnacona and took him to France to help them plead their case to King Francis I for another trip to "Kanata."

Word for the Day

When Jacques Cartier asked the Iroquois what the land on the north shore of the St. Lawrence River was called, they used the word *Kanata* (an Iroquoian word meaning a collection of houses). The French took this to be the name for the whole area and, over time, for the entire country.

While Chief Donnacona didn't live long enough to make the return voyage to Stadacona, five years later, in 1541, Cartier and his men convinced Francis I to underwrite the costs of a third expedition. When they reached Canadian soil, they had to contend not only with the harsh climate and another epidemic of scurvy, but with less-than-friendly relations with the Iroquois, who were not about to forget that these foreigners had abducted their beloved chief.

Cartier was determined to make something good come from what would be his final voyage. He and his men gathered 12 barrels of what they believed to be valuable gemstones. On their return to France, however, they discovered that they were carrying a cargo of worthless quartz crystal. Thereafter, the French used the expression *un diamant du Canada* (a Canadian diamond) to describe anything worthless.

The Search for the Northwest Passage

While a great deal of effort was expended during the 14th and 15th centuries trying to find the Northwest Passage to the Far East, it wasn't until the 20th century that a passage through Canada's arctic waters was eventually discovered.

Still, while they weren't successful in discovering the much-coveted Northwest Passage, Martin Frobisher and Henry Hudson certainly merit a mention in any Canadian history book.

In 1576, Queen Elizabeth I of England commissioned Frobisher to find the Northwest Passage. He set out with two small ships—the *Gabriel* and the *Michael*—eventually reaching Baffin Island and the large bay now named in Frobisher's honour. As if the hostile climate and navigational challenges weren't enough, Frobisher lost five of his men during conflicts with natives (believed to be of mixed Icelandic and Inuit descent). Frobisher returned to England that same year, carrying a black rock that many believed to be gold ore. He managed to attract enough interest to finance a second expedition in 1577 and a third in 1578. In the end, however, Frobisher not only failed to find the Northwest Passage, but discovered on his return to England that the "gold ore" he had prized so highly was, in fact, iron pyrites—"fool's gold."

However, Frobisher's experiences in Canada look like an absolute success story when compared to those of Henry Hudson, an Englishman who sailed for Holland. Hudson explored what is now known as Hudson Strait and Hudson Bay in 1610. Unfortunately, while Hudson was determined to make the most of the harsh conditions he faced in Canada, his crew was not willing to put up with the Canadian climate. They mutinied, threw Hudson, his son, and the remaining loyal crew members into a small open boat, and set them adrift. Hudson was never heard from again.

Samuel de Champlain

While some of the early explorers had been motivated primarily by fame and fortune, Samuel de Champlain had loftier ambitions. He wanted to establish a settlement in Canada "for the glory of God [and] for the renown of the French."

Champlain was an accomplished mapmaker and sea captain who was invited to join a party of adventurers led by a fur trader named Pierre du Guo de Monts. In exchange for his promise to establish permanent settlements on behalf of the French monarchy, he had been granted a monopoly over the fur trade in what the French monarchy was now calling "New France." While it probably seemed like a good deal at the time, the odds were clearly stacked against him: de Monts was the third Frenchman to be offered such a monopoly, and the first two attempts had been out-and-out failures. No wonder the French monarchy was so eager to find an entrepreneur to underwrite the costs of overseas colonization: it had nothing to lose and everything to gain!

While the French had been in the Americas in the 60 years following Cartier's misadventures, they were primarily there for commercial purposes—to acquire fish and furs—and had no interest whatsoever in establishing any type of permanent settlement.

However, when England claimed Newfoundland as an English colony, the French began to get nervous. They were worried that they would be cut out of any riches to be found in the New World, and they were anxious to establish a base from which they could continue to seek a passage to the Far East.

In 1604, with the blessing of the French monarchy, de Monts, Champlain, and their men set out for Canadian soil. They established a settlement at St. Croix Island, on the shores of the Bay of Fundy. (St. Croix Island is now called Dochet Island, and is part of the United States.)

While the group initially thought that they had chosen a good spot for their settlement, they soon discovered that their location was anything but ideal. It was marshy, with very little wood and no fresh water, and its sandy soil was thoroughly unsuitable for agriculture. What's more, it was too remote to be a promising location for any type of fur trading. In fact, its only advantage appeared to be that it was likely to be a safe refuge from unknown and hostile natives. (Obviously, the natives knew something that the explorers did not!)

While the group was convinced that they would fare better at St. Croix Island than along the infamous St. Lawrence River, this was not to be the case. They endured a particularly harsh winter during their first year in their new home (1604–05). By the end of winter, 35 of 79 men had died.

Not surprisingly, the survivors were unwilling to spend another winter on St. Croix Island. As a result, the settlement was relocated the following spring and summer to a place the adventurers named Port Royal (located in the southern part of present-day Nova Scotia). Champlain and de Monts hoped that Port Royal's more protected location would make it a much more pleasant place to live, but they weren't leaving anything to chance. Instead of relying on a series of flimsy dwellings—as they had done at St. Croix Island—they built a large weatherproof habitation for the entire group to share. They also decided to learn how to live off the land, rather than rely exclusively on supplies from France. This led Champlain to form "The Order of Good Cheer," a fraternal organization designed to encourage his men to organize banquets in which they would offer up the best fare that New France had to offer.

Port Royal became the first successful French settlement in Canada. The residents traded with local Micmac for furs and other goods, and quickly learned the art of surviving in the Canadian wilderness. While they enjoyed considerably greater success at Port Royal than they had at St. Croix Island—the winter was mild and fewer men died of scurvy—they were still faced with some major problems: the remote location made it difficult to explore inland, and there simply wasn't much territory in which fur could be obtained.

To make matters worse, poachers were beginning to cut into the fur trade and make off with great quantities of the best furs. This pirating was cutting into the profits needed to fund the settlement and undermining the monopoly that de Monts had been promised. The final blow came in 1607, when the French monarchy cancelled de

Monts's monopoly. By July, the settlement was deserted, and Champlain and de Monts were on their way back to France to try to convince the monarchy to reconsider.

After extensive lobbying, the King of France agreed to extend de Monts's monopoly for another year. Champlain convinced de Monts that the monopoly would be easier to enforce if they set up shop at Stadacona. Instead of having to defend the entire Atlantic seaboard, they would only have to safeguard the entrance to the St. Lawrence River, the only possible passage to the interior.

In the spring of 1608, Champlain, de Monts, and their men returned to New France. Despite the reluctance of certain members of their party, they established a new settlement at Stadacona. (The crew had heard about the gruesome deaths suffered by Cartier's men half a century earlier and weren't anxious to meet a similar fate.) By 1650, there were 70 people living at Stadacona, hardly enough to declare the settlement a metropolis, but more than enough to establish France's permanent claim to the area.

In 1610, Jean de Beincort de Poutrincourt—an adventurer who had been part of de Monts's original party and who had always dreamed of founding a colony—returned to Port Royal to reestablish the settlement as a combined mission, fur trade outpost, and agricultural settlement. Unfortunately, the revived settlement was plagued by both chronic lack of funds and major infighting. In the end, the residents of Port Royal were captured and the settlement was burned to the ground by Captain Samuel Argall, who had been commissioned by the Virginia Company to expel intruders from land claimed by England.

The Least You Need to Know

- The Vikings were the first Europeans to settle on Canadian soil (circa 1000), but their settlements were short-lived.
- The early European explorers were motivated by curiosity, the promise of fame and fortune, nationalistic fervour, and/or religious zeal.
- The first successful settlement in New France was Port Royal. Its success laid the groundwork for subsequent settlements on Canadian soil.

Chapter 3

Have Pelts, Will Travel (1600 to 1820)

In this chapter

- ➤ The origins of the fur trade
- ➤ The importance of the fur trade in New France
- ➤ The impact of European contact on Canada's native peoples
- ➤ The founding of the Hudson's Bay Company and the North West Company

While the fur trade in Canada clearly experienced its boom during the 16th and 17th centuries, historians believe that the native peoples of Canada had actually been trading furs long before that time, both with the early European explorers and fishermen and with other native groups.

It wasn't until beaver hats came into vogue in late 16th century Europe, however, that the fur trade really came into its own. Motivated by untold riches that seemed to be theirs for the taking, countless European entrepreneurs loaded their sailing ships with goods and travelled to the New World. They docked their ships on the St. Lawrence River or in Hudson Bay and transferred a smorgasbord of manufactured goods to canoes. They then headed inland to a variety of trading posts, where they exchanged these goods for valuable beaver pelts supplied by the various native groups in the area.

While the European traders made tremendous profits on these transactions, the natives with whom they traded were also extremely shrewd. They were very particular about the types of goods they were willing to trade for—primarily tools, weapons, utensils, iron pots, and luxury items such as cloth and European beads—and they knew how to use the competition between the French and English traders to obtain the best possible price for their pelts. The natives were also able to take advantage of the ongoing animosity between the French and English governments: at times, European trading partners paid exceedingly high prices for their pelts in order to keep the natives as allies!

Stats

Before the arrival of the Europeans, there were over 10 million beavers in North America.

The Fur Trade in New France

The importance of the fur trade in New France cannot be overstated. Without such a valuable commodity to offset the costs of exploration and settlement, Canada might never have come into being.

From the very beginning, the fur trade provided an economic basis for the creation of New France. It put money back in the pocket of the Mother Country—something that every good colony was expected to do.

Natives involved in the fur trade spent the winter months gathering pelts and then transported them to trading posts in the spring. Some natives acted as go-betweens, trading with other native groups who then brought the furs to the trading posts. Others were employed by the European traders, hunting, paddling supply canoes, making snowshoes, and performing a variety of other tasks.

Not surprisingly, native women played an active role in the operation of the fur trade. They dressed leather, made clothing and shoes, wove nets, mended birch-bark canoes, collected wood, erected tents, fetched water, and cooked for the traders. Some also acted as interpreters.

Because native women worked so closely with the traders, and because European women were an extremely scare commodity in New

Word for the Day

Over time, the Hudson's Bay Company gave official status to marriages between company employees and native women. These marriages *à la façon du pays* (in the custom of the country) were regulated by a marriage contract that emphasized the husband's economic responsibilities.

France, intermarriages between traders and native women became quite common. A trader who wished to marry a young native woman simply provided the father of the bride with goods such as a blanket, a gun, and/or a horse. In exchange for these gifts, the trader received the right to marry the young woman in question. Although many of these liaisons proved to be extremely long-lasting, the missionaries who came to New France in the early 17th century were generally disapproving. (Perhaps this was because native custom permitted these women to engage in a form of sexual comparison shopping before the wedding night!)

Over time, the nature of the fur trade began to change. As one area after another was depleted of beaver pelts, traders were forced to go further and further afield. What had previously been a part-time sideline involving only a few weeks of work per year soon became a full-time occupation. This led to increased conflict with native groups and other European traders, namely with the British.

The Impact of European Contact

While historians no longer view the fur trade as a tale of victims and victors, it is clear that the arrival of the Europeans did have a significant impact on the lives of Canada's native peoples.

As natives acquired tools and weapons from their European trading partners, they became increasingly dependent on these items and abandoned many of their traditional ways of doing things. Metal kettles replaced wooden vessels heated with stones. Guns replaced bows and arrows. Cloth replaced fur robes and skins.

The fur trade also affected where native groups lived and hunted, and their relationships with each other. Because beaver stocks were quickly depleted, native fur traders were forced to travel increasingly further afield to gather the goods that their European trading partners so desperately wanted. Over time, this forced migration led them into conflict with members of rival native groups, as well as their trading partners' enemies.

Perhaps the clearest example of the impact of European contact on Canada's native peoples is the effect of European diseases. Between 1634 and 1640, measles, influenza, and smallpox epidemics eliminated half of the Huron population as well as large numbers of Montagnais.

The Hudson's Bay Company

Until the mid-17th century, the fur trade was dominated by individuals—both native traders and French *coureurs du bois*. Then, the nature of the fur trade began to change.

In 1660, two young entrepreneurs, Pierre Radisson and Sieur des Groseilliers, asked the governor of New France for a licence to head north to seek furs. The fact that the governor of New France turned down their request didn't dampen their determination to go. They

Word for the Day

The *coureurs du bois* (runners of the woods) did the hard work of the fur trade. They were responsible for travelling long distances by canoe and transporting furs from the interior to the colony. Because they were independent traders in business to make a profit, they were willing to trade with anyone—French or English. Needless to say, their activities fell outside the officially sanctioned fur trade as controlled by the merchants of Montreal and Quebec.

So alluring was the life of a *coureur du bois* that authorities in New France soon found it necessary to discourage young men from neglecting their farms and families in favour of pursuing a life of adventure in the wilderness.

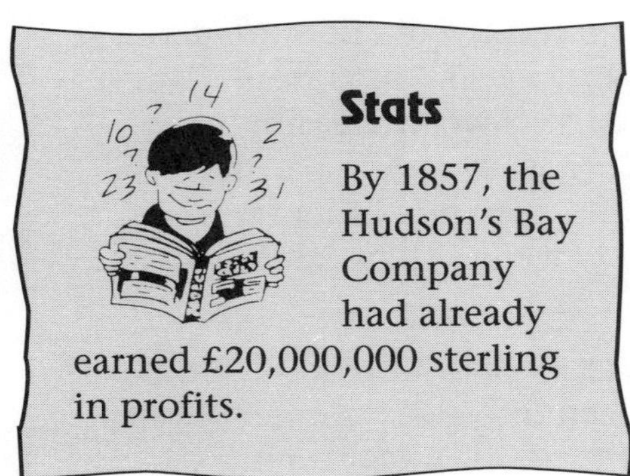

Stats

By 1857, the Hudson's Bay Company had already earned £20,000,000 sterling in profits.

headed north without his blessing, returning with a fleet of 300 canoes overflowing with valuable furs. Needless to say, the governor was not impressed. He seized 90 per cent of their take and threw the two looters in jail. As soon as they got out of jail, the two would-be traders slipped out of New France in 1661, and headed to England to seek backers for an even grander expedition.

Radisson and Groseilliers told interested merchants in England about the great "northern sea" that provided direct access to the heart of the new continent. They must have been good salesmen because they managed to convince British merchants to underwrite the costs of an expedition to test out their route. In 1668, the *Nonsuch* entered Hudson Bay, subsequently returning to England with a huge load of furs. Two years later, in 1670, the merchants who had backed this initial expedition decided to make their trading association permanent. They formed the Hudson's Bay Company to carry out trade in the Hudson Bay region of Canada.

The Hudson's Bay Company was in such favour with the King of England that it managed to win a trading monopoly that covered all areas drained by rivers flowing into Hudson Bay: an estimated 7.77 million square kilometres of territory! (Ironically, at the very time that the King of England was making this generous settlement, the territory in question theoretically belonged to France.)

The newly formed company began establishing posts around Hudson Bay. Because it relied on natives to transport furs from the interior to Hudson Bay, it found itself constantly besieged by French traders determined to intercept and steal its furs. These traders had set up a series of rival trading posts that stretched from Rainy River to the Saskatchewan River. Not surprisingly, the remaining years of the fur trade were a time of intense conflict between the French, the English, and their native allies.

The North West Company

Following the defeat of the French by the English at the Plains of Abraham in 1759, Montreal was overrun by a group of Scottish and English merchants who formed their own companies and hired experienced French traders. These independent fur trading companies were in constant conflict until 1779, when all of the independent traders in the area agreed to form one large company, the North West Company. This new company soon found itself in conflict with the Hudson's Bay Company. The two companies engaged in bitter competition until their eventual merger in 1821.

The Least You Need to Know

- ➤ The fur trade dates back to the arrival of the first European explorers and fishermen, but wasn't a powerful economic force until the late 16th century.
- ➤ The key economic activity in New France was the fur trade.
- ➤ The arrival of the European fur traders caused Canada's native peoples to abandon some of their traditional ways of life and to move to different hunting grounds as beaver stocks became depleted. This led them into conflict with other native groups and the enemies of their trading partners.
- ➤ The founding of the Hudson's Bay Company and the North West Company marked a significant departure from the days of the *coureurs du bois*.

Chapter 4

All This and Heaven, Too (1615 to 1649)

In this chapter

- The role of the missionaries in 17th century Huronia
- Native reactions to the missionaries
- The destruction of Sainte-Marie-Among-the-Hurons

It was nothing short of a calling from God that led Recollet and Jesuit missionaries to abandon the comforts of 17th century France for the opportunity to work in the rugged wilderness of New France.

The Recollets were the first religious group to set sail for New France. They left at the urging of Samuel de Champlain, who, upon his return to France in 1614, aroused their Christian consciences with tales of the unfortunate heathens on the other side of the world: heathens who had never even heard of God.

The Arrival of the Jesuits

By the end of their first decade in New France, the Recollets decided that they were in over their heads. They pleaded for help from other religious orders and, in 1625, the Society of Jesus (the Jesuits), one of the strongest religious orders of the day, agreed to take on some of this important overseas mission work.

The Recollets couldn't have asked for help from a more committed order of missionaries. The Jesuits firmly believed that Christianity—more specifically, Roman Catholicism—was the only legitimate religion. While it was clear to many of these early Jesuit missionaries that the Huron people had some sort of spiritual beliefs, they couldn't help but dismiss the Huron's non-Christian beliefs as nothing more than superstitions.

Voice from the Past

"...it is a great misfortune that so many poor creatures should live and die without any knowledge of God and even without any religion or law, whether divine, political, or civil, established among them."

—Samuel de Champlain, writing in his *Works* about the native people he encountered in Huronia in the early 17th century.

The Building of Sainte-Marie-Among-the-Hurons

The Jesuits felt that their chances of converting natives to Christianity would be greatly increased if the natives were less nomadic. They believed that if the natives lived in villages, learned how to farm, and sent their children to schools run by the Jesuits, it would only be a matter of time before they adopted the Roman Catholic faith.

To help them achieve this end, the Jesuits founded Sainte-Marie-Among-the-Hurons in 1638—a mission dedicated to serving the Huron people.

Separated from Quebec and Trois Rivières by more than 1300 kilometres of wilderness, Sainte-Marie-Among-the-Hurons had to become a self-sufficient community. Cattle, pigs, and poultry were brought from Quebec by canoe, and fields were cleared so that the community could grow its own corn, beans, and squash.

Initially, Sainte-Marie-Among-the-Hurons consisted simply of a residence and a chapel for priests. Over time, it expanded to include a church, hospital, workshops, a stable, barns, a cookhouse, a kitchen garden, and dwellings for layworkers and native converts. Fortified by a log palisade, Sainte-Marie-Among-the-Hurons was designed to provide the natives with an example of all the finer things in life that French culture and Christian living had to offer.

Setting a good example was very important to the missionaries in Huronia. That's why they were so eager to be rid of the *coureurs du bois*. They fervently believed that the *coureurs du bois*—with their untamed lifestyles and promiscuous ways—impeded their ability to convert the Huron to Catholicism.

Despite their concerns about the *coureurs du bois*, the missionaries did manage to win some converts to Christianity over time, although the motivations of some of the Huron who converted were often inspired by anything but religion! Some of the natives at the mission agreed to undergo conversion because they thought it was in their best interests to do so. They either believed that it would improve their relationships with the French (and therefore their trading fortunes) or were attracted by the ritual and ceremony of Catholicism. Participating in religious instruction at Sainte-Marie-Among-the-Hurons was a no-lose venture: the Jesuits rewarded those in attendance with gifts of trade goods and tobacco!

Trouble in Huronia

While the missionaries were initially accepted—or at least quietly tolerated—by the Huron people, their position became increasingly perilous during the 1630s. A devastating bout of measles or smallpox hit the Huron people between 1635 and 1640, reducing their population by 50 per cent. Because the missionaries made a point of baptising people on their death beds, segments of the Huron population began to conclude that baptism was, in fact, a particularly deadly form of witchcraft. Still, the fact that the Jesuits were not killed or expelled from Huronia at the height of the epidemic shows how dependent the Huron had become on the fur trade by this point, and how much their alliances with the French traders meant to them.

As if the epidemic was not enough to contend with, to add to the missionaries' problems, a decline in the beaver population was forcing the Huron to venture into the hunting grounds of other native peoples. This led the Huron into conflicts with other groups, most notably the Iroquois.

While the majority of Huron people continued to tolerate the missionaries, a highly vocal anti-French group began to make its presence

Voice from the Past

"...there are, altogether, many and considerable influences which not only hinder our work, but seem even to threaten the ruin of the whole mission. Some of these, indeed, are common to us with all the Huron—especially the enemy, whom we call by the name of Iroquois; they, on the one hand, close the roads and obstruct trade, and, on the other, devastate this region by frequent massacre; in short, they fill every place with fear. Other hindrances, however, are altogether peculiar to us—notably, the hatred towards us of certain infidel Hurons, which has grown to the degree that a few days ago they killed one of our domestics [Jacques Douart]. They were ready to offer the same treatment to us, if opportunity had occurred."

—Father Jean de Brébeuf in an excerpt from *Jesuit Relations* XXXII, 61, June 2, 1648.

felt. By 1645, a split had developed between the pagans and the Christians. The pagans were afraid that continued contact with the missionaries spelled a threat to their traditional ways of life. They felt that it was in their best interests to break off trading with the French and resume trading with the Iroquois. This would, of course, necessitate the expulsion of the Jesuits.

The Huron chiefs decided to bring the question of a continued Franco-Huron alliance to a head by killing a Frenchman. Jacques Douart, a French resident of Huronia whose only crime was being in the wrong place at the wrong time, was murdered by the Huron. At the same time, a proclamation was issued calling for the banishment of both the French and any Huron people who chose to practise Catholicism.

An emergency council was convened and the various proposals were debated. In the end, the pro-French contingent won and the Jesuits agreed to accept 100 beaver skins as compensation for the murder of Douart.

The situation in Huronia was serious enough to attract the attention of Charles Huault de Montmagny, the new Governor of Canada.

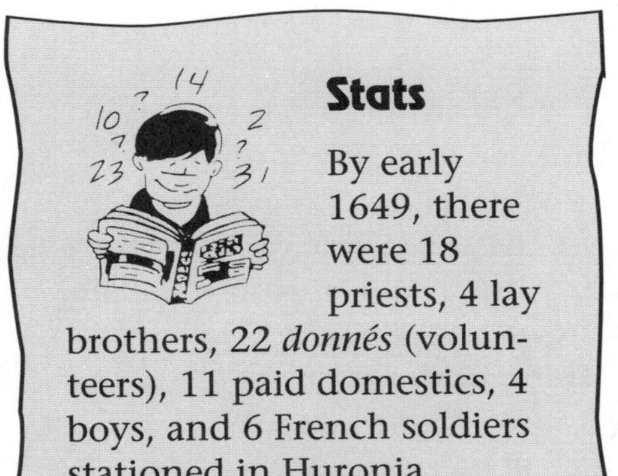

Stats

By early 1649, there were 18 priests, 4 lay brothers, 22 *donnés* (volunteers), 11 paid domestics, 4 boys, and 6 French soldiers stationed in Huronia.

He was determined to punish the Huron who came to Quebec for their poor treatment of the Jesuits. Montmagny made it clear that existing alliances between the French fur traders and the Huron had been terminated because of the natives' unacceptable treatment of the French missionaries, and that he'd only be willing to renew these alliances if the Jesuits were permitted to continue their work in Huronia undisturbed.

Fortunately for Montmagny and the missionaries, by this time the Huron were healthy and expecting a good harvest. As a result, many of their fears about the missionaries had been dispelled, and the missionaries were allowed to continue their work—at least for the time being.

Once the threats from within had been dealt with, the missionaries and the Huron people were forced to contend with an escalating series of attacks from the Iroquois. In 1648, the Iroquois attacked nearby St. Joseph, destroying the village. This brutal attack led thousands of Huron to take refuge at Sainte-Marie-Among-the-Hurons. The following year, the Iroquois attacked and demolished both Saint-Louis and Saint-Ignace. Two priests, Fathers Jean de Brébeuf and Jérôme Lalemant, were tortured and killed during these attacks and the Huron in the area were dispersed.

The Destruction of Sainte-Marie-Among-the-Hurons

Later that year, the Jesuits were forced to make a heartbreaking decision. They decided to abandon Sainte-Marie-Among-the-Hurons, the most successful mission in all of New France. To prevent the Iroquois from using the premises, the missionaries torched their beloved home and watched it burn to the ground. They then retreated to Saint-Joseph Island (now Christian Island in present-day Georgian Bay) with several hundred Christian Huron families in tow. They roughed it out for another year at their new premises before retreating to Quebec with 300 of their native followers.

Voice from the Past

"We, the Shepherds, followed our fleeing flock, and we too have left our dwelling place—I might call it our delight—the residence of Sainte-Marie, and the fields we had tilled, which promised a rich harvest. Nay, more, we even applied the torch to the work of our own hands, lest the sacred House should furnish shelter to our impious enemy [the Iroquois]; and thus in a single day, and almost in a moment, we saw consumed our work of nearly ten years, which had given us the hope that we could produce the necessities of life, and thus maintain ourself in this country without aid from France. But God has willed otherwise; our home is now laid waste."

—Excerpt from *Jesuit Relations*, XXXV, 25, written in the aftermath of the destruction of Sainte-Marie-Among-the-Hurons.

The destruction of Sainte-Marie-Among-the-Hurons was a serious setback for New France. It brought an end to the work being done by the missionaries in Huronia and led to a decline in the amount of fur trading being conducted in the colony.

The Least You Need to Know

- The missionaries in 17th century Huronia were motivated by a desire to bring Christianity to the "heathens" they encountered.
- The reaction of the Huron people was mixed. Some converted to Catholicism for purely material reasons, while others converted because they were genuinely interested in becoming Christians. Others refused to convert and worked to have the missionaries ousted from the colony.
- The destruction of Sainte-Marie-Among-the-Hurons brought an end to the work being done by the missionaries in Huronia and led to a decline in the amount of fur trading being conducted in the colony.

Chapter 5

Out with the Old and in with the New (1663 to 1760)

In this chapter

- The French government's methods of encouraging settlement in New France
- The seigniorial system
- The economy of New France
- The conflicts with the Iroquois and the British

To say that some people in 17th and 18th century France were less than enthusiastic about the potential of Canada is to drastically understate the case! Renowned philosopher Voltaire (1694–1778) dismissed the troublesome colony as nothing more than "a few acres of snow."

Even the French government (which professed to be interested in encouraging settlement in its distant colony) didn't always carry through on its plans. Over the years, the government had made a habit of conducting its colonization efforts at minimal effort and cost. A favourite technique was to arrange to have a group of explorers or entrepreneurs undertake the colonizing for them—a strategy that failed time and time again.

Such was the case in 1627, when Cardinal Richelieu, Louis XIII's Minister, formed the Company of One Hundred Associates. The Company was given a permanent monopoly on both the fur trade and other types of trading in New France for a 10-year period. In return, it was required to pay the administrative costs of the colony, send out 200 settlers each year, and have at least 4000 settlers established in the colony within 15 years. Because the French government was anxious to avoid a repeat of the religious conflicts it was experiencing at home, Huguenots (French Protestants) were barred from entering New France.

In 1628, the first group of 400 settlers left France, but unfortunately they didn't make it as far as Quebec. The ship on which they were travelling was captured by British raiders—including Captain David Kirke—as it entered the St. Lawrence River. (The next year, Kirke and his brother sailed to Quebec City and captured it. It remained in English hands for three years until a treaty returned it to France.)

By 1663, it was apparent that the Company of One Hundred Associates had failed to promote settlement in New France. Jean-Baptiste Colbert, Louis XIV's Minister of Finances, convinced the Company to voluntarily surrender its charter, and consequently, full authority over Canada returned to royal hands.

Given their experiences with the Company of One Hundred Associates, you would think that Louis XIV and Colbert would have been reluctant to subcontract the job of colony-building yet again, but that's exactly what they did. In 1664, they granted the Company of the West Indies a monopoly over French interests in both the Americas and the west coast of Africa. Once again, this strategy proved to be a failure. By 1674, it was clear that the French government was going to have to assume direct responsibility for promoting settlement in New France.

Government in New France

In 1663, New France formally became a royal colony. At that point, it had a population of 3000 (although a good proportion of the inhabitants were soldiers sent by Louis XIV to defend the colony against attacks from the Iroquois and the British).

Louis XIV appointed a Sovereign Council to assume responsibility for the day-to-day operations of the colony. The Sovereign Council consisted of a governor, a bishop, and an intendant. The governor was the King's representative in New France and, as such, was responsible for carrying out his orders. His areas of responsibility included defence and law enforcement. The bishop, on the other hand, was responsible for overseeing the work of the missionaries, churches, hospitals, and schools. Finally, the intendant was responsible for such practical matters as monitoring the fur trade and the flow of imports and exports; overseeing the courts, the roads, and social welfare; and encouraging settlers to come to New France.

While there were plenty of government officials in New France, life was anything but democratic. There was no parliament and there were no formal avenues for dissent. Anyone accused of a crime was assumed guilty until proven innocent, and the authorities had a variety of officially sanctioned methods of torture designed to encourage the accused to confess. (Fortunately, there are less than 20 recorded instances in the entire history of New France of torture being used to "facilitate the questioning" of the accused.)

The Great Intendant

The most famous intendant to rule in New France was Jean Talon, who was known as "The Great Intendant." Talon, who arrived in the colony in 1665, took some rather extraordinary steps to encourage population growth. In addition to offering free passage to anyone who was willing to relocate in New France, Talon implemented some innovative policies designed to boost the number of settlers in the colony.

In 1669, a royal decree was issued stating that girls were to be married by the age of 16 and boys by the age of 20. Those who complied with this decree would receive a royal gift of 20 livres each. Those who didn't head for the altar early enough in life risked seeing their parents fined.

There were also incentives to encourage a high birth rate. Families with 10 or more living children (those who became priests or nuns didn't count towards the total!) were given an annual pension of 300 livres. Those who really took their patriotic duty to heart and had 12 or more living children were rewarded with an annual pension of 400 livres.

One of the most memorable mechanisms of population growth of the time concerned the *filles du roi* (daughters of the King). Shiploads of marriageable young women were transported to New France so that the bachelors residing there could start families. If you were a bachelor less

Word for the Day

The *filles du roi* (daughters of the King) were sent to New France to help populate the colony. These young women, most of whom were between the ages of 12 and 25, were typically married off within 2 weeks of their arrival in New France.

Unlike immigrants to some parts of the world, the *filles du roi* were selected with great care. In some cases, they were asked to supply references from their priests, proving that they were of good character. Louis XIV's Minister of Finances, Jean-Baptiste Colbert, felt that you couldn't be too careful when choosing the people who would populate a new land: "In the establishment of a country, it is important to sow good seed." Jean Talon, the so-called Great Intendant, agreed. He felt that the *filles du roi* should not be "disgraced by nature" or have anything "repulsive about their external persons." They should be "healthy and strong for country work, or at least...have some inclination to work with their hands."

The *filles du roi* were given significant dowries by the King, a situation that gave them more than a little leverage when choosing suitors! In fact, approximately 11 per cent of the *filles du roi* entered into more than one marriage contract before going through with the final marriage ceremony.

The *filles du roi* immigration program was clearly a success. While only 230 single female immigrants had made it to New France between 1643 and 1663, 774 *filles du roi* arrived between 1663 and 1673. What's more, the settlement rate for the *filles du roi* was exceedingly high. Ninety per cent became permanent settlers, as compared to a mere 50 per cent for the immigrant population as a whole. This helps to explain why the colony grew so quickly in the subsequent century (its population increased to 70,000 by 1763) and why the ratio of men to women was roughly equal at the time of the Conquest.

than enthusiastic about the prospect of getting married, you were in for a rough ride: men who did not marry within 15 days of the arrival of the ships carrying the *filles du roi* were deprived of the right to participate in the fur trade. (Clearly, this was the 17th century equivalent of the shotgun wedding!)

While these may seem to be rather drastic measures, Talon was living in an extremely desperate time. The fate of New France was largely dependent on its ability to increase the number of settlers. In the end, Talon's strategies proved successful: by 1675, the population of the colony had risen to 8000—twice what it had been just seven years earlier.

Stats

At any given time, between 40 and 50 per cent of the inhabitants of New France were under the age of 15. As a result, young people were forced to shoulder many responsibilities that would otherwise have been performed by adults: barn cleaning, harvesting, and household chores.

The Seigniorial System

When King Louis XIV decided to play an active role in the life of the colony following the failures of the Company of One Hundred Associates and the Company of the West Indies to encourage settlement, he granted land to a series of lords known as seigniors. (Obviously, it never even occurred to the King that the land might actually belong to the natives who had resided on it for thousands of years!)

Each seignior was responsible for subdividing his land and settling farmers on it. He also had to provide his tenants with a few basic services, such as access to a flour mill and a chapel with a priest. The tenants, in turn, were responsible for constructing houses for themselves and cultivating the land, paying annual taxes, and providing three to four days per year of free labour to the seignior. While the seigniorial system prevented tenants from directly owning any property, this was not as much of a hardship as it might seem. The tenants were actually moderately well off, and the paternalistic philosophy behind the seigniorial system ensured that there were no landless poor in New France. The state—through the seigniors—was clearly prepared to take care of each and every citizen.

Trade in New France

Like other European colonies of the time, New France was valued both because it was a source of raw materials for France and because it provided a market for goods manufactured in the Mother Country. It was expected to produce far more wealth than was required to run the colony, and it was limited to trading with France and its colonies.

Given the limits that were placed on its economy, it's hardly surprising that the fur trade was the key economic activity in New France. While the colony exported some wheat, timber, and fish to Louisbourg and French colonies in the West Indies, most of its products were chiefly for the use of colonists: seal and whale oil, cod, eel, timber, iron products, tobacco, textiles, leather goods, and beer.

At the same time that it was exporting furs and other wares, New France imported a variety of goods, including cloth, salt, wine, brandy, sugar, molasses, spices, and weapons.

Occasionally, Peace Broke Out...

The history of New France is a story of a series of bitter conflicts. Throughout most of its history, the colony found itself battling two main enemies: the Iroquois and the British.

The conflict with the Iroquois was the result of fur trade turf wars. Champlain's decision a half century earlier to join the Huron in a raid against their traditional enemies the Iroquois led to a century of unrest in New France. While, strategically speaking, it might not seem to have been the wisest move, Champlain really had no choice but to participate in the raid. He wanted to firm up his alliance with the Huron and he was anxious to explore the area to the

Main Event

With the signing of the Treaty of Utrecht in 1713, New France surrendered control of Acadia, Placentia in Newfoundland, and a series of trading posts on Hudson Bay. While France lost a considerable amount of territory under the Treaty of Utrecht, its signing ushered in 30 years of peace, something New France badly needed at this point in its history.

south of the St. Lawrence River, something that this particular raid allowed him to do.

The governments of France and New France made a couple of efforts to bring the situation with the Iroquois under control. On two separate occasions, French troops spent the winter in Huronia, trying to protect French fur-trading interests. Similarly, in 1665, 24 companies of French regulars arrived at Quebec City and constructed 4 forts whose sole purpose was to help to defend the colony against the Iroquois and New France's other key enemy, the British.

By this time, the British and the Thirteen Colonies were causing New France nothing but grief. The Thirteen Colonies (located along the eastern seaboard of the present-day United States) were expanding inland and threatening France's control of fur country. The conflict was intensified by global commercial rivalries between France and Britain that often found themselves being played out in the New World. New France was expected to aid France by causing trouble for the British colonies, therefore forcing Britain to deploy troops to America and giving France an advantage in Europe. The conflict with the British was such a problem for New France that it's easier to single out periods of peace than periods of war! In fact, the only prolonged period of peace in New France occurred during the 30 years following the signing of the Treaty of Utrecht in 1713.

The Least You Need to Know

- The French government initially tried to involve private companies in the business of colonization. When that strategy failed, the government used a variety of other means to encourage population growth in New France.
- The seigniorial system ensured that there were no landless poor in New France. In exchange for a few minor duties, tenants were granted the right to live on the seignior's land.
- The fur trade dominated the economy of New France. Other types of industries were discouraged because they might compete with products manufactured by France itself.
- New France was almost constantly involved in conflicts with the Iroquois and the British.

Chapter 6

Hit the Road, Jacques (1710 to 1764)

In this chapter

- ➤ Who the Acadians were and what their lives were like prior to the expulsion
- ➤ Why the Acadians refused to swear the oath of allegiance to Britain
- ➤ The consequences of their actions

The expulsion of the Acadians could be considered a comedy of errors, if only the outcome weren't so tragic.

Played out over the first half of the 18th century, the drama reached its climax in 1755. At that point, a series of misunderstandings and poor decisions on the part of both the French-speaking Acadians and the British who had recently assumed control over their homeland culminated in Governor Charles Lawrence's decision to order as many as 10,000 Acadians to leave the colony.

In the Beginning...

The residents of Acadia (present-day Nova Scotia, Prince Edward Island, and New Brunswick) originally came from France. Arriving in the New

Word for the Day

In 1621, King James I of England gave the parcel of land known as Acadia to Sir William Alexander, who immediately named the area *Nova Scotia* (New Scotland). During the subsequent century, the area was passed back and forth between Britain and France as the two countries battled for much larger stakes elsewhere in the world.

World during the mid-17th century, they were mainly poor people with little, if any, farming experience. The fact that they were able to make a good living off the land is testament to the quality of the fertile soil they encountered in their adopted land. In fact, most Acadians were better fed and considerably healthier than their counterparts in France.

Regardless of whether the colony was in French or English hands—and it seemed to flip-flop continuously as the two countries battled for supremacy both in Europe and in the New World—Acadians had to be highly self-reliant. They learned how to dyke the marshlands off the Bay of Fundy so that they could grow a variety of crops, and they made their own furniture, tools, clothing, medicine, and food.

It wasn't until after the signing of the Treaty of Utrecht in 1713 that relative stability came to Acadia. Under the Treaty, France handed over Acadia, Newfoundland, and the Hudson Bay region to the British, retaining only Île Royale (Cape Breton Island) and Île Saint-Jean (Prince Edward Island). The region also came to be called Nova Scotia, the name the British had initially given it nearly a century earlier.

Stats

The number of Acadians living in Acadia (later Nova Scotia) grew from 200 in 1650 to 10,000 by 1750. During 1710 to 1749 alone, the population more than tripled, from 2500 to 8000.

The More Things Change…

While Nova Scotia was now back in British hands, day-to-day life didn't change much for the Acadians. They were initially told that they could remain on their lands and become British citizens or sell their possessions and move to other French colonies, but nothing was done to force the issue (initially, at least). The Acadians were also given a lot more slack than most newly conquered people. They were even permitted to continue to practise Catholicism, a highly unusual concession at a time when religious persecution tended to be the norm.

While some Acadians seriously considered relocating to the nearby French colony of Île Royale, they soon abandoned the idea. The land was rocky, the soil was poor, there was no land suitable for dyking, and the climate was far harsher than what they enjoyed in Nova Scotia. Because they were far more attached to their land than they were to France, many Acadians decided to stay in Nova Scotia, even though the colony was no longer controlled by the French.

A Question of Loyalty

Strange as it may sound today, it was standard practice in 17th and 18th century Europe for governments to require that their citizens swear oaths promising to serve their monarchs faithfully and to help defend their countries in the event of war. Such was the case for the Acadians. Not long after the colony passed into British hands, the Acadians met with a demand that they take such an oath.

You can't blame the Acadians for being less than enthusiastic about the idea of swearing an oath of allegiance. First of all, they had been handed back and forth from France to Britain and from Britain to France so often that they were understandably reluctant to align themselves with either country. Secondly, neither Britain nor France had proven itself particularly willing to rally to support the Acadians in their own times of need, so the Acadians certainly didn't feel honour-bound to put their own necks on the line.

The Acadians didn't out-and-out refuse to take the oath, however. They simply asked that it be modified. They stated that while they were not prepared to take up arms against the French, they were willing to guarantee to remain neutral in the event that Britain and France once again went to war.

Clearly, the two sides were at an impasse. The British felt that they were completely justified in asking the Acadians to take the oath, while the Acadians felt equally strongly that it wasn't in their best interests to comply. Fortunately for the Acadians, the British decided to let the matter drop for a number of years. The issue didn't surface again until 1729–30, when the British government began to pressure Governor Richard Philipps to resolve the matter once and for all.

Philipps realized that the Acadians were not about to swear the oath, so he came up with a clever solution that he managed to pull off because of the distance between the colony and the Mother Country. By making a verbal promise that the Acadians would be exempted from bearing arms, Philipps was able to convince a large number of Acadians to sign oaths of allegiance. Needless to say, the British government had no idea that Philipps was making these kind of promises and certainly would not have approved of his actions had they realized what he was doing. In the end, however, Philipps succeeded in satisfying both sides: the British were convinced that the Acadians had at last agreed to sign the oath, and the Acadians believed that they had taken a binding oath that guaranteed their neutrality. Everything was rosy for the Acadians...for a while.

Within a few years, the situation changed. By 1744, the 30 years of peace that had followed the signing of the Treaty of Utrecht came to an end and Britain and France were once again at war.

Given the tense climate at the time, in 1749, Britain decided to construct a military and naval base in Halifax, and brought in 2500 new settlers to populate it. Clearly, Halifax was intended to help counterbalance the noteworthy military force the French had built up at Louisbourg. (The massive fortress on the tip of Cape Breton Island named after the French King had been constructed some 30 years earlier.)

Clearly, the British were feeling anything but secure about their ability to maintain control over Nova Scotia—and for good reason. By the mid-18th century, the French-speaking Acadians outnumbered the non-French-speaking settlers by a ratio of nearly three to one. To make matters worse, the native population was clearly aligned with the French. In fact, Micmac in the area had raided Halifax, Lunenburg, and Dartmouth at the urging of their French missionary priest, the Abbé le Loutre.

An obvious solution was to encourage foreign Protestants to move to the area, thereby offsetting the overwhelming number of Catholic Acadians. Between 1750 and 1753, several thousand immigrants, mostly German-speaking, arrived from Germany, Switzerland, and Holland, as well as the Protestant areas of France. These immigrants mainly settled around Lunenburg. The colony also managed to attract settlers from England, although many of them were completely unsuited to pioneer life and left after only a few years.

Over time, these immigration initiatives began to backfire. Instead of increasing the number of Nova Scotians who were willing to rally behind the British Crown in the event of war, the British found themselves faced with an even larger neutral population. Like the Acadians, the German-speaking immigrants who had been encouraged to relocate to Nova Scotia liked to live apart from the British and wanted to be exempt from bearing arms.

The situation in Nova Scotia really heated up in the years following the signing of the Treaty of Aix-la-Chapelle in 1748. The British became increasingly determined to force the Acadians to swear an oath of allegiance, while the Acadians appeared oblivious to the increasing seriousness of the situation and chose to rely on the strategy that had served them well during the previous 40 years: neutrality.

Same Game, New Rules

The latest Governor of Nova Scotia, Charles Lawrence, decided that the Acadians posed a threat to the security of the colony. He suspected them of disloyalty and demanded that they swear an oath to the British Crown. According to Lawrence, neutrality was no longer an option.

While Lawrence had initially hoped to bully the Acadians into agreeing to take the oath, it soon became apparent that they were prepared to call his bluff. When large numbers of Acadians did what they had always done—refuse to take the oath—he had no other choice but to order them out of Nova Scotia. Of the 10,000 Acadians living in the area in 1755, approximately 8000 were forced to leave. Families were separated and many who were deported died at sea en route to Europe or the Thirteen Colonies.

Not all of the Acadians boarded ships, however. Some resisted deportation, fleeing into the woods with their families or heading off to P.E.I. or northern New Brunswick. Others headed to Louisiana, which had a large French-speaking population at the time.

Following the deportation, British soldiers toured the empty villages, torching the remaining homes and fields. If the Acadians somehow made their way back to Nova Scotia, the British didn't want there to be anything left waiting for them.

The Fall of Louisbourg

In 1758, the British sent a fleet of 160 warships carrying no fewer than 27,000 troops to Halifax. Their mission? To capture the fortress of Louisbourg. The troops descended on Louisbourg in June, and the fortress held firm for 49 days. Finally, the soldiers and citizens of Louisbourg surrendered. In the aftermath of the fall of Louisbourg, the 2000 to 3000 Acadians who had fled to Cape Breton Island and P.E.I. were ordered out of their new homes.

On the Road Again…

With the threat of Louisbourg under control, the government of Nova Scotia once again turned its attention to the perennial problem of immigration. The government was determined to boost the population of the colony. As a result of its efforts, between 1760 and 1776, more than 7000 New Englanders were encouraged to move to Nova Scotia. At the same time, the Pennsylvania Land Company brought approximately 25,000 Scottish settlers to the area.

By 1763, less than 1000 Acadians remained in the colony. Because they were no longer considered to be a threat, they were given official permission to resettle in Nova Scotia in 1764. Over the next couple of years, approximately 1000 returned, bringing the Acadian population in 1771 to approximately 20 per cent of what it had been prior to the expulsion.

Unfortunately, the Acadians learned the truth behind that old adage, "You can't go home again." While they were able to return to Nova Scotia, they weren't able to resettle on the marshlands that had previously provided them with their livelihoods. Settlers from New England had taken over the best land while the Acadians were away.

The Least You Need to Know

- The residents of Acadia (present-day Nova Scotia, Prince Edward Island, and New Brunswick) originally came from France, arriving during the mid-17th century.
- The Acadians were reluctant to swear an oath of allegiance to Britain because their policy of neutrality had served them so well in the past.
- As a result of their refusal to take the oath, approximately 10,000 Acadians were deported in the years immediately following 1755.

Chapter 7

You Win Some... (1760)

In this chapter

- The events leading up the Conquest
- The Battle of the Plains of Abraham
- The achievements of New France

By 1750, New France found itself coming into conflict with the Thirteen Colonies to the south.

The crisis came to a head when France decided to occupy the Ohio Valley and exclude the English from that region. It was France's way of protecting its fur trade interests in the face of ongoing expansion from the Thirteen Colonies.

Needless to say, the residents of the Thirteen Colonies were less than thrilled with this development. Governor Robert Dinwiddie of Virginia sent George Washington to Fort le Boeuf in 1753 to demand that the French withdraw from the area. When the French refused to heed the warning, Dinwiddie decided to take stronger action. In 1754, George Washington and some 300 men recruited by Dinwiddie set out to expel the French.

While Washington's expedition proved to be a complete and utter failure, it sparked off the final conflict in what had already become a prolonged and belaboured battle for North America. Although Britain and France, by some miracle, were at peace in Europe, they found themselves being drawn into conflict in the New World. What's more, both countries seemed, at last, to be willing to provide their embattled colonies with the support they so desperately needed.

New War, New Rules

In 1756, the outbreak of the Seven Years' War in Europe brought Britain and France into a formal state of war. At that point, the entire character of the conflict in the New World changed dramatically. Colonial forces led by rank amateurs were replaced with professional armies led by experienced commanders.

The two governments also seemed prepared to take this particular conflict more seriously than the ones that had come before it. Even before the war had been formally declared, France, for example, had taken steps to strengthen its defences in New France. Two regiments of regulars were sent out, and with them came Louis Joseph, the Marquis de Montcalm—the new commander of the French forces in North America.

Montcalm found himself faced with a challenging situation. While the self-confidence of those in New France had been boosted to new heights by recent successes against the British, political infighting and corruption at the highest levels of the civil administration threatened to

Real Life

François Bigot, the last of the intendants of New France, earned a reputation for being a corrupt and self-serving politician. Bigot sought to enrich himself—along with other equally dishonest, high-ranking officials—at the expense of both the treasury and the people. Bigot and his partners in crime engaged in the fraudulent sale of supplies, the filing of false claims, and other criminal activities designed to put money in their own pockets whenever possible.

derail the war effort. To make matters worse, New France was experiencing a food shortage that led to rationing, and the British were doing their best to disrupt the flow of supply ships between France and its colony.

Not surprisingly, by 1758, the military forces of New France seemed to be losing their competitive advantage. The recently reorganized British army was preparing to flex its muscles, and there seemed to be a newfound willingness in London to deploy enough forces to the New World to crush—not just repel—New France.

Everything Happens in Threes

The campaign of 1758 was designed to overwhelm the French forces on three fronts: at Duquesne, Ticonderoga, and Louisbourg. Faced with threats from all sides, Montcalm chose to concentrate his forces at Ticonderoga, which guarded the central and most direct approach to Canada. Although Montcalm managed to hold on to Ticonderoga, the French forces were forced to abandon Fort Duquesne, and Louisbourg fell after a seven-week siege.

The fall of Louisbourg on July 26, 1758, spelled disaster for New France. Without the bastion guarding the entrance to the St. Lawrence River, Quebec City was left vulnerable to attack.

Montcalm began to see the writing on the wall. Conditions in the colony had gone from bad to worse, and France had apparently resigned itself to the fact that the fall of New France was imminent. The King had, in fact, turned down Montcalm's recent appeals for aid, arguing that he couldn't possibly compete with the armies the British were amassing in the area. (There were already an estimated 50,000 British troops in America.) In a letter to the French minister of war, Montcalm spelled out the situation as he saw it: New France was doomed to be lost in the next campaign unless there was an unexpected turn of events. As a result, Montcalm's strategy became one of minimizing losses rather than attempting to win the war.

The Battle of the Plains of Abraham

Unfortunately for Montcalm, the change in circumstances that he kept hoping for never came. He gathered his forces together at Quebec City and awaited the inevitable attack from the British.

In June, General James Wolfe and 9000 men landed on the Island of Orleans and seized the town of Lévis, which was opposite Quebec City. It didn't take Wolfe long to decide that a direct assault wouldn't work. "The enemy," he complained, "has shut himself up in inaccessible entrenchments so that I can't get at him without spilling a torrent of blood."

Wolfe was forced to spend the rest of the summer waiting for the right opportunity. Motivated by his bitter hatred of the French and his frustration at the impasse he had reached with his enemies, he began burning houses in the area and destroying crops. He took settlers hostage, killing many of them.

By September, Wolfe was getting even more restless. He was worried that he would be forced to withdraw from New France before winter set in if his fortunes didn't improve soon. He decided to attempt a surprise attack on the French at the Plains of Abraham, an area adjacent to Quebec City that was guarded by a weak detachment led by an incompetent officer.

Voice from the Past

Following the Battle of the Plains of Abraham, Montcalm was taken back to Quebec City and told that he was going to die. His response? "Good. Then I shall not see the surrender of Quebec."

General James Wolfe was so overjoyed to hear that the enemy was fleeing that he managed to find the silver lining in his own personal situation: "God be praised," he said. "Since I have conquered, I will die in peace."

In a move of this nature, timing was everything. In the wee hours of September 13, 1759, the attack was launched. The first boats were able to deceive a French sentry who had been awaiting a shipment of supplies from Britain. By daybreak, Wolfe and his forces were making their way across the Plains of Abraham.

Montcalm was understandably horrified to discover that his defensive position had been pierced overnight. He found himself faced with two choices, neither of which were particularly appealing: maintain his defensive stance and risk seeing Quebec City fall under siege, or go on the offensive by meeting Wolfe and his forces in direct combat.

Montcalm chose the latter strategy, as Wolfe had hoped he would. Instead of calling in French forces, who were on standby and ready to attack the British from the rear, or forcing the British to assault the thick walls of the city, Montcalm led his men into battle. Within 15 minutes, both leaders had been mortally wounded and 1300 of their men had been killed. The British had seized control of Quebec City.

At moments, the winning side must have wondered whether the spoils were worth the victory. Quebec City certainly didn't seem like much of a prize at the time, but the British troops were honour-bound to hold on to it nonetheless. They spent a miserable winter in Quebec City, short on both adequate shelter and supplies.

As soon as spring arrived, the French made one last attempt to drive the British out of Quebec City. General Lévis besieged the city, which was now under the control of British General James Murray. While Lévis's forces managed to defeat the British troops in a skirmish outside the gates of the city, they lacked the strength to retake Quebec City. In the end, who would ultimately win control of New France came down to simple logistics: whichever country managed to get a supply ship in first was likely to be the winner. On May 9, 1760, British ships pulled into Quebec City, and the fate of New France was sealed. By the time the official surrender was signed that September, it was, for all intents and purposes, yesterday's news.

Factors That Led to the Fall of New France

Strategically speaking, New France was in a whole lot of trouble long before the British came calling.

The colony was dependent on a single access route: the St. Lawrence River. As a result, it was vulnerable to enemy blockade in the event of war.

It had not been allowed to develop and diversify because such development was inconsistent with the objectives of the Mother Country. As a result, its population remained small and dependent while the Thirteen Colonies to the south were experiencing tremendous growth.

The government of New France was divided in terms of strategy at the very time when it needed to operate from a position of strength. Montcalm wanted to fight the war using European-style military techniques, while the Marquis de Vaudreuil—the governor at the time—felt that it was best to stick to the strategy that had served the colony well up until that point: conducting swift raids against enemy outposts.

But while all of these factors contributed to the loss of New France, in the end it was Montcalm's decision to meet Wolfe in battle on the Plains of Abraham that sealed the colony's fate.

The Good News

While New France was ultimately conquered by the British, it is still deserving of a place of honour in Canadian history books—including this one! New France was home to the first permanent European settlers in Canada and the birthplace of the fur trade, and it managed to lay the groundwork for the country that was eventually to become Canada. At the end of the day, New France managed to do something that had never been done before: it provided European governments with living proof that a colony could survive in the St. Lawrence Valley after all.

The Least You Need to Know

- France's attempts to occupy the Ohio Valley led it into direct conflict with Britain and its colonies.
- The nature of war in New France changed dramatically with the outbreak of the Seven Years' War.
- The British victory in the Battle of the Plains of Abraham led to the end of New France and the beginning of British North America.
- New France's achievements were many: it was home to the first permanent European settlers in Canada and the birthplace of the fur trade, and it provided European governments with living proof that a colony could survive in the St. Lawrence Valley after all.

Part 2
Trials and Tribulations

During the years between the Conquest and the American Civil War, Canadians faced a series of conflicts from both without and within. On a number of occasions, tensions with the United States flared into out-and-out confrontation. Struggles between the two key players in the fur trade—the Hudson's Bay Company and the North West Company—forever changed the face of the fur trade in Canada. Conflicts in both Upper and Lower Canada threatened to throw the colony into a state of rebellion. And a growing desire for a closer economic and/or political association with the United States began to call into question just how long the British North American colonies could expect to remain distinct from the monolithic political entity to the south. The following chapters describe the forces that would ultimately drive the colonies towards Confederation.

Chapter 8

That Was Then, This Is Now (1760 to 1774)

In this chapter

- The aftermath of the Seven Years' War
- The Proclamation of 1763
- The Quebec Act of 1774

In the aftermath of the Seven Years' War, the British found themselves in possession of four new colonies: Canada, Grenada, and East and West Florida.

While the colonies hardly could have been more different from one another (and not just in terms of climate!), the British government's initial instinct was to treat all of the new possessions in the same manner, and to attempt to assimilate them into the existing British empire by establishing a uniform system of governance.

Unfortunately, the plan was a total flop. It failed to take into account the large French-speaking population in Canada and it ignored a series of equally complex problems in the other new colonies.

The Morning After

The British military governors who were put in charge of Quebec City, Trois Rivières, and Montreal were given the rather daunting task of holding together a newly acquired colony populated with people of a different religion, language, and culture than the Mother Country.

It wouldn't have been so bad if they could at least have felt confident that the colony would remain in British hands, but given the long history of war between Britain and France, it seemed unlikely that Quebec could actually be entering a period of relative stability.

As a result of this uncertainty, the military governors were reluctant to usher in drastic changes or do anything else that might rock the boat. Their chief motivation—like generations of bureaucrats both before and after them—was to avoid any actions that would cause civil unrest and make their task of governing even more difficult.

The military governors were also severely limited as to what they could do. Their authority was restricted by the terms of France's surrender, which were binding until the signing of the Treaty of Paris in 1763.

Main Event

The Treaty of Paris, signed in 1763, formally confirmed the outcome of the Seven Years' War. France abandoned all of its possessions in the Americas, while Britain walked away with Canada and the Spanish-acquired title to Louisiana.

Hard as it may be for our Canadian egos to take, neither the French nor the British particularly wanted Canada! There was intense pressure in England for the British to take the sugar island of Guadeloupe instead, while in France many people believed their country would be far better off without the troublesome colony that had proven to be such a drain on the financial and military resources of the Mother Country. (I guess you could say that the French lost the war, but won the peace!)

La Plus Ça Change...

During the five-year period between the end of fighting and the signing of the Treaty, Catholics were given the right to continue to practise their religion, and French-speaking settlers (habitants) were granted permission to remain on their land.

Because little of their day-to-day life changed dramatically during the first few years following the Conquest, the habitants weren't particularly upset by the fact that the colony had changed hands. If anything, the people resented France for abandoning the colony in its time of need and were grateful to the English for the improved economic prospects that accompanied the change of government.

A Blueprint for a Colony

Back in Britain, the Board of Trade was designing a blueprint for governing the new colony. Many of its plans for Quebec were based on the belief that it was just a matter of time before an influx of English-speaking Protestants began to offset the numbers of French-speaking Catholics in the colony, an assumption that would eventually prove to be a gross miscalculation.

The Board of Trade set out the specifics of its plans in the Proclamation of 1763. The Proclamation renamed New France "The Province of Quebec" and reduced its boundaries to the St. Lawrence Valley area, promised the establishment of British institutions and laws (in the hope of attracting American settlers), discouraged the traditional seigniorial system of land distribution in favour of a freehold system, and established a new set of rules for the fur trade. It also stressed the right of native peoples to make use of their land, which is why many present-day natives consider this document to be an early charter of rights. (This was very different from the policy exercised by the French, who, for the most part, had simply claimed the land as their own.)

Money Talks

On August 10, 1764, the mandate of the military government expired and a new civil government was ushered in. General James Murray, who had become commander at Quebec City following the death of Wolfe and who had served as the governor of that district during the military regime, became governor general of the entire colony.

Almost immediately, Murray came into conflict with members of the English-speaking commercial class in Montreal. These merchants were aggressive profiteers with strong ties to Britain. While they only numbered about 150 by 1770, they were clearly the most outspoken group in the new colony and honestly believed that the government was obliged to give their requests special consideration.

As you might expect, this attitude put them on a collision course with Murray, as well as his successor, Guy Carleton, both of whom tended to side with the French-speaking seigniors rather than the English-speaking merchants.

Almost from the beginning of his term of office, the merchants felt that Murray was unjustly and deliberately denying them their rights and opposing their interests. They felt he wasn't doing nearly enough for them, in terms of guarding their fur trade interests and providing them with the assembly that they had been promised. (Given the trouble they had already caused him, Murray was understandably reluctant to put any more power in their hands.)

In many ways, Murray was simply taking a realistic approach to the situation at hand. He had only 1500 soldiers to keep order in a colony that had 70,000 French-speaking Catholics, and was therefore reluctant to do anything that might upset the majority.

Wanted: English-Speaking Protestants

British dreams of repopulating Quebec with English-speaking Protestants were proving to be just that: mere dreams. An advertising campaign conducted in the Thirteen Colonies failed to attract an adequate number of settlers. Given the lousy weather, the large number of French-speaking Catholics, and the fact that the colony was being ruled by a military government that wouldn't allow elections, Quebec didn't have much to offer English-speaking Protestants who had already put down roots in the Thirteen Colonies.

Because the influx of English-speaking settlers was considerably less than the British government had hoped for, Murray began to conclude that the promises set out in the Proclamation simply could not be met. Many of the provisions of the Proclamation threatened to wreak serious injustice on the French-speaking people. Therefore, Murray's policy became one of protecting the "new subjects" (the French) against the overthrow of their familiar laws and customs while denying the "old subjects" (the English merchants) the rights that had been promised under the Proclamation, rights the merchants felt were owed to them because they were British subjects.

The merchants complained bitterly to the British government, petitioning for Murray to be replaced with a governor who was "acquainted with other maxims of government than military only." (Ouch!) Their pitch must have been persuasive because they succeeded in having Murray recalled in 1766.

The New Guy

Murray was succeeded by Sir Guy Carleton, a seasoned soldier and savvy politician. Initially, Carleton won the support of the English merchants by dismissing members of the pro-Murray faction from the governing council and relaxing some of the fur trade restrictions that were hampering the merchants' ability to profit from the fur trade. This initial action led the merchants to believe that they could count on their new governor for support. By the end of his first year in Quebec, however, Carleton concluded that Murray's take on the situation in the colonies really hadn't been that far off the mark.

The merchants soon realized that, like Murray before him, Carleton was more closely allied with the seigniors and the clergy than with them. What's more, he had refused to bring the long-awaited assembly into being (an assembly they expected to dominate because Catholics were ineligible to vote!).

The merchants weren't the only ones becoming restless, however. In 1769, impatient at the lack of progress in the colony, the British government issued a report calling for full implementation of the Proclamation of 1763, except for the provision that forbid Catholics from holding office.

Realizing that there was little hope of anglicizing Quebec and therefore that the provisions of the Proclamation were hopelessly out of touch with reality, Carleton recommended that the British government consider taking an entirely different tact. He suggested that the government reinstate French civil law, the seigniorial system of holding land, and the right of the Roman Catholic Church to collect the tithe from its followers. His rationale? Quebec was strategically important as a military base, and for the colony to remain secure, the British needed to earn the loyalty of their French subjects. (Carleton even went so far as to argue that Quebec was likely to become "the principal scene where the fate of America may be determined.") To earn the loyalty of the common folk, the government needed to win the support of the seigniors and clergy by reintroducing some of the social structures that had been present in New France.

Carleton's recommendations were accepted and, with the passage of the Quebec Act of 1774, England completely reversed its earlier policy of assimilation.

The Quebec Act was far-reaching and signified an abandonment of the British government's intent to govern all colonies in the British empire from the same blueprint. It gave Catholics in Quebec rights that they were denied in England (including the right to hold office), reestablished the seigniorial system, gave the Catholic Church permission to collect its tithe, and forbid the establishment of elected government. While the Act did contain some goodies for the English merchants—English criminal law was retained, a council to advise the governor was established, and the boundaries of Quebec were expanded considerably—they were furious about the ban on elected government.

Riots were held in Montreal and New England and, in Boston, the Sons of Liberty held rallies urging revolution. Clearly, rebels within the Thirteen Colonies felt that the measures in the Quebec Act hinted at what could be in store for them if they didn't get their own houses in order.

The Least You Need to Know

- ➤ The Proclamation of 1763 was designed to make Quebec a more attractive destination for the English-speaking settlers that the British government desperately hoped to attract to the colony.
- ➤ The Quebec Act of 1774 reversed many key provisions of the Proclamation of 1763. Its goal was to appease the French-speaking majority by addressing some of the grievances that had resulted from the Proclamation.

Chapter 9

The Giant Awakens (1763 to 1784)

In this chapter

- ➤ Canadian reaction to the American Revolutionary War
- ➤ The invasion of Canada
- ➤ The Loyalists

Now that the threat from the French had disappeared, residents of the Thirteen Colonies no longer needed Britain for security. As a result, they became less and less willing to accept any form of tyranny from the British government.

Between 1763 and 1774, the Thirteen Colonies repeatedly came into conflict with the Mother Country. When the British government asked the residents of these colonies to pay for a portion of the cost of running the garrisons that had protected them from the French during the recent Seven Years' War, animosity increased. The residents decried this as "taxation without representation," and widespread rioting broke out.

Following a series of uprisings, the British government decided it was time to get tough. They chose to make an example of

Massachusetts, placing the colony under martial law, suspending its assembly and constitution, and closing the port of Boston.

For the hot-blooded Patriots, who were infuriated by these acts, the final straw came when the Quebec Act was passed in 1774. They viewed the Act as yet another repressive piece of legislation from a distant imperial government, and feared it was simply a blueprint of what lay ahead for them if they remained a part of the British empire.

Taking Sides

Much as they would have liked to have sat on the sidelines and watched the British government battle it out with residents of the Thirteen Colonies, Canadians had little choice but to become involved. The Americans were eager to rally Canadian support to their cause. After all, there was power in numbers, and the last thing they wanted was a hostile British colony so close to their own border.

Governor Carleton was alarmed when he heard about American interest in getting Canadians involved in the rebellion. He immediately sought the help of local priests, who made a point of telling their parishioners just how anti-Catholic the American Patriots actually were.

Fortunately for Carleton, the American message met with only a lukewarm response in Quebec. While the French-speaking residents didn't feel any particular loyalty to Britain, they weren't about to embrace the Americans either. (For one thing, they disliked the Yankees and distrusted their "paper money"!) Probably the key motivation for staying loyal to the British, however, was purely economic: they realized that their livelihood in the fur trade depended on their relations with the British, and they weren't about to do anything to jeopardize those ties.

Still, while the residents of Quebec generally sided with the British during the ensuing conflict, they were certainly affected by the Patriotic spirit they wit-

Voice from the Past

"Your oaths, your religion lay upon you the unavoidable duty of defending your country and your king with all the strength you possess."

—Bishop Briand's message to Roman Catholics in Quebec, May 1775.

> **Main Event**
>
> 
>
> The American Revolution was significant for a number of reasons. In addition to breaking up the British Empire, it ushered in an era of revolution during which dominated peoples of the world demanded their freedom. It also helped to strengthen ties between Canada and Britain.

nessed in the American invaders. From 1776 onward, there would always be a "Patriot" movement in French Canada that sought protection for its own unique interests—in this case, its language and culture.

Maritime Response

The Americans were equally unsuccessful in attracting support in St. John's Island (later renamed Prince Edward Island), Newfoundland, and Nova Scotia.

St. John's Island was populated with recent arrivals from the British Isles. They had no desire to jeopardize their stake in the rich soil on which they had just settled, and therefore were not interested in siding with the Americans.

Newfoundlanders had similarly strong ties to Britain. Because permanent settlement in the area was forbidden, the majority of people who fished in Newfoundland maintained residences in Britain.

Nova Scotia was also reluctant to join the American cause. While the area had been populated by former New Englanders who tended to be more sympathetic to the cause of the Patriots than most Canadians at that time, they adopted a neutral stance almost immediately. Their reasoning was simple: they were miles away from the centres of discontent and didn't have the same grievances with the British government as the Thirteen Colonies did. What's more, the overwhelming British sea power in the area—Halifax was, after all, a British naval base—helped to keep any would-be rebels in line.

The Invasion of Canada

The Americans spent much of 1774 and 1775 trying to convince Canadians to join them. When that strategy failed, they decided that their only option was to beat them!

On June 27, 1775, the Continental Congress (the Patriots' decision-making body) agreed to an invasion of Canada. They believed that it was only a matter of time before the British government began recruiting Canadians to participate in border raids against them. As a result, the Congress began planning for a two-pronged strike that would see Montreal and Quebec City attacked simultaneously.

On September 6, an army of Patriots set out for Montreal. The initial commander became ill, however, and was forced to turn the command over to Richard Montgomery about 10 days later.

The Patriots encountered trouble at Fort Saint-Jean. It took the Patriots 55 days—until November 2—to take the Fort. They then began to advance to Montreal.

As Montgomery advanced, Carleton learned that Benedict Arnold was attacking Quebec City. He slipped out of Montreal and headed to Quebec City by boat, disguised as a farmer.

Montgomery occupied Montreal and then headed to Quebec City. Montreal was left in the hands of David Wooster of Connecticut. A rabid anti-Catholic, he encouraged his men to urinate on shrines and attack priests. Needless to say, this did little to endear him to the French-speaking Canadians who might otherwise have agreed to become allies of the American invaders.

At Quebec City, Montgomery joined Benedict Arnold and his forces. Arnold had arrived ahead of Montgomery, but hadn't had the strength of numbers required to take the city. The Patriotic forces in Quebec City still weren't in particularly good shape, even after Montgomery's arrival. The bitter cold, the hostility of the local population, and a high rate of desertions among his volunteers forced Montgomery to attempt an assault on December 31, even though his forces weren't what they should have been. In the end, Montgomery was killed, Arnold and 100 other men were wounded, and 400 rebels were captured.

Although the assault failed, the siege continued until May of 1776, when British General Burgoyne and 9000 men arrived. Faced with this show of British power, the Americans decided to retreat—and they kept on retreating. By June 19, all Canadian territory had been returned to British control. (The Patriots weren't particularly good losers, however; each year until the end of the American Revolution, they contemplated revenge on their neighbours to the north!)

While the British enjoyed these early successes, the tide ultimately began to turn against them. On July 4, 1776, the Continental Congress issued a Declaration of Independence. The British were forced to surrender at Saratoga (1777) and Yorktown (1781). After these two decisive losses, they began negotiating with the colonies to reach a settlement. At one point, Benjamin Franklin (a.k.a. the Father of Electricity) made a rather cheeky suggestion: that the British, in an effort to win back the goodwill of the United States, surrender Quebec as well. In the end, under the terms of the Treaty of 1783, the British agreed to cede some land south of the Great Lakes to their former American colonies and to recognize their independence. They managed to keep Quebec out of the deal.

The Coming of the Loyalists

Many Americans in the Thirteen Colonies remained loyal to Britain during the Revolutionary War. By 1783, however, persecution and charges of treason made it virtually impossible for them to remain in the United States.

While some migrated to Britain, the British West Indies, and Spanish Florida, the bulk of the 100,000 Loyalists leaving the United States chose to relocate in Nova Scotia and Quebec. In the spring and autumn of 1783 alone, British ships carried 30,000 Loyalists from New York to Nova Scotia.

You could hardly blame them for coming. The British government generously provided Loyalists migrating to Canada with land, provisions for the first year of settlement, and the tools needed to clear their land. The government also promised to compensate the Loyalists for the losses they had suffered when they abandoned their properties and businesses in the United States. While some found life on the frontier too difficult and returned to the United States or Britain, the majority of Loyalists decided to stay.

The Loyalists who settled in Nova Scotia located in the St. John Valley or along the Fundy shore. Feeling excluded from the centre of power in Halifax, the Loyalists asked the British government to establish a separate government for them. The imperial authorities were happy to oblige. They believed that small separate colonies were preferable to large monolithic ones. (Given their recent experiences, who could blame them?) As a result, New Brunswick and Cape Breton Island were established in 1784.

Voice from the Past

"And in as much as the said Associated Companies have for years past Nobly Contended for the support of that Constitution or Form of Government, under which they long have Enjoyed Happiness, and for which they have at least sacrifised [*sic*] their All. Tis Therefore their Earnest Wish and desire that His Excellency for their Better Government and Good order when they arrive at the Place destined for their Settlement would be pleased to establish among them a Form of Government As nearly similar to that which they Enjoyed in the Province of New York in the year of 1763 As the Remote situation of their new settlement from the seat of Government here will at Present Admitt of."

—Petition of the Associated Loyalists to his Excellency Lieutenant General Frederick Haldimand prior to their settlement at Kingston, January 1784.

The biggest problems caused by the influx of Loyalists occurred in Quebec. Right from the beginning, the British government was faced with a potential clash between the French and English peoples. The English-speaking Loyalists wanted the British government to provide them with the legal system and government institutions they had enjoyed in pre-Revolutionary America, but the government was understandably reluctant to do anything that might offend the French-speaking residents of Quebec. There was quite simply too much at risk.

The Least You Need to Know

- While Canadians attempted to remain neutral during the American Revolutionary War, they were drawn into the conflict when American forces decided to invade Canada.
- A large number of Loyalists migrated to Canada in the years following the war. They wanted the British government to provide them with the legal system and government institutions they had enjoyed in pre-Revolutionary America.

Chapter 10

A New Game Plan (1774 to 1791)

In this chapter

- Post-war grievances
- The Constitutional Act of 1791

It isn't easy to satisfy two groups of people with vastly different interests, but that's exactly what the British government tried to do in late 18th century Quebec.

The Quebec Act of 1774 had been written to satisfy the French-speaking majority and eliminate the grievances of the English-speaking minority. While the provisions designed to keep the French happy were obvious, what many in Quebec didn't realize at the time was that the Act actually gave local government (in this case, Governor Carleton and his cronies) the power to address some of the long-held grievances of the English merchants.

The citizens of Quebec weren't aware of these provisions because Carleton took whatever steps he could to hide this fact from them! In fact, he didn't even let the members of his council know about the discretionary powers they had been granted by the British government.

Carleton clearly believed that it was best to leave well enough alone: to continue to cater to the needs of the French majority and to ignore the protestations of the group he had long since dismissed as self-serving and overly aggressive—the English merchants.

Carleton's unwillingness to address the merchants' grievances led to a period of political struggle in Quebec that lasted throughout the American Revolutionary War. The merchants were not only upset by the fact that they were still being denied the representative government they had been promised under the Quebec Act, but they were also distressed because the war had interrupted the fur trade and other commercial activities.

By the end of the war, the tension between opposing groups in Quebec had escalated and Carleton's successor, Governor Frederick Haldimand, was forced to take action. During his office (1778 to 1784), he gave the English merchants some of what they had been asking for: *habeas corpus* (the right of an accused to be brought before a judge or court) and the right to have a jury present in a civil suit. Unfortunately, these reforms were too slow in coming to appease the English merchants, who once again campaigned to have the Quebec Act repealed.

He's Back...

The return of Carleton for a second term as governor in 1786 raised hopes among the so-called "French party" (a group of seigniors and other influential members of the French-speaking community) that they could once again count on his paternalism to uphold and extend their privileges.

But the times had changed, and Carleton had changed with them. (For one thing, he was no longer named Carleton; he'd recently been granted the title Lord Dorchester.) Dorchester's mission was to consolidate British colonial efforts in North America. Unfortunately, he had too much political baggage with him by the time he arrived. He was reluctant to break his ties with the old allies and supporters who were counting on him to defeat the reformers and the English party. At the same time, he saw the need for reform. Dorchester's indecisiveness left Quebec without the strong leadership it so desperately needed during the critical period from 1787 to 1790.

Post-War Griping

While the English merchants had been forced to keep their grievances to themselves throughout the American Revolutionary War, once the war ended, they were no longer willing to maintain their silence. Almost immediately, they began clamouring for change.

Fortunately, the recognition of American independence and the influx of Loyalists worked in their favour. Now that the colonial crisis was over, the British government could no longer justify its long-standing policy of inaction in the two Canadas. What's more, pressure from the Loyalist population for the same constitutional and legal rights that were enjoyed by other British subjects seemed to add weight to the merchants' cause.

In 1783 and 1784, the merchants petitioned the British government for the repeal of the Quebec Act, except for those portions of the Act that guaranteed the rights of the Catholic Church, upheld the use of the seigniorial system, and promised to provide an assembly and a legal system modelled after the British ones.

The merchants made one fatal error in their appeals: they claimed to speak for both French and English inhabitants of Quebec. Within a period of months, French leaders issued a petition repudiating the demands of the merchants and asking that the Quebec Act be upheld. The French believed that an assembly was simply a device that would be used to impose taxes on the province, and that the jury system would unjustly favour the rich over the poor.

The merchants also overstated their case in claiming to speak for the Loyalists. While eager to obtain representative government and a British-style legal system, the Loyalists were primarily concerned with economic matters at this time. Their main grievance concerned the seigniorial system. As a result, in 1784, the Loyalists petitioned the British government, demanding freehold grants, a system of English law, the establishment of local courts, and the creation of a separate government for the new settlements. In 1787, they reiterated their initial demands, and added a few new ones for good measure. They asked for aid in building roads, schools, and churches, and requested that restrictions be imposed on the importing of certain products from the United States, namely lumber and potash.

The Return of Carleton (a.k.a. Lord Dorchester)

Stats

Eighty-one per cent of the Loyalists coming to Canada after 1778 were farmers.

Imagine how the powers that be in Britain must have felt when presented with petition after petition from groups representing different interests within the province of Quebec. Their solution (in typical parliamentary fashion!) was to order a report.

They asked ex-Governor Dorchester and William Smith (the former chief justice of New York and present chief justice of Quebec) to suggest some solutions. Clearly, Dorchester was a poor choice for this task, because he was far too close to the problem. Not surprisingly, he was unable to come up with any concrete solutions. Smith wasn't much more successful than Dorchester, but he did make a rather noteworthy suggestion—and one that would prove truly prophetic. He suggested that London consider a federation of all of the colonies of British North America.

It was a great idea whose time hadn't come. The type of unifying forces at work in the United States simply weren't present in Canada. The colonies were separated by distance and divided by different interests. They had few economic ties and there was no common feeling of nationalism.

The British government itself was similarly unenthusiastic about the idea. Their experiences with the Americans had led them to conclude that when it came to managing colonies, small was better. They were understandably anxious to discourage any more outbreaks of colonial nationalism.

At the same time, however, they wanted to prevent Canada from being absorbed by the United States. If giving the English colonists representative government was what it would take to keep them happy, then that's what they were prepared to do. (Besides, they concluded, the colonists would be far more likely to accept taxes levied by a local government body in which they had a say than by the home government!)

Main Event

The Constitutional Act of 1791 divided Quebec into two provinces: Upper Canada and Lower Canada. It introduced changes to the structure of government while upholding many of the rights that French-speaking colonists had been granted under the Quebec Act of 1774.

Word for the Day

Bicameral means "two-chambered" and refers to a structure of government that consists of two groups of representatives.

The Constitutional Act of 1791: The Fine Print

The British government's solution to the growing dissent in Quebec was to pass the Constitutional Act of 1791.

The Act divided Quebec into two distinct provinces: Upper Canada (at the western end of the St. Lawrence River) and Lower Canada (at the eastern end of the St. Lawrence River). In Upper Canada, land would be granted in freehold (the owner would hold title to the land). In Lower Canada, the existing seigniorial system would be upheld, but new grants of land could be made in freehold, if the applicant wished.

The Act also spelled out a new system of government for the provinces—a bicameral legislature that provided for an appointed Legislative Council and an elected Assembly. Each province was to be granted an Assembly that would consist of not less than 16 members in Upper Canada and not less than 50 members in Lower Canada. The Legislative Council—the upper house—would be made up of at least 7 members in Upper Canada and 15 members in Lower Canada. The governor was given the right to veto bills or submit them for approval to the home government, if he saw fit, and London retained the right to overturn measures that had received the governor's assent, if necessary.

The British government also considered creating a Canadian system of hereditary titles that would be modelled on the British system. While this proposal was the source of much amusement in Britain, it was ultimately dropped.

The Act also addressed the issue of the Catholic Church and the introduction of English civil law. The rights of the Catholic Church were reaffirmed, but a new provision provided for the setting aside of land equal to one-seventh of future land grants for the support of a Protestant clergy. Also, the provinces were left to make their own decisions concerning the introduction of English civil law.

While the British government upheld the rights of their French-speaking subjects in the Act, they were simply biding their time until the French could be gradually assimilated into the Canadian population.

Reaction to the Act

Given the conflicting interests of the various factions within the province, it's hardly surprising that the Act met with mixed reviews.

The English merchants were opposed to the splitting of Quebec into Upper Canada and Lower Canada because it once again left them as an isolated minority in a largely French-speaking province.

The French-speaking residents, on the other hand, were generally pleased with the Act because it guaranteed that French civil law would remain in force, the clergy would retain the rights acknowledged by the Quebec Act, and the existing seigniorial system would remain untouched. They also welcomed the creation of Upper and Lower Canada.

Unfortunately for future generations, the Act didn't solve all of the colony's problems. It created two provinces divided along linguistic and religious lines, setting the stage for centuries of conflict between the two cultures.

The Least You Need to Know

- During the early 1780s, English-speaking merchants in Quebec petitioned the British government for the repeal of the Quebec Act. The British government asked Lord Dorchester (a.k.a. ex-Governor Carleton) to report on the situation in the province.
- In an attempt to balance the needs of the French-speaking majority and the new English-speaking settlers, the British government passed the Constitutional Act of 1791, which divided Quebec into two provinces: Upper Canada and Lower Canada. It upheld many of the provisions of the Quebec Act that angered the English merchants.

Chapter 11

Same Problem, New War (1783 to 1818)

In this chapter

- The War of 1812
- The Treaty of Ghent
- The aftermath of the War

Relations between the United States and Britain were tense during the years following the American Revolution, putting Canada in a rather difficult predicament.

By virtue of geography, she found herself situated next to a restless giant that seemed determined to flex its national muscles. To make matters worse, Canada's small population and scattered patterns of development only added to the problem. Clearly, she was extremely vulnerable to an attack from her neighbour to the south.

With Friends Like These...

The fact that the British were doing their best to antagonize the Americans only added to the problem. They refused to vacate the frontier forts in the northwest, despite their commitment to do so under

Main Event

Jay's Treaty, concluded by American Chief Justice John Jay and signed on November 19, 1794, was an attempt to prevent the volatile situation in the northwest from erupting. Under the terms of the Treaty, the British agreed to vacate the frontier forts and to refer outstanding boundary disputes to a joint American–British commission that would seek to resolve them. Because the British were still allowed to enter the west and trade with the natives there, the Americans continued to suspect them of encouraging the natives to resist American attempts at expansion. As a result, the Treaty only served to delay—not avoid—another conflict between the two sides.

the terms of the Treaty of 1783, a situation the Americans interpreted as further evidence that the British were actively encouraging natives in the area to attack American settlers. They had also begun seizing American merchant ships and forcing American sailors into service in the British war against Napoleonic France (common practice in that day and age, but despicable nonetheless).

The British also did their share of finger-pointing. They complained that the Americans had also breached the Treaty of 1783 by failing to pay pre-Revolutionary debts owed to British creditors and by refusing to compensate the Loyalists for property confiscated during the Revolution.

1812 Overture

As had been the case many times in the past, problems in Europe began to take their toll in the Americas. The Wars of the French Revolution had been fanned into the Napoleonic Wars, and Britain and France once again found themselves on opposite sides of the dispute. Unable to strike a decisive victory on the European playing field, the two countries began attacking the commerce of noncombatant nations, including the United States. After the British repeatedly seized American vessels attempting to enter French ports, U.S. President Thomas Jefferson retaliated by passing the Non-Importation Act, which prohibited the importation of many British goods.

On June 22, 1807, the crisis heated up even further. The British warship *Leopard* fired on the U.S. frigate *Chesapeake* off the coast of Virginia, spurring Jefferson to pass the Embargo Act of December 22, 1807, prohibiting all exports to Europe and restricting imports from Great Britain.

Still other forces were pushing the two nations to the brink of war. Ongoing problems with natives in the northwest convinced the Americans that the British were actively encouraging the natives to delay American expansion in the area. As a result, settlers in the American west began to believe that the solution to their ongoing security problems would be to eliminate the British presence in the area by conquering Canada.

Enter the "War Hawks"

The "War Hawks," a group of land-hungry rednecks spearheaded by Republican Henry Clay of Kentucky, were able to use the settlers' fears to their advantage. They were eager to go to war with Britain, and not just to gain relief from what they perceived to be British-backed hostile natives. They also thought that such a battle, which would pit them against Britain's ally in the Napoleonic Wars, Spain, might enable them to acquire Spanish Florida (a large tract of land extending westward from Florida to the Mississippi River).

U.S. President James Madison initially ignored the War Hawks' calls for war. His government relied on a series of diplomatic measures until June 19, 1812, when, faced with a tough re-election campaign, he agreed to ask Congress for a declaration of war.

Ironically, by this time, one of the causes of the war had already been resolved. On June 16, the British had agreed to stop forcing American sailors to participate on their behalf in the war with France.

This Means War

Once war was declared, strategists on both sides of the border sprung into action.

The Americans began planning for a three-pronged invasion of Canada via Lake Champlain, the Niagara frontier, and Detroit. They did not contemplate an invasion of the Atlantic provinces, as British sea power in that area was a deterrent.

While their plans may have looked good on paper, when it came time to execute them, the Americans began to flounder. Instead of coordinating their campaign operations (that is, attacking the line of communications along the St. Lawrence River that had served the Canadians well in previous conflicts and obtaining support from all U.S. states), the Americans became unduly preoccupied with land campaigns in the western portion of Upper Canada.

They also wrongly concluded that former Americans living in Canada would rally to their cause. Thanks to some brilliant strategizing by British General Isaac Brock, the opposite proved true. A few quick and decisive victories on the part of the joint Canadian and British forces managed to stifle any discontent in Upper Canada and convince those settlers who might otherwise have remained neutral to rally to the Canadian cause.

These early victories at Detroit, Niagara, and in the area around the Great Lakes largely resulted from Brock's ability to move his small forces by water. Not surprisingly, both sides became acutely aware of the importance of water transport in this conflict and began to devote considerable attention to shipbuilding. The Americans gained the advantage in the Great Lakes area during the spring and summer of 1813, capturing York, Fort George, and then the entire Niagara Peninsula.

More Tug of War

At that point, the situation of the British went from bad to worse. They suffered significant losses on the Great Lakes—mainly due to an unfortunate shortage of cannons—and were eventually forced to withdraw from the western portion of Upper Canada.

Then, the tide of war turned again. The British defeated the Americans in a daring nighttime attack at Stoney Creek and won a decisive victory at Beaver Dams. After a series of additional victories during the fall of that year, the British managed to go on the offensive, raiding and burning every American village along the Niagara River, reaching as far south as Buffalo.

The remaining months of the war were basically a stalemate, although the British forces under Major General Robert Ross did manage to burn down the White House and the Capitol, forcing President Madison and his government to flee. By the end of 1814, both sides were sick of the war and prepared to conclude that while each had been

Real Life

Laura Secord (1775–1868) overheard enemy officers who were billeted in her house planning a surprise attack on the Canadian forces at Beaver Dams. She set out at 4:00 a.m. on June 22, 1813, travelling 30 kilometres through swamps, creeks, and forests before she found the troops stationed along the Niagara Escarpment. As a result of her warning, the Canadians and their Six Nations allies brilliantly defeated the larger American forces and captured 400 of their men.

Main Event

The Battle of New Orleans—the final battle in the War of 1812—happened *after* the war had ended. Operating without benefit of cellular phones and other modern conveniences, both sides remained in the dark about the signing of the Treaty of Ghent until after the battle was over.

able to carry out strong defensive campaigns, neither had the forces required to mount a successful invasion.

End Game

The war officially ended with the signing of the Treaty of Ghent on December 24, 1814. When the resulting armistice took effect in February of 1815, it was clear that there had been no winner. For all intents and purposes, both sides had simply agreed to a return to the status quo. The key issues that had brought the two nations to war in 1812—maritime rights and native relations—were largely ignored.

The two sides agreed to send all outstanding issues to a joint commission, which ultimately helped to arbitrate some long-standing border disputes. In 1818, the two sides agreed that the eastern portions of New Brunswick and Maine would be divided by the St. Croix River (an inland boundary was not established until 1842), that the 49th Parallel should serve as the U.S.–Canada border between Lake of the Woods and the Rockies, and that Oregon should be jointly governed for the foreseeable future.

Another important agreement was signed a year earlier. The Rush-

Bagot Agreement of 1817 was designed to prevent a recurrence of hostilities. The Agreement limited each side's armed vessels to the number needed for policing and protecting its shores against smugglers.

The Aftermath of the War

While war brought prosperity to those areas of the British colonies that weren't directly involved in battle, other areas were devastated. To make matters worse, the British government was unreasonably slow in compensating those who had suffered property losses.

While there was clearly no "winner," both Canada and the United States emerged from the war with a heightened sense of national pride. Americans viewed the war as nothing short of a "second war of independence," while Canadians were proud of the way they had held up against a vastly superior enemy that—in their opinion, at least—had been solely motivated by vindictiveness and greed.

However, Canadians' feelings of pride were somewhat tempered by concerns about what was to come. They realized that the giant who had threatened to swallow their country hadn't disappeared, it had just gone back to sleep.

> **Stats**
>
> 
>
>
> The "Upper Canada Preserved" medal—issued by the Loyal and Patriotic Society of Upper Canada during the War of 1812—featured a British lion preventing an American eagle from seizing a Canadian beaver. When push came to shove and the government realized how much it would cost to award all the medals earned, it decided it couldn't afford to proceed and no medals were actually handed out.

The Least You Need to Know

- The War of 1812 was sparked by American fears that Britain was encouraging natives in the northwest to attack settlers.
- While neither side won, both countries emerged with a heightened sense of national pride.
- The Treaty of Ghent (signed in 1814), which ended the war, represented a return to the status quo.

Chapter 12

Rebels with a Cause (1830 to 1841)

In this chapter

- The causes of the Rebellion of 1837
- The Durham mission
- The first general election

The 1830s were a great time to be living in Upper or Lower Canada, provided, of course, that you were a member of the ruling elite.

In Lower Canada, members of the so-called Château Clique (a high-ranking group of government officials) worked closely with members of the English merchant class and the Anglican hierarchy to prevent the implementation of any truly representative form of government. By this time, the members of the old seigniorial class had fallen out of vogue; while they still played a role in the functioning of the Legislative Council and the Executive Council, they were by no means power brokers. They lacked the clout and connections required to make their voices heard.

The situation in Upper Canada was quite similar, where members of the so-called Family Compact dominated political affairs. Drawn from the administrative and professional classes and possessing strong ties to the Anglican Church, members of the Family Compact believed in "the British tie, a balanced government, and an established church." They were strongly in favour of efforts to promote the province's economic development, and could be narrow and vindictive when dealing with any challenge to their authority.

> **Stats**
>
> 
>
> In 1832, timber ships travelling to and from Europe brought cholera victims to America. A quarantine station at Grosse Île in the St. Lawrence River held 98,000 victims, but enough infected persons passed inspection to spread the disease to every Canadian village along the river. One of every ten residents of the St. Lawrence Valley died from the disease.

Both the Château Clique and the Family Compact maintained a monopoly on public office through a series of patronage appointments. Filling vacant government positions with like-minded individuals allowed them to block unfavourable legislation brought forward by the Assembly (the elected body) and to uphold the privileged positions held by the Anglican Church, the provinces' commercial and financial interests, and large land spectators. They expected the governor to rely on them for advice and support, and were quick to complain to the home government in Britain should the governor prove to be insufficiently deferential to their status and position.

Not surprisingly, popular opposition to these ruling elites began to build in each province. Reformers, who held the majority in the Assembly, were unable to obtain the legislative changes they sought because members of the Legislative Council and the Executive Council—who, coincidentally, tended to be friends of the ruling elite—could veto any legislation that they did not support. As a result, Reformers in both provinces began to clamour for a more democratic form of government. Unfortunately, the British government was not willing to pay much attention to their grievances until after the situation had reached crisis proportions.

Religious Discrimination

One of the key sources of discontent in both provinces was religious discrimination. Many people resented the special privileges that had been

Real Life

The urge for reform was not confined to Upper and Lower Canada. Reform fever also swept through the Maritimes during the 1830s. Joseph Howe, editor and publisher of the *Nova Scotian*, was the voice of dissent in Nova Scotia. Howe was tried for libel after he published an article critical of the government of the day, but his powerful speeches to the jury allowed him to win the case.

After being elected to the Assembly in 1836, Howe began demanding that Nova Scotians be allowed to enjoy the same political rights as Englishmen. His *Twelve Resolutions*, passed by the Assembly in 1837, criticized the government and recommended the disestablishment of the Anglican Church.

given to the Anglican Church. The Anglican Church was the only Protestant sect to be given the right to solemnize marriage. What's more, it was doing its best to monopolize the emerging field of education by establishing a series of Anglican educational institutions.

At the heart of the controversy, however, was the issue of the clergy reserves. Established under the provisions of the Constitutional Act of 1791, the clergy reserves were designed to provide for the support and maintenance of the Protestant clergy. The problem was that the Anglican Church wanted to be the sole beneficiary of these revenues, something that other Protestant sects were understandably unwilling to accept. While there wasn't a lot of money at stake, Strachan's insensitive handling of the issue kept it alive far longer than necessary.

The Reformers felt that the clergy reserves needed to be secularized for the good of the province. Because these reserves amounted to one-seventh of recent land grants and consisted of 200-acre tracts scattered throughout the provinces, they were becoming an economic nuisance, preventing the consolidation of settlement and, in some cases, the construction of roads. In 1827, an imperial Act allowed for the sale of one quarter of the lands in question. While this solved the economic problems posed by the clergy reserves, it failed to determine who would ultimately receive the revenues.

The Link Between Government and Business

Another source of unrest—and one that was particularly acute in Upper Canada—concerned the strong connection between business and government. Reformers believed that the government was spending money to further the position of the merchants rather than the public good. The founding of the Bank of Upper Canada (in which the government itself held an interest) and the scandal surrounding the construction of the Welland Canal did nothing to put these fears to rest.

Racial Conflict

In Lower Canada, the emerging discontent began to take on a racial character. French Canadians were determined to be recognized as members of a separate and distinct community with their own language, religion, and laws. They were interested in blocking any measure that might increase the strength of the English population, speaking out passionately against measures designed to promote the migration of additional English-speaking settlers as well as the Canada Tenures Act of 1825, which allowed proprietors to change from the traditional seigniorial system of landholding to one of freehold tenure.

While the French were clearly more interested in building a stable rural society than an expanding commercial state, the English were anxious to foster the province's economic development. In the end, the English ended up with a virtual monopoly over transportation, commerce, and banking.

The Seeds of Rebellion

It was in Lower Canada that the political divisions were to emerge first. When the need for additional revenue arose in 1805, the government asked that it be raised through a land tax. The Assembly rejected this proposal, suggesting a tax on imports instead. The merchants were indignant at what they perceived to be an attack on their livelihoods. As racial tensions intensified, the French founded their own journal, *Le Canadien*, which had the slogan, "Our language, our institutions, our laws."

By the end of the War of 1812, a charismatic member of the Assembly of Lower Canada was rallying support to the cause of reform.

Louis Joseph Papineau, a lawyer and former seignior, sought major reforms to the existing system of government, including an elected legislative council. In 1834, his Ninety-Two Resolutions were passed by the Assembly. They listed the key grievances and demands of his supporters: their desire for control over the government's revenue, their demands for an elected council, their insistence that changes to the system of land tenure not be permitted, and their call for the abolition of the British American Land Company (an organization whose mandate was to bring English-speaking settlers to the area). The Resolutions also made some rather damning personal accusations against the leading officials of the day and threatened rebellion.

At about the same time, the Reformers in Upper Canada were moving in a similar direction. When a would-be land developer, Robert Gourlay, distributed a questionnaire in various townships seeking information that would help him to obtain a large land grant and encourage immigration to the area, he was flooded with complaints about the haphazard land system and the lack of internal improvements. Gourlay organized a convention of township delegates in 1818 so they could discuss ways to petition the government for redress. Needless to say, his actions alarmed the members of the Family Compact. Never ones to let democracy get in their way, however, the members of the Family Compact secured legislation making such conventions illegal, arrested Gourlay, and had him expelled from the province.

In 1834, a group of Reformers who had been elected to the Assembly prepared a report detailing their grievances about the government of the day. These grievances included the lavish system of patronage, the poor handling of the clergy reserves issue, their frustration with ongoing economic abuses, and the fact that the Executive Council was completely unwilling to heed the will of the people. Not surprisingly, the report echoed what by that time had become a repeated call for an elected legislative council.

Cracks in the Movement

Over time, the Reformers in Lower Canada began to split into factions. Papineau's glorification of the American Revolution alienated the more moderate followers of John Neilson, who were hoping for constitutional reform along British lines. French Canadian moderates were similarly unimpressed with Papineau's increasingly pro-American stance; they feared that French language and culture would be lost if they were to partner with the United States. The clergy were also distressed, upset by the repeated threats of violence and the anti-clerical tone used by some of Papineau's younger followers.

The movement in Upper Canada experienced a similar split. While William Lyon Mackenzie advocated the introduction of an American system of government, Robert Baldwin and his more conservative followers hoped to see the introduction of the full British cabinet system.

From Bad to Worse

The tense situation in the two Canadas was heightened by the depression of 1837. Exports fell, prices declined, and the Bank of Upper Canada was forced to call in its loans. Bankruptcies, unemployment, and commercial paralysis resulted.

While the situation was bad enough in Upper Canada, it was even worse in Lower Canada. Overpopulation in the region of the old seigniories combined with the progressive exhaustion of the soil led to a decline in agricultural productions. A wheat fly plague in 1831 further reduced the harvest, leaving no surplus for export and reducing the inhabitants' overall purchasing power.

Real Life

William Lyon Mackenzie, publisher of a newspaper called *Colonial Advocate*, became the voice of Reformers in Upper Canada. He was quick to attack the merchants, churchmen, and high-ranking government officials who dominated the life of the province.

In 1826, the office of *Colonial Advocate* was attacked and its presses were destroyed by a mob led by sons of Family Compact members. Mackenzie managed to obtain damages that more than compensated him for his loss, and he used the publicity surrounding the incident to increase his political stature. In 1828, he was elected to the Assembly, representing the citizens of York.

By midsummer, both Papineau and Mackenzie were calling for a full-fledged revolt. Reformers in Toronto issued a virtual declaration of independence and farmers began to practise military drills.

The actual conflict started in Lower Canada. On November 7, 1837, a brawl between rival French and English organizations in Montreal showed how dangerous the situation had become. In an effort to prevent further trouble, Papineau and some of his followers left Montreal a few days later. The authorities concluded that they had left to find additional troops, issued warrants for their arrest, and pulled together some volunteer forces of their own. Papineau fled to the United States, but the rebellion continued without him. On November 25, a military force crushed a hastily assembled group of rebels at St. Charles, and in December, a gathering at St. Eustache was dispersed by 2000 troops. The rebellion in Lower Canada was virtually at an end.

The rebellion in Upper Canada was precipitated by the outbreak in Lower Canada. A group of farmers gathered at Montgomery's Tavern (just north of present-day Eglinton Avenue and Yonge Street in Toronto) and—under Mackenzie's leadership—began planning to capture the capital and overthrow the government. While their plans were doomed, the group shot itself in the foot when it decided at the last minute to move the date of attack ahead by three days to December 4. When they marched into town, just a few hundred strong, they were greeted by a force of 1000 volunteers. A few shots were fired, scattering the insurgents. Mackenzie fled across the border and tried to organize an invasion with the assistance of U.S. sympathizers, but aside from a few minor border raids, his plans never really got off the ground. By the end of 1838, the prospects for a rebellion had fizzled out entirely.

Stats

Nearly 46 per cent of rebels in Upper Canada were farmers, and 44 per cent were young men between the ages of 20 and 30. The majority of them were either American-born or the offspring of American parents.

The Durham Mission

While the rebellion failed, it helped to convince the British government that it needed to take drastic action to resolve the long-simmering unrest in its North American colonies. The government appointed John George Lambton, the first Earl of Durham, to investigate the situation and recommend possible solutions.

Durham was the right man for the job. Known as "Radical Jack" because of his exceptionally liberal views, he disagreed with the common sentiment in the Mother Country that the colonies were a burden. He believed that the colonies could become valuable outlets for British goods, and that the self-government they so obviously wanted was not incompatible with the principles of imperial unity that the British held so dear.

Durham believed that the racial problems in Lower Canada overshadowed all other issues. "I expected to find a conflict between a government and a people," he reported to London. "I found two nations warring in the bosom of a single state." He felt that the only solution to these problems was to extinguish any remaining hopes of French nationalism and to assimilate the French population as quickly as possible.

Word for the Day

Members of the U.S.-based *Hunters and Chasers of the Eastern Frontier* supported Mackenzie's and Papineau's calls for revolution in Canada. In autumn of 1838, a convention in Cleveland went so far as to organize a republican government for Canada, set up a bank, and raise an army for invasion. Nothing much came of these efforts and by the end of 1838, there was no more trouble along the border.

Durham wrote a series of reports to the British government, spelling out his suggested reforms. He criticized the system of land

Voice from the Past

"I entertain no doubts as to the national character which must be given to Lower Canada; it must be that of the British Empire; that of the great race which must, in the lapse of no long period of time, be predominant over the whole of the North American continent....

"If the population of Upper Canada is rightly estimated at 400,000 the English inhabitants of Lower Canada at 150,000 and the French at 450,000, the union of the two provinces would not only give a clear English majority but one which would be increased every year by the influence of English emigration."

—Lord Durham

Stats

By 1839, Upper Canada had a £1.2 million debt, most of it incurred during the construction of canals. Its annual deficit of £75,000 exceeded the province's entire annual revenue. The unification of the two Canadas led to a pooling of their debts, forcing Canada East (Lower Canada), which had a debt of just £95,000, to share the massive debt load of Canada West (Upper Canada).

grants in Upper Canada and the survival of feudal tenures in Lower Canada. He found fault with the justice system in Lower Canada and the powerful hold of the oligarchy over political life. And he called for a comprehensive system of primary education that would be jointly financed through local taxation and provincial grants.

His reports contained three key recommendations: that the two Canadas be unified and renamed Canada East and Canada West, that responsible government be implemented, and that Britain limit its involvement in colonial affairs to imperial rather than local matters.

Response to Durham's recommendations was mixed. The Reformers were pleased with the report, the Family Compact was stung by its criticisms, and the French were outraged by what they perceived to be a series of renewed attacks on their race.

In the end, the British government failed to carry out Durham's recommendations as fully as he would have liked. While they agreed to unify the two Canadas, they gave Canada East and Canada West equal representation in the Assembly, thereby perpetuating the situation of political deadlock. What's more, they refused to grant responsible government and they failed to keep their hands out of local affairs.

The First General Election

The union of the two Canadas was proclaimed on February 10, 1841, and the capital was established as Kingston. The general election that followed was among the most violent in Canadian history, with several people being killed in riots and many more being intimidated at the polls. The level of violence was understandable: the election took place in a time before secret ballots, when people voted by publicly stating which candidate they supported.

To make things worse, the new governor, Charles Poulett Thomson (Lord Sydenham), seemed determined to stir up trouble. He placed the polling stations for French candidates in the heart of English neighbourhoods and hired unemployed canal workers to harass potential voters!

In the end, the new Assembly was split among the various political factions and special interest groups. So while the Rebellion of 1837 was now behind them, considerable turbulence still lay ahead for Canada East and Canada West.

> **Stats**
>
> 
>
>
> The results of the election of 1841 show how fragmented the political scene truly was: 34% of those elected were moderate reformers, 28% were so-called "Sydenham men" (supporters of the colonial government), 24% were followers of Papineau, 8% were members of the Family Compact, and 6% were supporters of Baldwin's Ultra Reformers.

The Least You Need to Know

- ➤ The Rebellion of 1837 resulted from long-standing problems, such as religious discrimination, government corruption, and the conflicting desires of French- and English-speaking Canadians.
- ➤ Lord Durham recommended that the two Canadas be unified and renamed Canada East and Canada West, that responsible government be implemented, and that Britain limit its involvement in colonial affairs to imperial rather than local matters. He also stressed the importance of assimilating the French to avoid ongoing racial conflict.

Chapter 13

Friends and Neighbours (1840 to 1865)

In this chapter

- Boundary disputes and U.S. "Manifest Destiny"
- The Annexation Movement of 1849
- The Treaty of Reciprocity in 1854
- Canadian and American relations during the American Civil War

Throughout the first half of the 18th century, relations between Canada and its neighbour to the south were anything but friendly. At best, they were strained and characterized by mutual suspicion.

Just as Canadians were constantly fearful of the possibility of an American invasion, Americans were sceptical about Canada's supposedly neutral stance. They didn't like the fact that geography compelled them to share a border with a colony that was affiliated with their former Mother Country, a country with which they had recently been at war.

Border Disputes

Canada and the United States found themselves embroiled in a series of border disputes during the first half of the 18th century.

One of the hottest disputes concerned the boundary between New Brunswick and Maine. In 1818, in the aftermath of the War of 1812, Canada and the United States had agreed that New Brunswick and Maine would be divided by the St. Croix River. However, the St. Croix River didn't travel far enough inland to completely divide the territory. Rather than deal with the issue during the volatile post-war period, the two countries chose to leave the issue on the back burner, which they did for more than two decades.

By the early 1840s, however, the issue needed to be dealt with. Residents from both countries were moving into disputed areas, and timber in those areas was being cut under licences from both New Brunswick and Maine.

In 1842, negotiations between Lord Ashburton (the British envoy) and Daniel Webster (the American Secretary of State) resolved the dispute by giving Britain slightly less than half of the territory in question. The negotiations also resolved a border dispute involving a chunk of land between the St. Lawrence River and the Lake of the Woods. To the dismay of many Canadians, Ashburton handed over a large triangle of land west of Lake Superior without much protest.

Other border disputes were also causing problems. While Britain and the United States had agreed that the 49th Parallel would define the boundary to the Rockies, they had yet to decide on the boundary through Oregon (the western territory that included present-day British Columbia). Up to this point, the territory in question had been jointly occupied by the two countries. In 1846, the two countries agreed to extend the 49th Parallel as far as the coast and give Vancouver Island to the British.

These boundary disputes taught Canadians two important lessons. First of all, they learned that they needed to have a stronger voice in external as well as internal affairs. Secondly, they realized that if they were to retain the land above the 49th Parallel, they had to ensure that it was occupied—and soon. Otherwise, this land was likely to be swallowed up by an American public gone mad with ideas of Manifest Destiny.

Word for the Day

In 1845, *New York Post* editor John O'Sullivan wrote: "It is our *manifest destiny* to overspread and to possess the whole of the continent which Providence has given us for the development of the great experiment of liberty and federated self-government entrusted to us." Fortunately for Canada, most of America's expansion efforts were directed at present-day Texas and California.

Voice from the Past

"Between the abandonment by England of her former system of protection to Colonial produce, and the refusal of the United States to trade with us on a footing of reciprocity, Canada, to use the old proverb, is between the devil and the deep sea, and...we can see no way to get out of the scrape but by going to prosperity, since prosperity will not come to us."

—An excerpt from the *Annexation Manifesto* of 1849.

If You Can't Beat 'Em...

By the mid-18th century, some groups within Canada had decided that their best strategy in dealing with the United States would be to become a part of it through annexation. These pro-American sentiments reached their peak in 1849.

The Annexation Movement of 1849 was driven by a group of English merchants in Canada East who were dissatisfied with the results of the union of the two Canadas. They felt that the French still possessed far too much political power and were discouraged because the economic upturn they had been waiting for simply hadn't happened.

On October 11, 1849, they issued an Annexation Manifesto, which stated their desire to become a part of the United States. They believed that annexation would lead to higher farm prices, lower import costs, new sources of credit, and access to American capital (something that seemed critical for the growth of Canadian-based transportation systems and industries). They also believed annexation would provide Canada with a stronger political voice than it presently enjoyed in its colonial relationship to Britain, and would help stamp out the fires of

French nationalism that kept igniting. In short, annexation appeared to be the cure for all that ailed Canada.

Almost immediately, the English merchant group found themselves some rather strange bedfellows. While their reasons for supporting annexation were quite different from those expressed by the English-speaking merchants, a group of young French-speaking radicals believed that annexation to the United States was not necessarily a bad thing. In fact, they argued, French-speaking citizens would be guaranteed better protections under the U.S. system of government than they presently enjoyed under the British system.

While this rather articulate group of young people attracted a great deal of attention, for the most part, French Canadians were opposed to annexation. Support from Canada West was similarly lacking. Even the Americans were lukewarm to the idea, fearing that they would add to their rather precarious problems at home if they were to antagonize the South by adding more territory to the north. Not surprisingly, by the early 1850s, the idea of annexation had largely fallen out of fashion.

Give and Take

While Canadians were no longer talking about the possibility of annexation, they were still looking for a special type of relationship with the United States. What they were now proposing was reciprocity, a form of "free trade" between the two countries.

William Hamilton Merritt, a milling and transportation magnate, is credited with starting the talk about reciprocity in 1846. He felt that Canadian companies such as his would benefit from access to the larger American market.

The new governor of Canada, Lord Elgin, also supported the idea, but in his case, for political reasons. He believed that closer economic ties between the U.S. and Canada would increase the overall level of prosperity, thereby increasing Canadians' satisfaction with their colonial status and reducing the risk of annexation.

Stats

During the years that the Treaty of Reciprocity was in effect (1854 to 1866), trade between the U.S. and British North America tripled.

Despite interest on the Canadian side of the border, initially there was little interest from the Americans. In fact, a vocal group in the northern United States was far more anxious to exclude Canadian companies from their market than to gain access to the limited Canadian market.

What ultimately brought the Americans to the negotiating table was...fish. In recent years, the two countries had experienced an escalating series of crises over territorial fishing rights off the coasts of Newfoundland and Labrador. In 1852, the British sent a naval force to guard its fishing rights, while the United States sent a warship to protect its fishermen. Clearly, the right to fish in the cod-rich waters off the Maritimes was something that Canada had and that the United States wanted.

The only way that the British negotiators handling the talks were able to get the Americans to agree to reciprocity was by putting the issue of fishing rights on the table. In the end, under the terms of the Treaty of Reciprocity (signed in 1854), Americans gained access to all fisheries north of 36° latitude as well as the right to use the canals along the St. Lawrence River. Canadians gained access to Lake Michigan. Both countries gained free entry to each other's markets for principal natural products such as farm produce, fish, timber, and coal. (A few other goodies were thrown in to appease the American South, such as turpentine, rice, and raw tobacco.)

Stats

During the American Civil War, British colonies provided a safe haven to $30 million worth of escaped slaves. This was a sore point with southerners, who resented this loss of their "property."

Anything But Civil

The outbreak of the American Civil War once again changed the nature of relations between Canada and the United States. The atmosphere went from lukewarm to outright chilly.

Americans in the north were concerned that the British might intervene in the war. They had already expressed their sympathy for the southern cause on a number of occasions, and had even gone so far as to consider granting formal recognition to the southern Confederate government.

Their sense of outrage at what they perceived to be British interference in an internal U.S. matter extended to Canada. They ignored the fact that most

Canadians were supportive of the North's position and that tens of thousands of Canadians had joined the armies of the North. (It didn't help, of course, that the South began plotting to use Canada as an entry point from which to attack the North, or that members of the Canadian manufacturing class talked about how they might benefit from the destruction of the U.S. industrial north.)

Tension between Canada and the United States escalated to the point where it looked as if Canada might once again be invaded. Britain brought in 15,000 reinforcements to safeguard its colony.

At the same time, opposition to the Treaty of Reciprocity was gaining strength. In January 1865, the United States government approved a resolution demanding that the Treaty be cancelled. A year later, it was allowed to expire.

Pro-annexation sentiments once again began to emerge. As a result, many Canadians began to believe that the collapse of reciprocity would lead their country into the arms of the Americans.

The Least You Need to Know

- A series of boundary disputes during the first half of the 18th century taught Canadians that they needed to have stronger control over external affairs and to occupy all lands above the 49th Parallel to safeguard their territory against American expansion.
- In 1849, certain groups of Canadians spoke out in favour of annexation (that is, having Canada join the United States). Americans were less than enthusiastic about the idea.
- Americans were similarly reluctant to discuss reciprocity (a form of "free trade" between the two countries) until Canadians agreed to include valuable fishing rights to sweeten the deal. The result was the Treaty of Reciprocity in 1854.
- The American Civil War further strained relations between Canada and the United States. At one point, it looked as if Canada might be invaded by hostile U.S. forces.

Part 3
The Business of Nation-Building

Sir John A. Macdonald was a man with a mission. More than anyone else, he was responsible for guiding the country towards Confederation and holding it together during its turbulent first quarter century.

If it hadn't been for Macdonald's single-minded vision and his extraordinary political skills, Canadian history might have followed an entirely different path. While John A. was certainly no saint—as his opponents would have gleefully declared at the time!—he was just what Canada needed during its formative years: a man with the guts and determination to make Confederation work, no matter what the price.

Chapter 14

From Sea to Shining Sea (1850 to 1867)

In this chapter

- The forces leading to Confederation
- The Charlottetown Conference and the Quebec Conference
- Pro- and anti-Confederation sentiment
- The threat from south of the border
- The British North America Act

By the early 1860s, certain colonies within British North America were beginning to consider the idea of a federation. In the Atlantic colonies, there was talk of a possible Maritime union, while in Canada, there was discussion of a much wider union—one that would bring together all of British North America.

There were many reasons for this sudden interest in federation: the ongoing political deadlock in Canada East and Canada West, the problem of the railways, the drastic change in the trade situation following the cancellation of the Treaty of Reciprocity, and growing concerns about defence.

Political Deadlock

The whole reason for unifying Canada West and Canada East had been to promote harmony and assimilation, but neither of these goals were achieved. Instead, the new united Assembly found itself paralyzed because no single party had adequate support to form a government. As a result, during a single two-year period, there were no fewer than five different governments in power.

To make matters worse, there were still two systems of justice headed by two attorneys general, as well as separate educational systems. Canada East and Canada West hadn't merged their identities. If anything, they had become even more aware of their linguistic, religious, economic, political, and cultural differences.

Voice from the Past

"One hundred years have passed away since these provinces became by conquest part of the British Empire. Here sit today the descendants of the victors and vanquished in the fight of 1759, with all the differences of language, religion, civil law, and social habit nearly as distinctly marked as they were a century ago."

—George Brown, during the Confederation debates in the Assembly of the two Canadas.

Railway Fever

During the first half of the 19th century, the colonies relied on water for transportation. While shipping had always been a way of life in the Maritimes, large-scale water transportation only came to the land-locked Canadas during the 1820s and 1830s. Both the Rideau Waterway (which ran between the Ottawa River and Lake Ontario) and the Welland Canal (which ran between Lake Ontario and Lake Erie) were constructed during this period. While the canals were ideal for moving goods during the summer months, they weren't of any use at all during the long Canadian winter. As a result, the commercial community began to look to the railways for the solution to their transportation woes.

Stats

By 1851, the populations of Canada West and Canada East had reached 890,000 and 952,000 respectively.

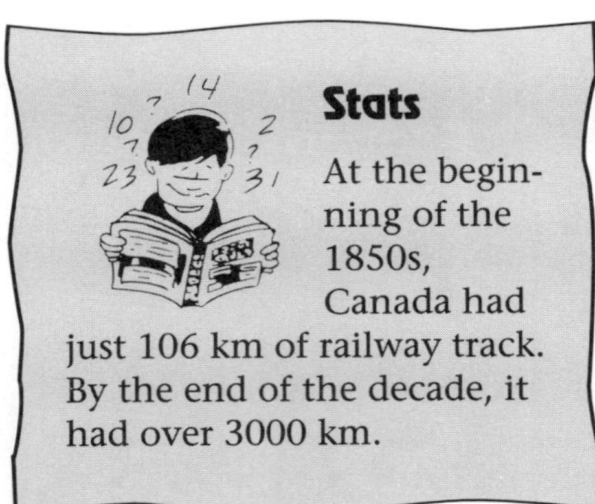

This isn't to say that the railways offered the ideal situation: sparks from passing trains were known to cause forest fires during the summer months, and the hardy few who ventured out on the trains in mid-winter often found themselves being asked to help clear snow off the tracks! But given the alternatives (and frankly there weren't all that many!), railway transportation seemed to have a lot to offer.

The problem, of course, was money. Railways were a costly venture, and even the magnificent Grand Trunk Railway—at one point the largest railway in the world!—had not been able to turn a profit. The residents of Canada East and Canada West began to dream of a railway that would link the various colonies in British North America, providing increased opportunities for trade and allowing for their mutual defense. The dreaming actually got to the talking stage in 1861 and 1862, with the two Canadas, New Brunswick, and Nova Scotia meeting to discuss the possibility of building such a railway together. Unfortunately, much to the anger of the other colonies, representatives from the two Canadas pulled out of the venture at the last minute. Having just been forced to raise taxes in order to keep the Grand Trunk Railway afloat, they were understandably reluctant to become involved with another railway project.

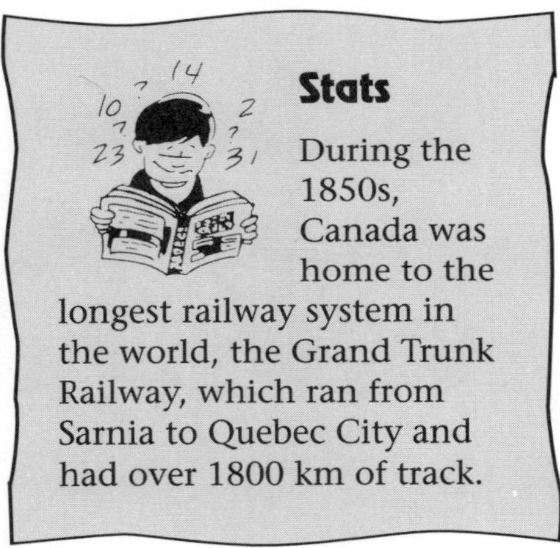

This isn't to say that Canada had abandoned its love affair with the railway. It was simply looking for a better way to finance a project of this magnitude. That's why, when it began to look as if a union of the colonies of British North America might allow for the construction of an intercolonial railway, Canadians began to throw their support behind the idea of Confederation.

Trade Woes

Another factor making Confederation look increasingly attractive in the two Canadas was the trade situation. The colonies were no longer receiving preferential treatment in their trade with Britain, as the Mother Country was more interested in purchasing goods at the best possible price than in supporting her colonies' economies.

To make matters worse, the Treaty of Reciprocity with the United States was cancelled by the Americans in 1865. As a result, the idea of joining the colonies together to increase the size of the market for one another's goods began to have considerable appeal.

Fears About Defence

The long-standing fear of invasion by the United States continued in the two Canadas, even after the end of the U.S. Civil War. Canadians were particularly fearful of their situation because Britain had made it clear that they were retreating from the burden of imperial defence, and that they expected the colonies to play an increasing role in ensuring their own security. Clearly, a federated British North America would be in a better position to fend for itself against the larger American forces.

Charlottetown Conference

By the mid-1860s, the three Maritime provinces—Nova Scotia, New Brunswick, and Prince Edward Island—were talking about the possibility of union. Delegates from Nova Scotia, New Brunswick, and Prince Edward Island decided to meet in Charlottetown, Prince Edward Island, on September 1, 1864, to discuss the pros and cons of such a federation.

When politicians from Canada West and Canada East heard about the Charlottetown Conference, they asked if they could attend to present their proposals for a wider union. The Maritimers agreed.

Despite the fact that they were merely invited guests, the Canadians played a dominant role in the proceedings. George Brown, a politician from

Voice from the Past

"The United States have frightful numbers of soldiers and guns. They wanted Florida and seized it. They wanted Louisiana and purchased it. They wanted Texas and stole it. Then they picked a quarrel with Mexico and got California. If we had not the strong arm of England over us, we too would be part of the states."

—Confederation supporter
D'Arcy McGee of
Lower Canada

Voice from the Past

"...all matters of general interest are to be dealt with by the general legislature, while the local legislatures will deal with matters of local interest, which do not affect the confederation as a whole."

—John A. Macdonald, describing the Fathers of Confederation's vision for the Dominion of Canada

Canada West, made a convincing argument for the benefits of a union of all of the colonies in British North America. To alleviate Maritime fears about having their voices lost in such a federation, he explained how regional representation and "representation by population" could be combined and balanced in a two-house legislature, and how power could be divided between the federal and provincial governments.

In the end, the Maritimers agreed to abandon the idea of a Maritime union in favour of a broader form of union, concluding that a broader federation was preferable "if the terms of union could be made satisfactory." The delegates to the Charlottetown Conference agreed to meet the following week in Halifax, at which point they decided to hold another conference in Quebec City in October.

Quebec Conference

The Quebec Conference was attended by delegates from all five eastern colonies: Canada, Nova Scotia, New Brunswick, Prince Edward Island, and Newfoundland. The proceedings got underway on October 10, 1864.

During the subsequent three weeks, the delegates hammered out a blueprint for Confederation. John Alexander Macdonald's proposal that the separate provincial governments be eliminated was shot down by the delegates from the Maritimes and French Canada. They agreed, instead, to a federal structure that would see both a strong central government and an ongoing role for the various provincial governments, which would maintain their autonomy in matters of "a merely local or private nature." The delegates' ideas were articulated in a document called *Seventy-Two Resolutions*. The delegates left the Conference promising to take the *Resolutions* back to their various governments and to promote the cause of Confederation.

The Reaction in the Colonies

Given that the colonies had very little in common, it's hardly surprising that the idea of Confederation met with varying degrees of enthusiasm.

Pro-Confederation sentiment was strongest in Canada West, where people were eager to find a solution to such problems as political deadlock, trade problems, and military insecurity. Because much of Canada West was cut off from the rest of the world during the long, harsh winters, the idea of pooling resources to create a transcolonial railway had particular appeal. What's more, the area had experienced a period of tremendous population growth, and was eager to see more land opened up in the unsettled area to the west.

There was considerably less enthusiasm in Canada East. French Canadian nationalists were concerned that Confederation represented yet another attempt to assimilate them, while members of the English-speaking elite were fearful that their interests would be ignored in a French-speaking province. While there was plenty of anti-Confederation rhetoric in the province, in the end, the pro-Confederation forces came out on top.

In Newfoundland and Prince Edward Island, the idea of Confederation was rejected outright. The benefits of such a union appeared to be vastly outnumbered by the disadvantages, the most significant of which was the fact that the smaller provinces would be left with, at best, a very small voice in the new government.

In Nova Scotia and New Brunswick, the response was lukewarm, largely because they had the least to gain. Nova Scotia was particularly difficult to entice into the scheme, because it had a balanced economy and excellent transportation systems.

Voice from the Past

Catharine Parr Traill and Susanna Moodie were two British gentlewomen who wrote about what life was like in Upper Canada during the early 19th century. The picture the two sisters painted was anything but rosy. In the concluding paragraph of *Roughing It in the Bush* (first published in 1852), Moodie writes: "If these sketches should prove the means of deterring one family from sinking their property, and shipwrecking all their hopes, by going to reside in the backwoods of Canada, I shall consider myself amply repaid for revealing the secrets of the prison-house, and feel that I have not toiled and suffered in the wilderness in vain."

Main Event

On July 1, 1867, the British North America Act came into effect, uniting Ontario, Quebec, Nova Scotia, and New Brunswick as the Dominion of Canada.

It looked like Confederation was doomed to go nowhere until a series of threats from south of the border convinced the colonies that it would be better to pool their resources than to continue to go it alone.

The Threat from South of the Border

Two separate crises served to remind British North America of the ongoing threat posed by their neighbour to the south.

On October 19, 1865, a handful of American Confederate soldiers raided St. Albans in Vermont, robbed its banks, and escaped into Canada. When a judge in Montreal agreed to set the bank robbers free (arguing that he had no jurisdiction over the case), Americans in the northern states were furious and began talking about invading Canada.

Then, in early 1866, members of the Fenian Order, a group of Irish nationalists, began recruiting members of the disbanded U.S. Union Army to help them strike at Britain by attacking British North America. In June, the Order invaded Canada with a force of 1000 men.

Convinced by these two incidents that Confederation was, in fact, in their best interests, delegates from Canada, New Brunswick, and Nova Scotia met in London, England, to draft a bill that could be submitted to the British Parliament. Using the resolutions from the Quebec Conference as their starting point, the delegates increased subsidies to the provinces, gave minorities the right to appeal to a federal authority if they felt they weren't being treated satisfactorily by the province, and mandated participation in the construction of an intercolonial railway.

They had no problem getting the bill approved by the British Parliament, which apparently took far greater interest in a bill debating a new dog tax than the one dealing with the Confederation of Canada. Parliament ignored a 30,000-name petition submitted by anti-Confederation forces in Nova Scotia and passed the British North America Act. The passing of the Act meant that, as of July 1, 1867, the colonies joined together to become "one Dominion under the name of Canada" led by Prime Minister John A. Macdonald.

Voice from the Past

"Died. Last night at twelve o'clock, the free and enlightened province of Nova Scotia."

—Advertisement in the Halifax *Chronicle* on July 1, 1867.

The Least You Need to Know

- Political deadlock, the desire to construct a transcolonial railway, trade woes, and defense concerns were the key factors leading to Confederation.
- The Charlottetown Conference—initially planned to discuss the possibility of Maritime union—was dominated by talk of a wider union.
- Delegates at the Quebec Conference passed the *Seventy-Two Resolutions*, detailing their plans for Confederation.
- Response to the idea of Confederation was mixed. Canada West was strongly in favour of it, while support in Canada East was more guarded. Nova Scotia and New Brunswick were lukewarm to the idea, while Newfoundland and Prince Edward Island were completely opposed to it.
- On July 1, 1867, the British North America Act came into effect, creating the Dominion of Canada.

Chapter 15

Walking Papers (1867)

In this chapter

- ➤ The role of the monarchy, the Senate, and the House of Commons
- ➤ The judicial system
- ➤ Provincial vs. federal powers
- ➤ Differences between the Canadian and American systems of government

When the Fathers of Confederation sat down to draft a constitution for the Dominion of Canada, they borrowed from both the British and American systems of governments. The result was the British North America Act, which came into effect on July 1, 1867, after being proclaimed by the British parliament.

The purpose of the British North America Act was to create a strong national government that could act directly on behalf of individual citizens, without the intervention of the provinces; and that would have adequate powers to deal with any matters of truly national concern. The Act provided for a federal government consisting of a representative of the British Crown, a Senate made up of regional (not

Word for the Day

The word *Dominion* was chosen as an alternative to *Kingdom* because neither the British nor Canadian governments wished to use a term that might offend the Americans. It was also a term that Britain had used to refer to its overseas colonies. The expression *Dominion from sea to sea* originates in the *Bible* in *Psalm 72*.

provincial) members who were to be appointed for life, and a House of Commons to be elected on the basis of "representation by population."

A Constitutional Monarchy

Under the terms of the British North America Act, Canada became a constitutional (or limited) monarchy, which meant that the head of government was technically the British monarch.

In addition to being an affirmation of Canada's ongoing desire to maintain its strong imperial connection, the clause of the British North America Act that assigned executive power to the sovereign was meant to guard against democracy gone wild, something Canadians perceived to be the key failing of the American system of government.

Stats

The Fathers of Confederation felt that a key function of the Senate should be the upholding of individual property rights. As a result, the British North America Act required that all senators own at least $4000 of property, a considerable amount at that time.

The Senate

The British North America Act created a Senate, which was to be made up of regional representatives appointed for life. Initially, Quebec and Ontario were each given 24 members, while Nova Scotia and New Brunswick had 24 members between them. (Nova Scotia and New

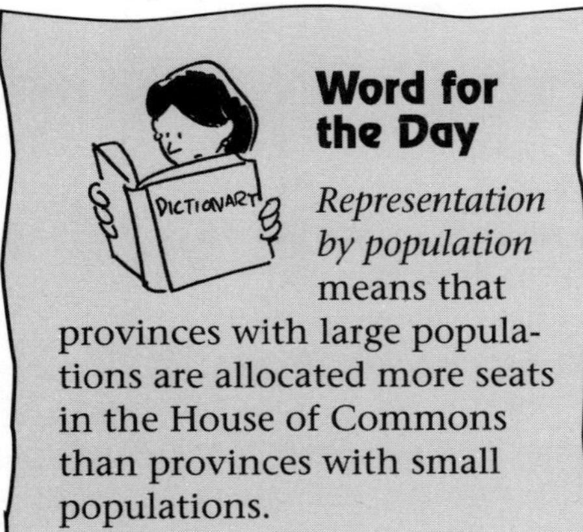

Word for the Day

Representation by population means that provinces with large populations are allocated more seats in the House of Commons than provinces with small populations.

Brunswick also agreed to relinquish two seats each, should Prince Edward Island decide to join Confederation.) When the western provinces joined Confederation later on, an additional 24 seats were set aside for them.

The House of Commons

The Act also created a House of Commons, whose members were to be elected. Seats in the House of Commons were to be assigned on the basis of population. Quebec was given 65 seats; the other provinces were assigned seats on the basis of how their populations compared to that of Quebec.

The Act also stated that seats in the House of Commons were to be reassigned once per decade, following a census, but that no province would have its representation reduced unless its proportion of population to that of the entire Dominion declined by at least 5 per cent.

The Judicial System

Under the terms of the British North America Act, criminal law became a federal matter while civil law rested with the provinces. This allowed for the continuation of French civil law in Quebec.

The Dominion, however, retained the right to establish a court of appeal and "any additional courts for the better administration of the laws of Canada."

Provincial vs. Federal Powers

In an effort to avoid the types of problems they had recently witnessed among their neighbours to the south, the Fathers of Confederation sought to define clearly the types of powers that were to rest with the provinces and those that were to rest with the federal government.

Section 92 of the Act listed the areas over which provinces had exclusive control (that is, public lands, municipal institutions, licences, local public works, prisons, hospitals, charitable institutions, the solemnization of marriage, plus "all matters of a merely local or private

Voice from the Past

"It shall be lawful for the Queen, by and with the Advice and Consent of the Senate and House of Commons, to make Laws for the Peace, Order, and good Government of Canada, in relation to all Matters not coming within the Classes of Subjects by this Act assigned exclusively to the Legislatures of the Provinces...."

—Section 91 of the British North America Act

Word for the Day

Residual power is the right of the federal government to assume any powers not specifically granted to provinces under the terms of the British North America Act.

nature in the province"). The provinces also acquired jurisdiction over education in Section 93.

Section 95 identified areas of shared provincial and federal jurisdiction (that is, agriculture and immigration), but clearly indicated that in the event of a conflict, the federal government had ultimate decision-making authority.

Section 91 dealt with the issue of residual powers. It gave jurisdiction over all areas not specifically assigned to the provinces to the federal government, and provided the federal government with the right to disallow provincial legislation within a one-year period if it was contrary to federal policy or if it went

Stats

Section 133 of the British North America Act allowed for the use of both English and French in Parliament and in the Quebec Legislature.

beyond the powers given to the provinces. Section 91 also spelled out some of the areas that fell under federal jurisdiction (that is, regulation of trade and commerce; right of taxation; and currency, banking, interest, and bankruptcy).

Differences Between the Canadian and American Systems

The Fathers of Confederation set out to create "a constitution similar to that of the United Kingdom." Because the British had a unitary system of government (that is, one central administration for England, Ireland, Scotland, and Wales), they were forced to incorporate elements of the American federal system as well.

The Fathers of Confederation were anxious to improve on the American system of government which, they felt, left too much power in the hands of the states. As a result, the Canadian system was designed to provide for a federal legislature that combines both regional (Senate) and proportional (House of Commons) representation. What's more, the British North America Act clearly spelled out how power was to be distributed between the federal and provincial governments.

The Least You Need to Know

- The Canadian system of government provides for a sovereign head of state (the Governor General), an appointed Senate that relies on regional representation, and an elected House of Commons that relies on representation by population.
- Criminal law is a federal matter, while civil law is handled by the provinces.
- The Fathers of Confederation drew from both the British and American models to create a uniquely Canadian system of government.

Chapter 16

More Room at the Table (1867 to 1873)

In this chapter

- The Red River Rebellion
- Manitoba, British Columbia, and Prince Edward Island enter Confederation

The ink hadn't even dried on the British North America Act before Prime Minister John A. Macdonald started dreaming about "a Dominion from sea to sea." He believed that there was strength in numbers, and that the only way that Canada would thrive in the decades ahead was if she had the territory and population required to hold her own against her restless neighbour to the south.

In the six years after Confederation, Macdonald saw his dreams for Canada realized as he welcomed Manitoba, British Columbia, and Prince Edward Island into Confederation.

Macdonald Looks to the West

While Macdonald had originally hoped that Britain would purchase the Canadian West and give it to the Dominion, there was little enthusiasm in Britain for the idea. Instead of giving the territory to Canada, Britain agreed to lend Canada the £300,000 it needed to purchase the land from the Hudson's Bay Company, and helped arrange a deal in which Canada would allow the Hudson's Bay Company to keep 45,000 acres around its posts and give it one-twentieth of all future lands surveyed for settlement.

By November 19, 1869, when the deal was signed, all that remained to be done was to formally transfer authority from the Hudson's Bay Company to the Canadian government and to establish a provisional government that would administer the territory as a colony of the Dominion until its population increased enough to warrant provincial status.

At least, that's what the federal government thought.

The Red River Rebellion

Unfortunately, the architects of the plan for the new colony had neglected one small detail: the wishes of the people who were already living in Rupert's Land (present-day Manitoba). The Métis and other native people who had been living in the area for hundreds of years were anything but thrilled about the prospect of being dragged into

Real Life

Louis Riel (1844–1885) was a highly charismatic leader who believed he had a divine mission to defend the Métis' way of life. He believed that the people of the Red River settlement should have been consulted about entering Confederation and, assuming they had agreed to join, should have been brought in as a province rather than a colony. Following the Red River Rebellion, Riel was exiled to the United States. In 1885, a group of Métis in Saskatchewan asked him to return to Canada to lead them in a revolt against Ottawa. The result was the Rebellion of 1885. Tried in Regina, where he refused to plead insanity, Riel was found guilty and sentenced to death. He was hanged on November 16, 1885.

Voice from the Past

On January 19 and 20, 1870, 1000 people gathered at Fort Garry to hear speeches from politicians on both sides of this issue. Donald Smith, an official with the Hudson's Bay Company, assured the crowd that Canada sought union "peaceably" and without prejudice to "any class of people of this land." Louis Riel made an impassioned speech in which he stated: "Most of us are half-breeds, but we all have rights. We claim no half rights...but all the rights we are entitled to. Those rights will be set forth by our representatives, and what is more...we will get them."

political union with Canada without being consulted, especially since union seemed to threaten their traditional way of life. A group of Métis led by Louis Riel seized Fort Garry (present-day Winnipeg) and prevented William McDougall, the colonial governor, from entering the colony. In early December 1869, Riel and his followers proclaimed a provisional government.

Prime Minister John A. Macdonald found himself faced with a crisis that threatened to rock the Dominion. He could either declare war on Riel and his followers or he could negotiate with the Métis in an attempt to reach a peaceable settlement. He chose to negotiate.

In the meantime, the provisional government began to come into conflict with Canadian settlers in the area who refused to recognize Riel's authority. The situation culminated in the Métis' decision to execute a Canadian, Thomas Scott, for insubordination. Scott was executed by firing squad on March 4, 1870.

The reaction from the rest of Canada was immediate. The Protestant majority in Ontario felt that Riel should be brought to justice for his part in Scott's execution, and there were repeated cries for "Riel's head in a sack." In Quebec, however, there was considerable sympathy for the French-speaking Catholic leader and his followers.

By the time federal forces arrived in Red River in August 1870, Riel was long gone, the resistance had subsided, and the remaining Métis leaders had gone into hiding.

Real Life

Sir John Alexander Macdonald (1815–1891) was the Prime Minister of Canada from 1867 to 1873 and from 1878 to 1891. Prior to becoming a member of the federal Conservative party, he was a lawyer, a businessman, the alderman of Kingston, and one of the leaders of the coalition government of the Province of Canada. A committed federalist, Macdonald is remembered for his skill as a politician, the role he played in the construction of the Canadian Pacific Railway, and his handling of the Red River Rebellion (1870) and the Northwest Rebellion (1885).

In 1875, the fate of the Métis leaders was decided. Everyone except for Riel and another leader, Ambrose Lépine, received an unconditional pardon. Riel and Lépine received a pardon on the condition that they stay out of Canada for the next five years. Clearly, Macdonald wanted the problem to go away.

The Manitoba Act

Manitoba entered Confederation on July 15, 1870. Under the terms of the Manitoba Act, 570,000 hectares of land were set aside for the Métis, the French language and Catholic religion were protected, and Manitoba was guaranteed both a cash grant and annual subsidies. The

Word for the Day

Manitoba is thought to be either a Cree word meaning "the Great Spirit" or an Assiniboine word meaning "lake of the prairies."

remainder of the West was to be administered as the Northwest Territories under an appointed governor and council.

Word for the Day

Originally, the first British settlements on the northwest coast were called New Caledonia. However, in the 1860s Queen Victoria renamed the area *British Columbia* in honour of explorer Christopher Columbus.

British Columbia Enters Confederation

The next province to join Confederation was British Columbia. Feeling more than a little drained by the Manitoba negotiations, Macdonald decided to sit this round out and let his long-time political ally George Étienne Cartier handle the situation for him.

British Columbia was eager to talk to Cartier. The colony was experiencing a bad case of post–Gold Rush letdown. The earlier period of prosperity had ended, the colony's population was in decline (and what was left was badly scattered), there were few markets for its natural products, and it was struggling under a back-breaking debt load.

Stats

By 1870, half of British Columbia's income was being spent to service the interest on its $1 million debt.

British Columbia felt that it had two alternatives: to seek annexation to the United States or to enter Confederation. When the Americans proved lukewarm to the idea of welcoming British Columbia, talk turned to joining Canada.

In the end, British Columbia agreed to join Confederation in exchange for a rather generous bundle of goodies. The provincial debt would be assumed, a favourable subsidy would be granted, full responsible government would be introduced in the province, and—last but not least!—an intercontinental railway would be started within two years and completed within ten. British Columbia was happy to agree to these terms, which were far more attractive than those it had originally asked for, and officially entered Confederation on July 20, 1871.

Real Life

One of the most enthusiastic proponents of Confederation in British Columbia was the editor of *British Colonist,* a fellow by the name of Amor de Cosmos. (Cosmos had actually been born "Smith," but decided to opt for a name that was a little more colourful.) He organized a series of mass meetings throughout the province to press for entry into Confederation.

Meanwhile, at the Other End of the Continent...

By the early 1870s, Prince Edward Island was beginning to regret its decision not to join Confederation. Like British Columbia before it, Prince Edward Island had learned a hard lesson in the economics of running a colony, and had been left with a crushing debt load as a result of its efforts to construct a railway.

To make matters worse, the colony was faced with the ongoing problem of absentee landowners. Back at the time of the Conquest, the majority of land in the colony had been given to friends of the home government. These landlords had made little effort to settle the colony, and had been unwilling to make even the most rudimentary improvements to their property on behalf of their unfortunate tenants. By the 1870s, the situation had gone from bad to worse.

Word for the Day

Originally known as Île St-John, *Prince Edward Island* was renamed in 1800 in honour of Prince Edward, who would later become the father of Queen Victoria.

Then Canada came calling. The Dominion offered to give Prince Edward Island $800,000 to buy back land from absentee landowners, to pay off the colony's railway debt, to start and maintain a steamer service between the island and the mainland, and to grant a generous subsidy of $50 per person.

On July 1, 1873, Prince Edward Island entered Confederation. Within two years, under the terms of the Compulsory Purchase Act, it had managed to buy back much of the land held by absentee landowners.

Stats

Prince Edward Island's debt had grown from $250,000 in 1863 to $4 million in 1873.

The Least You Need to Know

- ➤ The Red River Rebellion was led by Louis Riel, a charismatic politician determined to protect the Métis' traditional way of life and ensure that Manitoba receive provincial (rather than colonial) status upon entry into Confederation.
- ➤ Manitoba joined Confederation on July 15, 1870. Under the terms of the Manitoba Act, it received 570,000 hectares of land for the Métis, guarantees that the French language and Catholic religion would be protected, a cash grant, and annual subsidies.
- ➤ The remainder of the West was to be administered as the Northwest Territories under an appointed governor and council.
- ➤ British Columbia joined Confederation on July 20, 1871. It negotiated for the assumption of its provincial debt, a favourable subsidy, full responsible government, and the construction of an intercontinental railway that was to be started within two years and completed within ten.
- ➤ Prince Edward Island joined Confederation on July 1, 1873. The Dominion gave Prince Edward Island $800,000 to buy back land from absentee landowners, agreed to pay off the colony's railway debt and to start and maintain a steamer service between the island and the mainland, and granted a generous subsidy of $50 per person.

Chapter 17

Iron Horses (1871 to 1885)

In this chapter

- The Pacific Scandal
- Mackenzie's railway program
- The Canadian Pacific Railway's financial difficulties
- The last spike

One of the key components of the agreement that brought British Columbia into Confederation in 1871 was the Canadian government's promise to build an intercontinental railway.

While Macdonald was convinced of the political and economic benefits the railway represented for the rest of Canada, others were not so sure. Given the mammoth price tag of the project, it's hardly surprising that the railway emerged as the central issue in the election of 1872.

Even before the election was called, the railway issue was heating up. The government had introduced a railway bill that provided $30 million in cash plus 40 million acres of property to the private company that committed to constructing a railway from the Pacific

Ocean to a point 200 miles north of Toronto within 10 years of July 20, 1871. (Canada had promised British Columbia that construction would be completed by this date.) The bill also gave the federal Cabinet the right to decide who would receive the contract.

Two rival groups emerged, each of which was interested in obtaining the contract. One group based in Montreal centred around Sir Hugh Allan. The other based in Toronto centred around Senator D.L. Macpherson. While Macdonald hoped that the two groups would join together, they didn't appear willing to do so. Reluctant to alienate the well-placed supporters of either group, Macdonald did what any savvy politician would do: he postponed the decision regarding the granting of the contract until after the election.

> **Stats**
>
> 
>
> The bulk of Canadian industry in the 1870s consisted of small shops of less than five employees that were producing consumer goods for local markets. Typical products were woollen textiles, boots, shoes, and harnesses. The completion of the transcontinental railway promised to open up new markets and stimulate the Canadian manufacturing sector.

Allan and his American supporters attempted to sway the matter in their favour by contributing $350,000 to the Conservative campaign. While the Conservatives used the money to win the election, they refused to be bought. They granted Allan's group the charter for the Canadian Pacific Railway in 1872, but refused to name Allan president of the railway until he disassociated himself from his American backers. The Americans were furious and leaked details of their political contributions to members of the opposition.

In 1873, Liberal member of parliament L.S. Huntington stood up in the House of Commons and charged that the government had been bought—and with American money, no less! He was able to back up his allegations when G.W. McMullen, a representative of the American financial interests that had been excluded from the final railway contract, provided the press with copies of letters and telegrams between his group and members of the Conservative party. The evidence was damning; it proved that both Cartier and Macdonald had been involved personally in the negotiations. A motion of censure was made in Parliament. Before it could be formally passed, Macdonald and his

Real Life

Alexander Mackenzie (1822–1892) was the Prime Minister of Canada from 1873 to 1878. Prior to entering politics, he worked as a stonemason, a building contractor, and as the editor of *Lambton Shield*. Mackenzie headed up the first Liberal administration of the Dominion of Canada. During his years in power, he introduced the secret ballot (1874), founded the Royal Military College (1874), and created the Supreme Court of Canada (1875). Mackenzie also served as the Leader of the Opposition from 1878 to 1880, following his defeat to Sir John A. Macdonald in the election of 1878.

government chose to resign. Liberal leader Alexander Mackenzie assumed the role of prime minister and called an election almost immediately. Not surprisingly, the Conservatives were roundly defeated and the Liberals won a resounding majority in the 1874 election.

A subsequent investigation into the so-called Pacific Scandal helped to clear Macdonald's name somewhat, but not enough to change his short-term political fortunes. The commission conducting the investigation concluded that while Macdonald had acted quite properly in his dealings with Sir Hugh Allan, Macdonald's sidekick George Étienne Cartier had damaged his party's credibility and reputation by making unreasonable promises to Allan regarding the railway charter.

Mackenzie and the Railway

One of Mackenzie's first acts as prime minister was to cancel the contract that had been awarded to Allan. While it was clearly the right thing to do, the cancellation left the government in an awkward situation. The poor state of the economy was making it difficult to attract private capital, so no other company had stepped forward to bid on the contract. As a result, the Mackenzie government was faced with a difficult choice: abandon the railway and forsake its promise to British Columbia or undertake the construction on its own.

Mackenzie chose to pursue the latter option, building the railway in sections as settlement warranted and using water routes and American railway lines to fill in the missing stretches. While it was a frugal approach to the business of railway construction, it was too slow and too cautious for British Columbia, which began to talk about seceding from the union.

When the Liberals went back to the polls in 1878, they were defeated. The strongest reason for their defeat was their inaction concerning the railways.

Stats

In the election of 1873, the Liberals won 133 seats and the Conservatives won 73. Within five years, their fortunes were reversed: in the election of 1878, the Conservatives won 137 seats and the Liberals won 69.

More Financial Woes

For the first few years after his government's return to power, Macdonald continued with the piecemeal program of railway construction. Then, in 1880, a new railway syndicate with connections in London, Paris, and New York was given the contract for the Canadian Pacific Railway. The principals of the company were railway promoter J.J. Hill, Donald Smith of the Hudson's Bay Company, and George Stephen of the Bank of Montreal.

The new syndicate still relied on government subsidies and land grants but, initially at least, the amount they asked for was less than what the Conservative government had previously been offering. They asked for $25 million in cash and 25 million acres of the prairies' most fertile land. The government also agreed to allow them to assume ownership of the existing 700 miles of railway, import their materials duty-free, and avoid paying taxes on their land for 20 years and on their property forever. What's more, the government forbade the construction of any competing line to the south or southwest during the next 20 years, and promised that rates would not be regulated until the company was consistently in the black. In exchange,

Stats

The $25 million that the Canadian Pacific Railway received was equivalent to two years of Canada's national revenue.

Stats

With 5000 men and 3500 horses working from sunrise until sunset, CPR General Manager William Van Horne was able to meet his commitment to construct 400 miles of track during 1882.

the government asked that all work on the railway be completed by 1891.

The terms of the agreement were so generous that a rival syndicate, encouraged by the Liberals, put forward a competing proposal. The Conservatives chose to disregard the second proposal, however, and used their majority to push the first contract through Parliament.

Work had no sooner begun on the 1900-mile stretch of railway when problems arose. There were additional expenses involved in securing the eastern lines connecting to Montreal and Toronto. Construction was more difficult than anticipated. And the company was running out of money.

In late 1883, the company asked the government for a loan of $22.5 million. Macdonald initially turned down the request, but was convinced by those in his party that the failure of the Canadian Pacific Railway would mean the end of the Conservative Party. Macdonald forced the loan through Parliament—and, in the process, had to placate interests in both Quebec and Ontario with additional subsidies. Unfortunately, the influx of money did not end the railway's financial problems. Within a year, they didn't even have enough money left to meet their payroll obligations, and the company went back to Ottawa to request another $5 million.

Main Event

The so-called "last spike" in the construction of the Canadian Pacific Railway was driven into the ground on November 7, 1885, at Craigellachie, in the interior plateau of British Columbia.

At this point, the Canadian Pacific Railway was technically bankrupt, and the federal government was reluctant to bail it out again. The outbreak of the Northwest Rebellion (also known as the Rebellion of 1885) proved to be the company's salvation. Military personnel were transported to Saskatchewan in just six days and were able to quash the Rebellion.

Now that it was able to justify the existence of the railway on military grounds, the Canadian government was willing to approve the loan. Later that year—on November 7, 1885—the last spike was driven into the Canadian Pacific Railway.

The Least You Need to Know

- During the election of 1872, the Conservative party accepted political donations from one of the two groups vying for the railway contract. When the so-called Pacific Scandal came to light, the newly elected Conservative government was forced to resign.
- Alexander Mackenzie was unable to find another private backer for the transcontinental railway, so he opted to construct the railway as government finances permitted. The pace was too slow for British Columbia, which threatened to secede. In 1878, the Liberal government was easily defeated by Macdonald's Conservative party.
- The construction of the Canadian Pacific Railway proved to be an expensive venture for the federal government, which was repeatedly asked to pour more money into the project. The project might have been axed during the final months of construction had it not been for the Northwest Rebellion, which provided a military justification for the railway.
- The last spike was hammered into the ground on November 7, 1885, signalling the completion of the Canadian Pacific Railway.

Chapter 18

Sibling Rivalry (1867 to 1896)

In this chapter

- Macdonald's National Policy
- Regional discontent
- The Northwest Rebellion (a.k.a. The Rebellion of 1885)
- The second Quebec Conference (1887)
- Commercial union
- The Conservative party after John A. Macdonald

The decades following Confederation were a time of disappointed hopes. While the West had been acquired and the plans for a transcontinental railway were well underway, the prosperity and the flood of settlers that the Dominion had anticipated simply hadn't materialized.

To make matters worse, the economy was sluggish, and attempts to renew reciprocity with the United States had failed. Prices were falling, markets were contracting, and there was a decline in both the value and volume of exports. In a nutshell, the country was experiencing an economic crisis at the very time it needed substantial revenues to finance its railway programs.

Word for the Day

In the years following Confederation, a small group of federalists adopted the motto *Canada First* and attempted to elicit among their fellow Canadians a strong outpouring of "national sentiment" that would unify the country as "one nation of brothers." They felt that it was important to develop a strong national identity that would set the Canadians apart from the British and the Americans. Despite some rather creative arguments concerning the strengths and virtues of the Canadian people (they argued that Canadians were much stronger than Americans because they had been nurtured at "the icy bosom of the frozen North"), their efforts were mostly in vain. By 1880, the Canada First movement had fizzled out.

But that wasn't all. People were leaving Canada in record numbers and heading to the more prosperous United States to seek their fortunes. Between 1871 and 1881 alone, over 1 million people left the Dominion.

Macdonald's National Policy

Throughout the 1870s, Macdonald continued to believe that the key to the success of the Canadian federation was economic prosperity. His National Policy (1879) was an attempt to stimulate the Canadian economy by providing a series of protective tariffs of up to 35 per cent on imported goods. Macdonald believed the tariff would provide a remedy for the economic depression Canada had been experiencing and increase Canada's chances of regaining reciprocity with the United States.

His logic went like this. The railway would make east-west trade possible for the very first time. The growing population in the West would create a market for Canadian manufactured goods as well as provide a ready source of raw materials for the growing industries of central Canada. And the high tariff would encourage Canadians to shop at home, thus encouraging economic growth within Canada.

The National Policy was politically attractive because it represented the next logical step from colony to nation within the empire. Unfortunately, it didn't reap the economic benefits that Macdonald had hoped for, and the Dominion continued to suffer from regional inequality and conflict.

Discontent in British Columbia

The reason for discontent in British Columbia was simple: the federal government had not only failed to deliver on its promise of having the transcontinental railway completed by July 20, 1881, but had also come dangerously close to abandoning the project midstream. Is it any wonder that many in British Columbia began to second-guess their decision to enter Confederation?

Nova Scotia's Grievances

Stats

In September 1867, 36 of the 38 seats in the Nova Scotia legislature were won by separatist candidates. What's more, the first post-Confederation throne speech in the province called for dissolution of the union.

Nova Scotia shared British Columbia's belief that Confederation had brought with it more burdens than advantages. Many in Nova Scotia had been sceptical about joining Canada from the very beginning. In fact, 18 of the 19 members of Parliament elected by Nova Scotia in the first federal election in 1867 were separatists!

In 1868, a group of Nova Scotians led by Joseph Howe went so far as to ask the British government to permit them to withdraw from Confederation. When the imperial government turned down their request, Howe convinced the Canadian government to increase Nova Scotia's annual subsidy from $63,000 to $82,000 for a 10-year period. (The only condition that Macdonald demanded in return was that Howe sit in the federal Cabinet!)

By the 1870s, the situation in Nova Scotia was becoming even more dismal. The days of shipbuilding were coming to an end, and the coal mining industry was proving a poor substitute for the province's maritime economy.

In 1886, another resolution in favour of secession was introduced in the Nova Scotia legislature. Even though it failed to pass, it signalled that Nova Scotia was anything but content with its lot within Confederation.

Complaints from Central Canada

While the provinces at either end of the country were quick to point out the many privileges enjoyed by central Canada, Ontario and Quebec also had their share of grievances. They didn't like the fact that their taxpayers were constantly being forced to subsidize other regions of the country, and they resented what they viewed as federal intrusions into provincial affairs.

The provinces were so determined to protect their autonomy, in fact, that they were prepared to take minor cases to the highest judicial authority to prove their point. One of the key disputes over provincial jurisdiction related to an incident in a pool hall. At the time, Ontario had a law that tavern games must end when drinking stopped. On Saturday, May 7, 1881, customers at Archibald Hodge's pool hall continued shooting pool after the 7:00 p.m. limit on drinking. The tavern owner was fined $25, but appealed his case to the Judicial Committee of the Privy Council of Great Britain, arguing that the province had no jurisdiction to make such a law. Much to the tavern owner's disgust, the Privy Council pointed out the extent of provincial power under the terms of the British North America Act and upheld Ontario's right to regulate the playing of pool in taverns. It was clearly a victory for provincial rights, but one that the citizens of Ontario could not publicly toast after 7:00 p.m. on a Saturday night!

The Wild West

While the people of Ontario were busy grappling with such earth-shattering issues as pool hall curfews, the people of Manitoba had a few beefs of their own.

First of all, there was a shortage of fertile land in the province, thanks to a series of deals made by the federal government. Because of the Dominion's agreements with the Hudson's Bay Company and the Canadian Pacific Railway, only one quarter of the land in the province's fertile belts was actually available for settlement.

And then there was the problem of the Métis and the natives.

While Manitoba hadn't experienced the same degree of conflict between natives and settlers that had been seen south of the border, there were problems nonetheless. The virtual extinction of the buffalo had forced the province's native peoples to conclude a series of treaties that

Stats

Under the homestead system in the Canadian West, a settler could secure 160 acres of land by cultivating and living on it for three years and then paying a $10 patent fee.

Stats

Between 1874 and 1877, most of the native-owned land between Manitoba and the Rocky Mountains that fell south of the 60th Parallel was transferred by treaty from the native people at virtually no cost to the federal government. The native people were being decimated by both outbreaks of smallpox and the disappearance of the buffalo. The 60 million buffalo that had wandered the prairies a century earlier were nearly extinct.

they might not otherwise have agreed to sign. These treaties provided for the surrender of most of the fertile belt in exchange for land on reserves, the payment of annuities, and government assistance with education and agriculture.

In the aftermath of these treaties, a large number of Métis moved west from Manitoba and settled in the Saskatchewan River Valley. Here they found themselves faced with the same problem the Red River Métis had faced: a central government that was blatantly disregarding their needs and posing an ongoing threat to their way of life.

The Métis decided to turn to the leader who had helped them 15 years earlier: Louis Riel.

Riel was, by this time, living in the United States, having been exiled for five years for his part in the execution of Thomas Scott and then having been bribed by the Macdonald government to continue to stay away. (However, being in exile didn't stop him from getting elected to the Canadian Parliament on three separate occasions!)

Following a brief stint in a mental institution, Riel had obtained work as a school teacher in Montana. Over the years, he had become increasingly delusional and had come to believe that he was, in fact, an instrument of divine revelation.

Riel agreed to return to Canada and, within a matter of months, helped the Métis and white settlers in the area to draft a petition to Ottawa. The petition demanded more generous treatment of natives, more favourable land terms for all settlers, local control over natural resources, lowered tariffs, a railway to Hudson Bay, local self-government, and adequate representation in Ottawa.

Macdonald (who by this time had acquired the nickname "Old Tomorrow" because of his tendency to ignore problems in the hope that they would go away!) chose not to respond to the petition. The situation escalated, and Riel proclaimed a provisional government in March of 1885.

By this time, Riel had lost the support of both the white settlers and the clergy. (The clergy had abandoned him when he decided to found a new church and declare himself a prophet!) His support among the Métis and the natives, however, continued to be strong. When the Métis attacked police at Duck Lake (March 26), pillaged a Hudson Bay post and laid siege to the town of Battleford (March 30), and attacked a settlement at Frog Lake, massacring its inhabitants (April 2), the federal government decided that it was time to intervene. They sent a force of 5000 troops into the area by railway. On May 12, General Frederick Dobson Middleton captured the rebel headquarters at Batoche. The leaders scattered. Riel was captured on May 15, Poundmaker on May 26, and Big Bear on July 2.

In the aftermath of the Rebellion, Riel was charged with high treason. The issue during his trial was his sanity. In the end, the jury found him to be both sane and guilty, but recommended mercy. The Canadian government, however, was not about to allow Riel to get off once again.

Voice from the Past

"The hanging of Riel is a bloody concession made to Orange fanaticism; it is the explosion of a blind rage against the French-Canadian nationality....If the English united against us to crush us, let them know that we are not a national of slaves who will allow those of our own people who battle heroically for the rectification of grievances to mount the scaffold. French Canadians too know how to unite, not to quelch in blood a fierce hatred but to make their rights respected.... It's quite clear that the intention is to destroy the French Canadians; but the French Canadian nationality is too strong and healthy a tree for fanaticism to blow it down."

—*Le Monde*, November 17, 1885

The justice minister instructed the magistrate to disregard the recommendation for clemency and ordered that Riel be executed by hanging.

When Riel was hanged on November 16, 1885, the country was thrown into crisis. While residents of Protestant Ontario felt that Riel had finally got what he deserved, French Catholics in Quebec argued that Riel had deserved to be pitied, not punished, and that he should have been pardoned. Like similar incidents in the past, the hanging of Riel served to increase the tension between French- and English-speaking Canadians.

Talk, Talk, Talk

In October of 1887, representatives from Nova Scotia, New Brunswick, Quebec, Ontario, and Manitoba met in Quebec City to consider "questions which have arisen or may arise as to the autonomy of the provinces, their financial arrangements, and other matters of provincial interest." Basically, the provinces were anxious to increase their share of the national revenue and to put an end to the all-too-common federal practice of disallowing provincial legislation.

Stats

The Conservative party was eager to defend federal rights against encroachments from the provinces. As a result, 68 provincial laws were disallowed between 1867 and 1896.

The second Quebec Conference passed a resolution demanding the readjustment and stabilization of provincial subsidies, provincial input regarding the selection of senators, provincial consent for the transfer of local works to Dominion jurisdiction, clearer criteria for determining the validity of provincial laws, and the removal of the power of disallowance from the Dominion to the imperial government.

Macdonald not only chose to sit out the proceedings (along with both British Columbia and Prince Edward Island), but also chose to ignore the resolutions the conference produced.

Commercial Union

At about the same time the provinces were meeting to discuss their grievances, staple producers began to express their desire for commercial union with the United States. The movement was encouraged by U.S. President Grover Cleveland, who had pledged to seek reductions in the tariffs that were limiting trade between Canada and the United States.

In the end, nothing came of the talk about commercial union. Not only were Canadian manufacturers against it, fearing that they would be unable to compete in a larger continental market, but the American public had little interest in additional trade opportunities with Canada.

The End of an Era

The campaign of 1891 was Macdonald's last political battle, but he fought the good fight until the end. The key issue in the election was commercial union with the United States, an issue Macdonald masterfully turned to his advantage.

When Macdonald got his hands on a pamphlet written by a prominent Liberal who was strongly in favour of commercial union, he was able to use it as an excuse to make an impassioned plea to loyalty: "As for myself, my course is clear. A British subject I was born—a British subject I will die. With my utmost effort, with my latest breath, will I opposed the 'veiled treason' which attempts by sordid means and mercenary proffers to lure our people from their allegiance."

Rallying under the cry of "The Old Flag, The Old Man, and The

Voice from the Past

"When this man is gone, who will there be to take his place? What shepherd is there who knows the sheep or whose voice the sheep know? Who else could make Orangemen vote for Papists, or induce half the members for Ontario to help in levying on their own province the necessary blackmail for Quebec? Yet this is the work which will have to be done if a general break-up is to be averted. Things will not hold together of themselves."

—Goldwin Smith, one of Macdonald's most outspoken critics, commenting on John A.'s superb political skills.

Old Policy," the Conservatives won a slim majority once again. Unfortunately, the election took a lot out of Macdonald; within three months, he was dead. (Ironically, Macdonald was buried in an American-made casket that strongly resembled the one used to bury U.S. President Ulysses S. Grant, something of which "The Old Man" most certainly would not have approved!)

Macdonald had dominated the Conservative party for so long that choosing a successor proved to be extremely difficult.

The first person to attempt to step into his shoes was Sir John Joseph Caldwell Abbott. A mediocre politician, Abbott was ill-suited to the position of prime minister. "I hate politics. I hate notoriety, public meetings, public speeches, caucuses, and everything I know of that is apparently the necessary incident of politics," he declared. He didn't have to put up with the job for very long. Ill health forced him to retire in 1892.

Following in Abbott's footsteps was Sir John Sparrow David Thompson. His term in office was unremarkable except for one fact: he died suddenly on December 12, 1894, while visiting Queen Victoria at Windsor Castle!

The next Conservative up to bat was Sir Mackenzie Bowell, a former Grand Master of the Orange Master and the last Canadian prime minister to be drawn from the ranks of the Senate. Bowell got himself

Real Life

Sir John Joseph Caldwell Abbott (1821–1893) was the Prime Minister of Canada from 1891 to 1892. He assumed power when the leader of the Conservative party, Sir John A. Macdonald, died in office. Within 18 months, he was forced to resign due to his own ill health. Prior to entering federal politics, Abbott was a lawyer, president of the Canada Central Railway, a member of the Board of Directors of the Canadian Pacific Railway, the mayor of Montreal, and a member of the Senate.

into trouble over the Manitoba Schools Question verdict, and found himself subjected to a lengthy filibuster by opposition MPs.

Real Life

Sir John Sparrow David Thompson (1845–1894) was the Prime Minister of Canada from 1892 to 1894. He assumed power when his fellow Conservative Sir John Joseph Caldwell Abbott was forced to resign due to ill health. Thompson died during a visit to Windsor Castle, where he was visiting Queen Victoria. Prior to entering federal politics, Thompson was a lawyer, the alderman of Halifax, and a justice in the Supreme Court of Nova Scotia.

Real Life

Sir Mackenzie Bowell (1823–1917) was the Prime Minister of Canada from 1894 to 1896. He assumed power when Prime Minister John Sparrow David Thompson died suddenly while in office. Prior to entering politics, Bowell was the printer, editor, and later owner of *The Belleville Intelligencer* and a businessman. He handed control of the government over to Sir Charles Tupper following a lengthy filibuster concerning the Manitoba Schools Question.

Word for the Day

Filibuster refers to the use of irregular or obstructive tactics, such as exceptionally long speeches, to prevent the adoption of a measure or to force a decision.

Main Event

In 1890, Manitoba decided to abolish separate schools in favour of non-denominational schools. The legislation in question—the Manitoba Schools Act—was upheld by the Privy Council, but the federal government was determined to provide for separate schools in Manitoba. A compromise between the federal government and the province was finally reached in 1897 during Sir Wilfrid Laurier's term as prime minister. Separate schools were not restored, but provisions were made for denominational religious teaching and bilingual instruction in schools in which 10 or more pupils spoke a language other than English. The Manitoba Schools Act not only stirred up the French-English question, but also represented the ongoing struggle for provincial autonomy.

In the end, a fellow Conservative—Sir Charles Tupper—assumed the office of prime minister and called a general election on the Manitoba Schools Act question. The Conservatives were defeated in that election by a powerful new Liberal leader, Sir Wilfrid Laurier. The Macdonald era was over; the Laurier era had just begun.

Real Life

Sir Charles Tupper (1821–1915) was the Prime Minister of Canada for a few months in 1896. He assumed control of the government from fellow Conservative Sir Mackenzie Bowell following a filibuster on the Manitoba Schools Question. Prior to entering federal politics, he was a physician, the head of the Canadian Medical Association, and the premier of Nova Scotia. Tupper also served as Leader of the Opposition (1896–1901) following his defeat to Sir Wilfrid Laurier in the 1896 election.

The Least You Need to Know

- Macdonald's National Policy (1879) was an attempt to stimulate the Canadian economy by providing a series of protective tariffs.
- Regional discontent continued to be a problem. Each province had its own unique grievances.
- The Northwest Rebellion (a.k.a. The Rebellion of 1885) resulted in the hanging of Louis Riel. Debate about whether Riel had been treated fairly threatened to divide the country.
- The provinces were anxious to increase their share of the national revenue and to put an end to the all-too-common federal practice of disallowing provincial legislation. Five provinces met in Quebec City in October 1887 to discuss their grievances. (British Columbia, Prince Edward Island, and the federal government chose not to participate.) Unfortunately, the resolutions resulting from the second Quebec Conference were ignored by the federal government.
- Staple producers were anxious for commercial union with the United States; manufacturers were not.
- The Conservative Party went through a period of crisis following the death of Macdonald. The Dominion was led by four different Conservative prime ministers during the five years following his death.

Part 4
Canada's Century

The first part of the 20th century was a time of unprecedented prosperity for Canada. There was tremendous demand for the country's exports, and immigrants were being attracted to Canada in record numbers. Unfortunately, the new century also brought with it some new problems. Cities sprung up and became overcrowded overnight, necessitating government and church involvement in urban reform. Great Britain suddenly developed a newfound interest in Canada, seeking her cooperation in matters of defence. Labour unions began to come into conflict with big business. Women began to assert themselves in public life and to demand the right to vote. And after decades of disinterest, the United States expressed a sudden willingness to renew talks about reciprocity. Clearly, these were times that could make or break a politician....

Chapter 19

Happy Days (1896 to 1914)

In this chapter

- The booming Canadian economy
- The Fielding tariff

"The nineteenth century was the century of the United States; the twentieth century will be the century of Canada."

When Sir Wilfrid Laurier made this bold declaration shortly after winning the election of 1896, his fellow citizens were inclined to believe him.

Many of the problems that had plagued Canada since Confederation seemed to be disappearing, and Canada was beginning to benefit from the worldwide prosperity that had been triggered by the discovery of gold in South Africa.

Prior to 1896, however, the Canadian economic situation had been anything but rosy. The West had not experienced the boom in agricultural production and settlement that the Fathers of Confederation had anticipated, largely because many potential emigrants from Britain and continental Europe had chosen to seek their

Real Life

Sir Wilfrid Laurier (1841–1919) was the first French Canadian to serve as the Prime Minister of Canada. He headed the federal government from 1896 to 1911 and led the Liberal party from 1887 to 1919.

Prior to entering federal politics, he worked as a lawyer, an editor, an ensign in the infantry, and from 1871 to 1874 served as a member of the Legislative Assembly of Quebec.

Laurier is remembered for his skills as an orator, and for his efforts to reach compromise solutions that would hold the country together rather than tear it apart. His major accomplishments in office included the resolution of the Manitoba Schools Question (1896), the creation of the provinces of Saskatchewan and Alberta (1905), and the formation of the Departments of Labour (1900) and External Affairs (1909). He was less successful in his handling of Canada's involvement in the Boer War (1899), the Alaska Boundary Dispute (1903), and the infamous Naval Service Bill (1910), which created his so-called "tin-pot" navy.

fortunes in the United States or Australasia instead. The East was, at best, progressing slowly towards its goal of industrialization, with less than 20 per cent of the Canadian population engaged in manufacturing. In addition, the volume of Canada's exports had fallen by 20 per cent during the 1870s and had shown no signs of recovery during the subsequent 15 years.

Boom Times

Fortunately, 1896 marked the beginning of a worldwide boom that would help to stimulate Canada's economy. Canada was able to benefit tremendously from this general economic upturn because the prices of raw materials (its key exports) rose much more quickly than the prices of manufactured goods (its key imports). Between 1896 and 1914, Canadian exports enjoyed an average price increase of 32 per cent (with grain prices jumping a phenomenal 66 per cent because of increased demand from European countries). During this same period,

Stats

Between 1891 and 1916, the gross value of manufactured goods increased from $368 million to $1.381 billion, and the value of field crops more than quadrupled.

In this period, Canada's exports of grains increased from 2 million bushels to 150 million bushels. Much of these exports went to Europe, which desperately needed foodstuffs to feed its growing urban population.

the cost of Canada's imports rose by only 24 per cent. What's more, a sharp decline in ocean-freight rates made Canadian exports much more competitive in the international marketplace, leading to boom times for the Canadian economy.

At the same time, the Canadian economy began to diversify. Technological change led to the creation of new staples such as silver, nickel, and wood fibre. Canada's mineral wealth became apparent during the early decades of the new century when copper and nickel reserves were discovered in the Sudbury area and silver was discovered near Cobalt. By 1914, Canada had acquired a near-monopoly over world nickel production. New techniques for using wood pulp (rather than costlier linen and cotton rags) to make paper allowed Canada to become the leading exporter of wood fibre after 1900.

During the first few decades of the 20th century, various provinces were able to capitalize on their natural resources. In Ontario, hydroelectric power opened up a wealth of new opportunities. In British Columbia, a rapidly increasing fishing industry

Stats

Not all parts of the country shared equally in the newfound prosperity. Declining markets for fish and timber combined with the decreased need for coal in the new age of hydroelectric power took their toll on the Maritime provinces. Between 1891 and 1911—a period during which Canada's population grew from 4.8 million to 7.2 million—Nova Scotia's population increased by just 42,000, New Brunswick's population increased by just 30,000, and Prince Edward Island's population decreased by 16,000.

(the value of which doubled between 1900 and 1914) fuelled economic growth in the province.

> **Stats**
>
> One of the prime beneficiaries of the newfound prosperity was the West. Between 1891 and 1916, the population of Manitoba increased from 152,000 to 554,000, the population of British Columbia increased from 98,000 to 456,000, and the population of the Northwest Territories (which by 1905 had become the provinces of Saskatchewan and Alberta) grew from 100,000 to 1 million.

The Boom in the West

The manufacturing and natural resource sectors weren't the only ones to benefit from technological change. The turn of the century also saw numerous agricultural advances. Studies into so-called "dry farming" techniques showed prairie farmers how to maximize their agricultural output despite the arid conditions. Improved technology (that is, improved ploughs, harrows, and seed drills and gas-powered tractors) enabled farmers to tend to their crops more efficiently, the only downside being the increased debt load they were forced to carry to acquire these agricultural bells and whistles. Most significant of all, however, were the improvements to the actual varieties of grain. The introduction of Marquis wheat—which required eight fewer days to mature than Red Fife yet maintained the desired hardness and protein content—enabled farmers to dramatically increase their yields. As a result of these advances, during the 15 years between 1896 and 1911, wheat acreage tripled and wheat production quadrupled.

> **Stats**
>
> 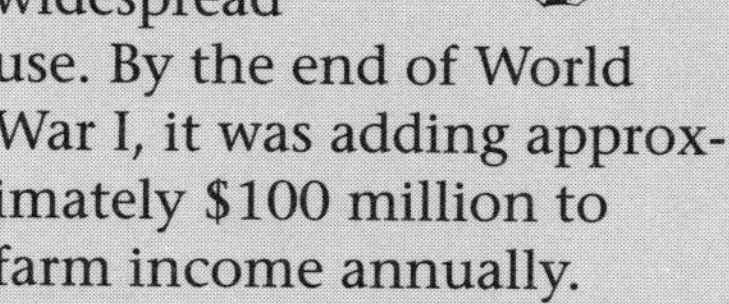
>
> By 1911, Marquis wheat was in widespread use. By the end of World War I, it was adding approximately $100 million to farm income annually.

Foreign Ownership and Other Perils

The improved economic conditions in Canada attracted a great deal of interest from foreign investors (primarily British and American), who poured their money into the country's newly discovered resources (that is, the mining sector) as well as a number of manufacturing enterprises.

By 1912, Coca-Cola and 200 other products from around the world were being made in Canada.

Not everyone was happy about the amount of foreign capital being poured into the country, however. Quebec nationalist Jules Fournier expressed the fears of many Canadians in 1908 when he said, "We will be working to enrich the foreigner in our very own forests, at our very own waterfalls, in all of our own resources. They will have the money and consequently the power and we, we will be the drawers of water and hewers of wood."

The early 20th century was also a time of mergers and acquisitions. To prevent too much power and wealth accumulating in too few hands, the Dominion government introduced the Combines Investigation Act in 1910. The purpose of the Act was to strengthen existing antitrust legislation.

The Fielding Tariff

While the economy was clearly booming (something that the Laurier government was only too happy to take credit for!), the country was anxious to see what the new Liberal government would deliver in its first budget.

After campaigning on the merits of free trade with the United States, the new government was committed to showing some movement in that direction in its 1897 budget. Finance Minister William S. Fielding was able to save face with the farmers, who had been particularly outspoken in support of free trade, by proposing a rather novel solution. Because free trade with the United States had become an impossibility ever since the American government had introduced its own protective tariff (the Dingley tariff), Fielding introduced a two-tiered tariff that basically put responsibility for the negotiation of free trade in the hands of the Americans. Those countries that had tariffs designed to exclude Canadian goods would receive one rate; those that admitted Canadian goods at preferential rates would receive reduced tariff rates from Canada.

While the budget more closely resembled the Conservative protectionist budgets of years gone by than the free trade system the Liberals had promised to deliver, it contained enough goodies to win the support of imperialists (who felt that the budget would increase trade with Britain), farmers (who were satisfied by changes to the tariff rates for fence wire, cream separators, and similar items), and the business community (who, for once, were not unduly alarmed by the direction taken by the federal finance minister). Somehow, Fielding had managed to do the impossible: introduce a budget that didn't produce an outcry from Canada's many interest groups.

The Least You Need to Know

- The election of the Laurier government coincided with a period of worldwide prosperity. Because the price of raw materials rose much more quickly than the price of manufactured goods, Canada was able to benefit tremendously from the boom.
- The early 20th century was a period of technological change that allowed Canada to develop some new staples for export (that is, nickel and wood fibre) and to improve its agricultural output.
- The Fielding tariff—introduced as part of the Laurier government's first budget—provided preferential tariff rates for countries who admitted Canadian goods at reduced rates.

Chapter 20

On the Grow (1896 to 1914)

In this chapter

- ➤ Immigration and western settlement
- ➤ French-Canadian reaction to immigration
- ➤ The farmers' grievances
- ➤ The need for more railways
- ➤ The creation of Saskatchewan and Alberta

During the first years of the new century, the Laurier government devoted considerable energy to attracting settlers to the Canadian West.

The architect of the government's immigration programs was a rising political star named Clifford Sifton who had made a name for himself because of his astute handling of the Manitoba Schools Question.

After joining the federal Cabinet as the Minister of the Interior, Sifton launched a massive immigration campaign designed to bring settlers to Canada. His campaign targeted both the United States and Europe.

In the United States, Sifton advertised in thousands of farm journals and rural newspapers, promoting the benefits of the cheap, fertile

Real Life

Clifford Sifton joined the Laurier Cabinet following a distinguished career as the Attorney General of Manitoba, a position he assumed at the tender age of 30. His boundless faith in the potential of the West made him the ideal choice for the position of Minister of the Interior. Believing that the West needed to be developed in an orderly, businesslike fashion, Sifton simplified the homesteading process and forced the railways to select their land. (Up until that time, large portions of the West were untouchable because of the agreements that various governments had made with the railroads.) His greatest claim to fame, however, were his immigration campaigns, which attracted large numbers of settlers to the Canadian West.

land available in Canada. He provided newspaper editors with free trips to the Canadian West, in the hope that their favourable reports would encourage settlement. He organized tours of the West for prospective settlers, with the government and the railways picking up the tab. He published a series of pamphlets with such catchy titles as *The Last, Best West, The Evolution of the Prairie by the Plow, The Wondrous West, Canada in a Nutshell, Where and How and All About It, Information and Facts for the Prospective Settler*, and *One Thousand Facts About Canada* (which was later reissued as *Five Thousand Facts About Canada*!). While the pamphlets were designed to be persuasive, they tended to stick to the facts. The last thing Sifton wanted was to populate the Canadian West with a large number of disgruntled settlers.

Voice from the Past

"The best way you can help the manufacturers of Canada is to fill up the prairie regions of Manitoba and the Northwest with a prosperous and contented people who will be consumers of the manufactured goods of the east."

—Finance Minister William S. Fielding

Sifton's campaign in Europe was equally comprehensive. Sifton

Voice from the Past

"If a settler is one who has been engaged in agricultural pursuits in the old land, is possessed of his full faculties, steady, honest, sober, and willing to work whether he be rich or poor, Galician, Austrian, Russian, Swede, Belgian or French, we believe it most desirable to encourage him to occupy our land and to break up our soil and assist in developing the resources of the country, and in this way enrich himself and Canada."

—Deputy Minister of the Interior James Smart

appointed immigration agents in a variety of countries, printed handbills and pamphlets in a number of languages, and sent successful western settlers on speaking tours overseas. Perhaps the best measure of the European campaign's success was the resistance that it encountered. Many European governments made it clear that Canadian immigration agents were not welcome in their countries. The French government actively campaigned against immigration to Canada, while Germany prohibited immigration agents and levied heavy licensing fees on steamship companies that transported emigrants.

The results of Sifton's efforts speak for themselves. Between 1897 and 1911, nearly 2 million immigrants poured into Canada, swelling the population by nearly one third. While the majority of these immigrants ended up in cities (a problem Sifton's program had not anticipated), enough located on agricultural land to create 30,000 new farms each year. As a result, Canada's wheat production tripled every five years between 1896 and 1911.

While Sifton's campaign was undeniably successful, the situation south of the border also worked in his favour. The exhaustion of free homestead land in the United States meant that a steady stream of settlers who might

Voice from the Past

"I think a stalwart peasant in a sheep-skin coat, born on the soil, whose forefathers have been farmers for ten generations, with a stout wife and a half-dozen children, is good quality."

—Minister of the Interior Clifford Sifton

Stats

A new settler needed $250 to establish a farm. This included $180 for a yoke of oxen, $30 for a cow, $20 for a wagon, and $14 for a breaking plough. He also needed enough funds for a house and household effects. Depending on the level of comfort he was accustomed to (and this did vary considerably!), the total cost for a farm and homestead could run anywhere from $500 to $1500 and beyond.

otherwise have settled in the American West headed for Canada instead. The opening of the Canadian West was, as Sifton himself said at the time, the last great North American land rush.

Some Were More Welcome Than Others...

In many ways, Canadian immigration policy was quite liberal for the time. Because Canada was badly in need of settlers, minority groups were able to negotiate a series of special privileges that they might not otherwise have been granted. Groups such as the Doukhobors, the Hutterites, the Mennonites, and the Mormons were, for example, promised freedom from persecution, guaranteed the right to practise their religion, and given permission to establish their own schools (provided they did so at their own expense).

This is not to say that all immigrants were welcomed equally, however. Some ethnic groups, such as African Americans, the Chinese, the Japanese, and East Indians, were discouraged from coming to Canada because they could not easily be assimilated into the Canadian population.

Voice from the Past

"Slabs of sod were placed around the lumber shack and another room was added—all sod. The inside was plastered with mud, with a nice smooth finish. As the years passed the mud plastering was papered over with building paper. The sod walls were three feet thick. There was a good shingle roof and board floors. It was a warm cosy place."

—A settler's description of her first home in the Canadian West.

Whenever these so-called "undesirables" arrived in large numbers, the backlash from Canadian citizens was considerable. The Asiatic Exclusion League, for example, was formed in Vancouver in August 1907 because of fears that the large waves of Asian immigrants would overtake the Canadian population in the area. Likewise, in May 1914, a Japanese immigrant ship, the *Komagata Maru*, spent two months sitting in Vancouver harbour before the 376 East Indian would-be settlers on board were escorted back out to sea by the *HMCS Rainbow*.

Fear and intolerance of immigrants were not confined to British Columbia, however. It was a problem in most of the country's largest cities, where large numbers of immigrants settled while they saved towards the purchase of their first homestead or where they fled following agricultural failures. Immigrants were accused of being the cause of everything that ailed these urban areas, including prostitution, alcoholism, and the slum-like conditions in the inner cities.

The majority of Canadians believed that foreigners needed to assimilate into Canadian society. The views of reformer J.S. Woodsworth were typical: "If Canada is to become in any real sense a nation, if our people are to become one people, we must have one language."

Stats

By 1911, the majority of Winnipeg residents were foreign-born. As a result, the compromise of the Manitoba Schools Question reached in 1896 began to cause problems. By 1907, Winnipeg schools offered instruction in 13 different languages. Those who had come from Ontario began to call for an end to what they saw as an absurd situation, and began lobbying for instruction in one language and one language only: English.

French-Canadian Reaction to Immigration

While English Canadians may have been less than enthusiastic about the large number of immigrants who arrived during the first decade of the new century, French Canadians were positively hostile. They feared that they were going to be vastly outnumbered by the new arrivals, and that they would no longer be able to defend their interests against the non-French-speaking majority. Their fears were not unreasonable: by this time both English-speaking Canadians and new immigrants had become quite outspoken about the position of French-speaking Canadians,

Voice from the Past

"It never was in the minds of the founders of this nation, it never was in the minds of the fathers of confederation, the men whose names these present so-called Liberals are so fond of evoking, that in order to be broad—or even in order to make land speculators rich—we ought to change a providential condition of our partly French and partly English country to make it a land of refuge for the scum of all nations."

—Quebec nationalist Henri Bourassa,
speaking in the House of Commons in 1904.

stating repeatedly that French Canadians were no more deserving of special rights and privileges than members of any other ethnic group.

To counter this threat to the French-Canadian culture and way of life, a number of nationalistic groups emerged in Quebec during the early 20th century. Organized by young people from middle-class professional backgrounds, their mission was to preserve the French-Canadian culture and to protect the special rights they had been given at the time of Confederation.

One of the most significant of these nationalistic groups was *La Ligue Nationaliste Canadienne*, founded in 1903. The group was heavily influenced by the ideas of Henri Bourassa, an independent federal politician who had broken with the Laurier government over the issue of Canadian participation in the Boer War. *La Ligue* stood for the preservation of Canada within the British Empire; the maintenance of the rights guaranteed to the provinces under the terms of the British North America Act; respect for linguistic dualism and separate school rights; and the intellectual and economic development of Canada by and for Canadians.

Another noteworthy group was the *Association Catholique de la Jeunesse Canadienne-Française*, founded in 1904. The *Association*'s constitution stated that the "French-Canadian race has a special mission to fulfil on this continent and that it must...guard its distinct character from that of other races" and that "the progress of the French-Canadian race is in special fashion attached to the Catholic faith, which is one of the essential and specific elements." The *Association* circulated petitions demanding the greater use of the French language in the economic life of Quebec, and spoke out strongly against both the Autonomy Bill of 1905 (which created the provinces of Alberta and Saskatchewan) and the Naval Service Bill of 1910 (which established a Canadian navy).

Other groups, such as the *Société du parler français* and *La Ligue des Droits français* (later renamed *La Ligue d'Action française*), sought to promote the French language and to protect it from any perceived "corruption."

Growing Pains

Despite the challenges posed by the emergence of a multicultural society, the West was experiencing an unprecedented boom. A large number of acres were being farmed, and wheat production was at an all-time high.

With these boom times, however, came some inevitable growing pains. Farmers in the West had a lengthy list of grievances: there was a shortage of freight cars at harvest time, the men controlling the grain elevators were offering unreasonably low prices for wheat and other products, and the protective tariff forced them to buy manufactured goods at artificially high prices and to sell their products in an unprotected and highly competitive marketplace.

The farmers responded by pulling together. By organizing, they were able to win some important concessions from the Dominion government. Freight rates were lowered on many of the railways serving the West, and the various cooperative grain growers' associations (formed in the prairie provinces after 1902 to handle grain sales) were increasingly recognized by government as the voice of the western farming community.

More Railways

One of the farmers' key grievances was the need for more railways. Within a few years of coming to power, the Laurier government found itself pressed to subsidize not one but two new transcontinental railway systems: the Canadian Northern Railway and the Grand Trunk Pacific.

Main Event

In 1901, western farmers experienced a bumper crop. Instead of being the source of celebration, however, the crop caused considerable grief. It was so large that the railways were only able to carry out one third of the crop before winter arrived; the rest was left to rot.

As a result, a group of western grain growers formed the Territorial Grain Growers' Association to fight for better rail service and fairer pricing methods. The Association grew quickly, soon spreading to Manitoba, where the Manitoba Grain Growers' Association was formed in 1902.

The Manitoba Grain Growers' Association also formed the Grain Growers' Grain Company, a farmer-owned cooperative company that purchased grain from farmers and sold it to a central marketing agency, the Winnipeg-based Grain Exchange. By 1912, the Company had 27,000 shareholders, owned several grain elevators, published a newspaper, and was beginning to supply its members with farm equipment and supplies.

Initially, the government of Manitoba had provided financial support to the Canadian Northern Railway. As a result, by 1903 the railway stretched from Port Arthur to Portage La Prairie and connected with the Northern Pacific in the United States, making it the third largest railway system in Canada. The forward-thinking entrepreneurs behind the enterprise then acquired lines in the Maritimes, Quebec, and Ontario, as well as a westward extension that reached as far as Edmonton. At this point, there were only two gaps in what otherwise would be Canada's second transcontinental railway. The Canadian Northern Railway turned to the federal and provincial governments for assistance,

Stats

The railways were built by poorly paid immigrant labourers who were brought to Canada by the railway companies. Between 1907 and 1914, 60,000 workers were involved in railway construction each year.

and walked away with $105 million in federal guarantees plus another $130 million in provincial guarantees.

The backers of the long-established Grand Trunk system convinced the Laurier government to build another line from the Maritimes to Winnipeg. This new line would be leased to Grand Trunk's subsidiary, the Grand Trunk Pacific. At the same time, the Grand Trunk Pacific would lay track from Winnipeg to the Pacific coast, aided by a government guarantee of bonds of up to $13,000 per mile in the prairies and up to 75 per cent of the cost through the mountain region.

Initially, the federal government tried to get the two railways to work together, but neither was prepared to cooperate. In the end, the government decided to subsidize both railway systems. Laurier argued that Canada's growth would be sufficient to justify investment in both projects: "This is not a time for deliberation, this is a time for action. The flood-tide is upon us that leads to fortune; if we let it pass it may never recur again."

Unfortunately for Canadians, Laurier was a little too optimistic. Canada was not yet ready to support three transcontinental railway systems. It wasn't long before both the Canadian Northern Railway and the Grand Trunk Pacific collapsed into bankruptcy.

Two New Provinces

The boom in the West also led to the creation of two new provinces, Alberta and Saskatchewan. The two new provinces were established in 1905, with the passage of the Autonomy Act.

Since 1875, Alberta and Saskatchewan had been part of the Northwest Territories. While Manitoba had initially hoped to extend its borders and absorb the 164,000 settlers living in this area, the federal

Word for the Day

Alberta was named after Princess Louise Caroline Alberta, the daughter of Queen Victoria and the wife of the Marquis of Lorne (Canada's Governor General from 1878 to 1883).

Word for the Day

The Cree referred to the river that flowed across their prairie lands as *Kisikatchewan,* meaning "swift current." Early explorers recorded the name of the river as *Saskatchewan.*

government had other plans for the West. It decided to create two new provinces and maintain control over their natural resources, as had been done in Manitoba. While Laurier had hoped to provide for a separate school system in the two provinces, public outcry from Manitoba and Ontario forced him to reconsider. In the end, a secular school system was introduced in each province, with time allocated for religious instruction during the school day.

The Least You Need to Know

- The Canadian government devoted considerable resources to attracting settlers to the Canadian West. As a result, more than 2 million immigrants entered Canada between 1897 and 1911.
- The backlash against the new immigrants was considerable. French Canadians were particularly concerned that they would be so badly outnumbered by these new immigrants that they would lose the special rights and privileges they had been guaranteed at the time of Confederation.
- Farmers began to organize to ensure that they received the best possible price for their grain and to lobby the federal government for the redress of some long-standing grievances.
- The boom in the West highlighted the need for more railways. The federal government agreed to subsidize the cost of building two new transcontinental systems: the Canadian Northern Railway and the Grand Trunk Pacific. In the end, both railways went bankrupt.
- The Autonomy Act of 1905 created the provinces of Saskatchewan and Alberta.

Chapter 21

Them vs. Us (1887 to 1910)

In this chapter

- The colonial conferences
- The Boer War
- The Alaska Boundary Dispute
- The Naval Service Bill

Throughout the Laurier years, the aim of the Canadian government was to maintain its connection with Britain but prevent the British government from interfering in Canadian affairs. Often that meant resisting subtle—and not so subtle—pressure from Great Britain, which was anxious to forge stronger economic and military ties with Canada.

The Colonial Conferences

In the late 19th and early 20th centuries, the British government organized a series of colonial conferences that it hoped would promote closer ties among the various countries within the British Empire. While there was considerable talk about establishing free trade and sharing imperial defence costs, nothing concrete resulted from the discussions.

The Boer War

In 1899, the Boer (or "farmer") republics of Transvaal and the Orange Free State declared war on Great Britain. The Boers were Dutch settlers living in South Africa. While they had only come under British control in the late 1870s, they had been farming in South Africa for 200 years. When huge quantities of gold and diamonds were found on Boer lands, the British and the Boers came into conflict over who had the right to these riches.

As soon as war had been declared, Britain turned to its colonies for support. It asked Canada, Australia, and New Zealand to send troops. Laurier's first response was that as the war posed no direct threat to Canada, Canadians should not become involved.

The outcry from English-speaking Canadians was immediate: they thought Canada should back Britain in the war. In an effort to appease the imperialists, Laurier agreed to send a volunteer contingent of 1000 men to help in the war, provided that Britain paid for and maintained the troops while they were in South Africa. In the end, 7300 Canadians served in the Boer War.

French Canadians were not pleased to see Canadians involved in the war, which they viewed as an act of British aggression against a linguistic minority. Tensions between French- and English-speaking Canadians over the issue increased the growing rift between the two cultures.

> **Stats**
>
> The Klondike gold rush peaked in 1903, when $12 million of gold was discovered. By 1914, that quantity had dropped to $5 million. The value of the discoveries continued to decline thereafter.

The Alaska Boundary Dispute

When gold was discovered in the Klondike in 1896, the long-standing dispute with the United States over the Alaska boundary suddenly heated up.

The boundary issue had been on the back burner since the United States purchased Alaska from the Russians back in 1867. What was being disputed was who owned the Alaska panhandle—a thin strip of land running along the coast of British Columbia, just south of Alaska. The panhandle's proximity to the gold fields made it very valuable land. Whichever country had control of it stood to gain the most from the gold rush. Basically, the prosperity of Vancouver versus the prosperity of Seattle was at stake.

In an attempt to resolve the dispute, in 1903 the Americans, the British, and the Canadians agreed to form a six-person tribunal to examine the issue. The three countries agreed to appoint "impartial jurists of repute," but when push came to shove, U.S. President Theodore Roosevelt stacked the deck in his favour by appointing three Americans who were anything but impartial: Secretary of War Elihu Root, Senator Henry Cabot Lodge, and Senator George Turner. The tribunal was rounded out with two Canadians, Lieutenant Governor Sir Louis Jetté of Quebec and lawyer A.B. Aylesworth of Ontario, and one representative from Great Britain, British Chief Justice Lord Alverstone.

In the end, Lord Alverstone ended up with the deciding vote, and he chose to side with the Americans. Jetté and Aylesworth were so disgusted with the outcome that they refused to sign the award, calling it "a grotesque travesty of justice." The Canadian public was similarly outraged. Articles in Canadian newspapers angrily declared that Canada had once again been "offered as a sacrifice on the altar of Anglo-American friendship." Even Clifford Sifton added his two cents, complaining bitterly that Britain had decided "to sacrifice our interests at any cost, for the sake of pleasing the United States."

The outcome was actually more reasonable than the Canadian government or the public as a whole were prepared to admit at the time, as the Americans probably had the stronger case. What made the outcome so hard to stomach, however, was the obnoxious behaviour of President Roosevelt, who threatened to forcibly seize the Alaskan border if Canadians would not come around to his way of thinking. Because of the high degree of dissatisfaction among Canadians, Robert Borden and his Conservatives were able to score political points against the Liberals by accusing them of grossly mishandling the situation.

The Naval Service Bill

In 1909, Britain discovered to its horror that Germany was building a navy that threatened to challenge Britain's supremacy on the seas. It called an emergency imperial conference (previously known as a colonial conference) to discuss the issue.

At the conference, the British made it clear that they wanted financial support from the colonies to allow them to build on the strength of the British navy. Rather than agreeing to provide Britain with financial support, Laurier agreed to create a Canadian navy that would consist of five cruisers and six destroyers and feature a permanent naval force of reserves and regulars. While the navy would be under Canadian command, it could be placed under imperial control in the event of war.

When Laurier introduced his Naval Service Bill in the House of Commons on January 12, 1910, the messy question of imperial relations was once again brought to the forefront. This time, nobody was happy. Staunch imperialists viewed the creation of such an insignificant navy as an insult to Britain in her hour of need, while French Canadians viewed the creation of any navy at all as a surrender to imperialism. What's more, Maritimers—whose shipbuilding industry had long been in decline—were furious that the ships were to be built in Britain!

Although the Conservatives took great delight in taunting the Liberals about their so-called "tin-pot" navy, the Naval Service Bill passed nonetheless, and the Canadian navy—small as it was—officially came into being.

The Least You Need to Know

- Canada was anxious to maintain her place within the British Empire but wanted to prevent Britain from interfering in Canadian affairs.
- The Boer War was the first foreign war in which Canadian soldiers participated. More than 7300 Canadians served in the war, which was strongly supported by English-speaking Canadians and strongly opposed by French-speaking Canadians.
- The Alaska Boundary Dispute came to a head when gold was discovered in the Klondike. Both the Canadians and the Americans wanted claim to the thin strip of land known as the Alaska panhandle. Canadians were outraged when an "impartial" tribunal consisting of three Americans, two Canadians, and one Brit awarded the panhandle to the Americans.
- After discovering that Germany was increasing its navy, Britain turned to its colonies for support. Rather than agreeing to provide the British with financial support, Canada offered to create its own navy. Because the navy consisted of just five cruisers and six destroyers, the Conservatives took great pleasure in ridiculing Laurier about his "tin-pot" navy.

Chapter 22

Bright Lights, Big Problems (1896 to 1914)

In this chapter

- Urban reform
- The temperance movement and the emergence of the women's movement
- The roots of the labour movement

The cities were a terrific place to live in turn-of-the-century Canada—provided, of course, that you belonged to the upper class.

The wealthiest citizens enjoyed moonlit pleasure cruises and drives in motor cars, belonged to exclusive social clubs, and lived in fine city homes designed to showcase their owners' wealth and achievements.

The story was quite different on the other side of town, however, where members of the poorer classes were housed in substandard accommodations and forced to struggle for their very survival.

Urban Reform

By the first decade of the new century, conditions in the cities had deteriorated to the point that something had to be done. Both government officials and the churches were concerned about the slum-like conditions that could be found in the underbelly of the country's largest cities.

As a result, city governments began to introduce a wide range of municipal improvements: they established parks, improved sewers, cleaned streets, installed better lighting, created more efficient forms of public transportation, and

Stats

By 1921, the population of Canada was roughly 50 per cent urban and 50 per cent rural.

Stats

Between 1891 and 1908, the population of Montreal grew from 268,000 to 373,000; the population of Toronto increased from 181,000 to 314,000; the population of Winnipeg went from 26,000 to 140,000; and the population of Vancouver jumped from 14,000 to 93,700.

Real Life

H.C. Hocken was the mayor of Toronto from 1912 to 1914. During that time, he introduced a comprehensive urban reform program aimed at improving the quality of life for inner city residents.

Hocken established recreation facilities, introduced public baths, constructed a new sewage treatment and filtration plant, extended the city's sewer system, formed a housing company to build houses that could be rented out at cost, provided for a public health nursing program, and distributed fresh milk to infants living in the slums.

Hocken also introduced a minimum wage for municipal workers ($15 per week), created separate courts for women and children who found themselves in conflict with the law, and established a series of correctional farms for young offenders.

began to offer their citizens access to hydroelectric power.

While the city governments focused on the physical aspects of city life, the churches were more concerned about what they perceived as growing evidence of moral decay. Motivated by a desire to improve the quality of city life for the good of all, they established missions designed to minister to the needs of inner-city residents.

The All Peoples' Mission in Winnipeg, founded by the Methodist Church in 1892, was typical. J.S. Woodsworth, a minister and social activist who would later become a Member of Parliament and the leader of the Co-operative Commonwealth Federation (the predecessor of the New Democratic Party), assumed responsibility for the mission in 1907. He organized a series of activities for residents of the city's poverty-stricken North End, including kindergarten programs, summer camps, English classes, free legal clinics, poor relief programs, and Sunday schools.

Prohibition

At the same time that city governments and the churches were busy establishing urban reform programs, middle-class Anglo-Saxon Protestants were becoming increasingly convinced that alcohol was the root of all evil. They blamed liquor for a smorgasbord of evils, including mental illness, family breakdown, poverty, prostitution, problems in the workplace, disease, crime, and accidents.

The driving force behind the movement was middle-class Protestant women who became involved because they saw alcohol

Voice from the Past

"Public affairs, the social and political business of the country must be brought under the Commandments and the Sermon on the Mount...temperance is but one of the social, we might say, national questions which the Church must consider."

—Rev. H.R. Grant, leader of prohibition forces in Nova Scotia, speaking at the Synod of the Presbyterian Church in 1907.

Stats

The first local chapter of the Women's Christian Temperance Union was founded in 1874. By 1900, the organization had 10,000 members and had established chapters throughout the Dominion.

consumption and the evils that it represented as a threat to their way of life. They joined organizations such as the Women's Christian Temperance Union (WCTU) where they worked to achieve a common goal: prohibition.

While the focus of the WCTU was undeniably prohibition, at times the organization became a little overzealous, widening its focus to other threats to "pure living," such as certain styles of evening dress, round dances, nude art, gambling, the theatre, prize fights, and the employment of women as bar maids. Even novels were identified as a source of moral decay. (A mere peek at today's fiction bestseller list would be enough to make any self-respecting WCTU member roll over in her grave!)

For the most part, the members of the WCTU relied on petitions to pressure the government to act. In 1896, Laurier agreed to hold a national plebiscite on the issue of prohibition. The members of the WCTU, who had worked so long and hard to obtain this victory, felt that they should be able to vote in the plebiscite. When the government refused their request, the outcry was considerable; "Dear women, are we free and intelligent citizens of a civilized

Voice from the Past

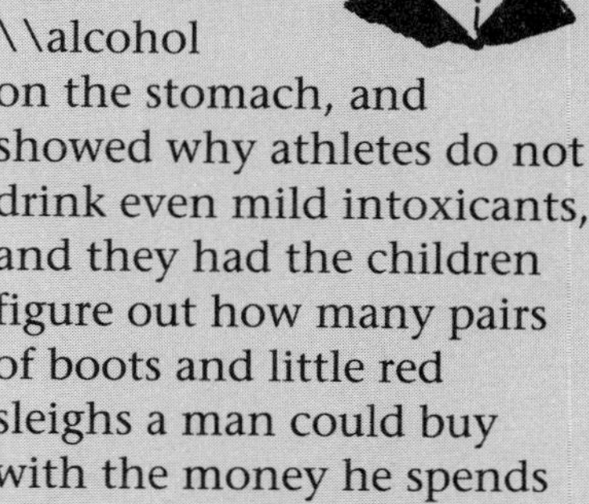

"They explained the circulation of the blood, and the effect of \\alcohol on the stomach, and showed why athletes do not drink even mild intoxicants, and they had the children figure out how many pairs of boots and little red sleighs a man could buy with the money he spends on a daily glass of beer."

—Nellie McClung, member of the Women's Christian Temperance Union (WCTU) and early feminist, talking about the WCTU's education programs.

nonentities that our government reckons us?" the Nova Scotia WCTU asked its members.

The long-anticipated plebiscite took place on September 29, 1898. Every province but Quebec voted in favour of prohibition, but the Laurier government—which relied on Quebec for its political support—refused to heed the results of the plebiscite.

The members of the WCTU were outraged. Having lost their faith in government, they concluded that the only way in which women would be able to make their voices heard and exercise their role as "the moral guardians of society" would be by obtaining the right to vote.

The National Council of Women of Canada

Another women's organization that played an important role during this period was the National Council of Women of Canada, which was founded in 1893 by Lady Ishbel Marjoribanks Gordon, the Countess of Aberdeen and the wife of Canada's Governor General. Within six years, there were 23 Local Councils up and running in cities from Charlottetown to Victoria.

The Council's aim, as stated in its constitution, was to encourage women to play a larger role in their communities: "We, Women of Canada, sincerely believing that the best good of our homes and nation will be advanced by our own greater unity of thought, sympathy, and purpose, and that an organized movement of women will best conserve the greatest good of the Family and State, do hereby band ourselves together to further the application of the Golden Rule to society, custom and law."

From the beginning, the Council recommended reforms in the areas of dental and medical health, the provision of recreation facilities, truancy, prostitution, "the white slave trade," and immigration policy. While the Council initially ignored the suffrage issue, it eventually came on board, arguing that women—as the purist part of the species—were, in fact, *more* deserving of the vote than men!

Because the Council was deliberately non-partisan and non-denominational, it was able to attract women from a number of different walks of life. Ironically, because of its policy of encouraging silent prayer, it was unable to attract support from the ranks of the Women's Christian Temperance Union! It was, however, able to attract consider-

Voice from the Past

"The woman who aspires to make home a place for rest after work and for strengthening before labour, a centre of holy associations and inspiring memories has need herself to be in touch with every side of our manifold life. She must realize that no walls can shelter her dear ones from the temptations, sorrows and discouragements of life. She must learn that if the poor around her doors are not cared for, the orphans not housed, the erring not reclaimed, because she was too much engrossed in her own house to lend a helping hand, the results of her self-absorption may be in the future to provide pitfalls for her own children whom she so desires to cherish. The high ideal of a pure and holy family life is the chief strength of all nations."

—Lady Aberdeen, speaking to the founding convention of the National Council of Women of Canada.

able support from other women's organizations, including the Victorian Order of Nurses, the Girls' Friendly Society, the Dominion Women's Enfranchisement Association, the Dominion Order of King's Daughters, the Lady Aberdeen Association for Distribution of Literature to Settlers in the West, the Women's Art Association of Canada, and the National Home Reading Union, all of whom were affiliated with the Council by the turn of the century.

The Roots of the Labour Movement

Canadian women weren't the only people interested in reform. Members of the working class were anxious to see improvements in their working conditions. As a result, there was a tremendous interest in unions during the Laurier years.

Stats

By 1914, 100,000 Canadians belonged to unions.

While trade unions and working men's associations had been around since the mid-19th century, until the early 20th

Stats

Between 1901 and 1914, there were 420 strikes in Ontario involving 58,356 men and women.

Stats

In 1908, Ontario became the first province to pass a child labour law. The new law established 14 as the minimum age for working in a factory.

century they were primarily limited to members of skilled trades. By 1900, however, two large unions—the American Federation of Labour and the Labour Congress of Canada—had emerged.

While Canadian manufacturers didn't like any type of union, they were particularly fearful of the U.S.-based American Federation of Labour. They feared that union leader Samuel Gompers and his followers would come to Canada and attempt to stir up labour unrest. (To a certain extent, their fears were justified. Gompers repeatedly warned Canadian workers that they were in danger of being exploited by the Americans who controlled the factories in which they worked.)

Some employers were so frightened of the prospect of unionization that they introduced a series of workplace improvements designed to lessen the appeal of unions. They installed baths and showers, organized company excursions and picnics, introduced profit-sharing programs, and—in a very few cases—even established pension plans.

While the unions managed to attract large numbers of members and made tremendous strides during the early 20th century, they tended to ignore those most in need of protection: the men who cleared the bush and put down road beds for Canada's railways. These unfortunate souls were not only paid poorly, but were also completely dependent on the railways for transportation, food, clothing, and accommodation. It was the closest thing to slavery that could be found in Canada at the time.

The unions also ignored female workers—no small feat, considering that there were 100,000 of them in the Canadian labour force by 1900! Working in the canning and textile industries or as domestic servants, women were almost invariably paid less than their male counterparts. In fact, as an article in the Toronto *Globe* pointed out, women were typically paid one third to one half less than men for performing identical tasks.

Their Mission, Should They Choose to Accept It...

Clearly, the first decade of the 20th century was a time of considerable unrest. The task that fell to Laurier and his fellow politicians was to find a way to meet the ever-evolving needs of a rapidly changing population.

Stats

By 1911, every province except Prince Edward Island had introduced worker's compensation legislation.

The Least You Need to Know

- Poor conditions in urban areas encouraged both local governments and the churches to introduce a series of urban reforms.
- Believing that alcohol was the root of all evil in society, many middle-class women joined the Women's Christian Temperance Union and began lobbying for prohibition.
- Over time, women concluded that the only way they could fulfil their role as the "moral guardians" of society was by obtaining the vote.
- Labour unions attracted many members in turn-of-the-century Canada. The two biggest unions were the U.S.-based American Federation of Labour and the Labour Congress of Canada.

Chapter 23

Laurier's Swan Song (1910 to 1911)

In this chapter

- The renewed quest for reciprocity
- The election of 1911

After 50 years of attempting to reestablish reciprocity with the United States, the Canadian government had pretty much given up on the idea of ever seeing free trade with the Americans by the time Laurier came to power. Rather than focusing its attention on its neighbours to the south, the new Liberal government chose instead to focus its efforts on negotiating favourable tariffs with Britain.

Memories As Long As the Transcontinental Railway

Unfortunately for Laurier, prairie farmers were not about to let him forget the rhetoric about reciprocity that had propelled him to office in the election of 1896 or his subsequent failure to deliver what they wanted most: free trade with the United States. In the fall of 1910, 1000 farmers travelled to Ottawa to demand an end to price-fixing by eastern industrialists and to insist that the government negotiate North American–wide reciprocity in farm products.

Their protest attracted a great deal of attention. It even caught the eye of the new U.S. president, William Howard Taft. During an interview with the editor of the Toronto *Globe*, Taft signalled his interest in reopening the discussions about free trade: "I am profoundly convinced that these two countries, touching each other for more than 3000 miles, have common interests in trade."

Washington Bound

Laurier wasn't about to let an opportunity like that slip away. Finance Minister William S. Fielding and Customs Minister William Paterson were dispatched to Washington to hammer out an agreement with the Americans. By January of 1911, the two were back in the House of Commons, gleefully reporting on the deal they had negotiated: free trade in farm, forest, fishery, and mine products, and drastically reduced duties on a number of manufactured articles. All that was left to be done was for the American and Canadian governments to ratify the agreement.

At that point, Laurier made a serious tactical error. He decided to delay Canadian parliamentary approval until the U.S. Senate had passed its bill.

Laurier's decision gave the Conservatives enough time to muster up opposition to the agreement. Business interests, manufacturers, the banks, and the railways joined the Conservatives in denouncing reciprocity as a threat to both Canadian independence and imperial solidarity. In the end, Laurier was forced to call a general election on the issue. Clearly, the issue of reciprocity would make or break the Liberal government.

Other Issues in the Election of 1911

While reciprocity was at the forefront of everyone's mind throughout the election campaign, there were a number of other equally controversial issues on the table. Both French- and English-speaking Canadians were still stirred up about the school disputes in the Prairie provinces and Laurier's decision to establish a Canadian navy. All the carefully crafted compromises that Laurier had negotiated during his

Voice from the Past

"I am branded in Quebec as a traitor to the French, and in Ontario as a traitor to the English. In Quebec I am branded as a Jingo [a supporter of a warlike imperial policy], and in Ontario as a Separatist. In Quebec I am attacked as an Imperialist, and in Ontario as an anti-Imperialist. I am neither. I am Canadian...."

—Sir Wilfrid Laurier, on the campaign trail during the election of 1911.

years in office were coming back to haunt him. Instead of winning him the support of the majority of Canadians, as he had hoped, his compromises had backfired by alienating more people than they satisfied.

Anti-American Sentiment

As expected, the reciprocity issue set the tone for the campaign.

The economic benefits that reciprocity seemed to promise to fishermen, miners, forest workers, and farmers were virtually ignored because of the Conservative opposition's repeated warnings that reciprocity would not merely jeopardize Canada's position within the British Empire, but would likely mean the end of Canada as well. (The depth of the anti-American sentiment that the reciprocity issue aroused is indicated by a cartoon that appeared during the election campaign. The cartoon showed a large tiger labelled "annexation" lurking behind a smaller tiger called "reciprocity.")

The tide really began to turn against the Laurier government when Clifford Sifton resigned from the Cabinet and organized the "Revolt of the Eighteen," a public repudiation of reciprocity by 18 prominent Toronto Liberals who claimed that reciprocity would "weaken the ties which bind Canada to the Empire."

As if that weren't enough for Laurier to contend with, the American Speaker of the House of Representatives James Beauchamp "Champ" Clark was quoted as saying that he hoped "to see the day when the American flag will float over every square foot of the British North American possessions, clear to the North Pole."

If Canadians hadn't been alarmed by the intentions of the Americans up until this point, they certainly were after Clark contributed his two cents. They couldn't get to the polls fast enough. Canadians decided to get back at the American government by doing the unthinkable: rejecting an agreement they had been clamouring for since the middle of the previous century.

In the end, the Laurier government was humiliated, holding on to just 87 seats. The Conservatives—under leader Robert Borden—were only too happy to use their 134 seats to form the next government.

> **Stats**
>
> 
>
> While the Conservatives won a majority government in the election of 1911, the split in the popular vote was actually very close. The Liberals picked up 623,554 votes to the Conservative's 666,074.

The Laurier Years in a Nutshell

The Laurier years had been a time of considerable change for Canada. The country had welcomed two new provinces and absorbed more than 2 million new people. It had evolved from a largely rural-based society into a country that was basically half urban and half rural. It had begun to assume its place on the international stage and to pull itself out of Britain's shadow. The Canadian economy was booming, and Laurier's prediction that the 20th century would be "Canada's century" didn't seem that far off the mark. Little did Borden know, however, when he took over the reigns of power that he would be faced with the daunting task of leading Canadians through World War I.

The Least You Need to Know

- Prairie farmers continued to lobby for reciprocity throughout the Laurier years. Manufacturers, on the other hand, remained opposed to free trade with the United States.
- In the fall of 1910, the Americans expressed a willingness to renew talks on reciprocity. Within a few months, the two sides had drafted an agreement to bring before their respective governments.
- The Laurier government was soundly defeated in the election of 1911 due in large part to the emotionally charged issue of reciprocity.

Part 5
War and Peace

The years 1914 to 1945 were tumultuous ones for Canadians. Not only did the country find itself faced with two World Wars, but it was hit hard by a world-wide depression that wreaked havoc on its economy for an entire decade. (It was hard to say which was worse: the war or the peace!)

As if global events weren't enough for Canadians to contend with, the country was forced to deal with the growing unrest of women, labourers, farmers, and anyone else who decided to hop on a soapbox and have his or her say. Consequently, by the end of this period, you needed a program to keep track of the growing number of political parties....

Chapter 24

Canada at War (1914 to 1918)

In this chapter

- The War Measures Act
- The wartime economy
- The homefront
- The Conscription Crisis
- Ypres and Vimy Ridge
- Canada's role in making the peace

While Britain didn't actually declare war on Germany until August 4, 1914, Britain and its colonies had been anticipating the possibility of war for some time. As early as 1912, Prime Minister Robert Borden had travelled to London to discuss what Canada's role might be in the escalating tensions between Britain and Germany.

When war actually broke out, Borden confirmed that Canada was willing to contribute to the war effort, but stressed that it wanted to do so on its own terms. It was an argument he would continue to make throughout the duration of the war.

Real Life

Sir Robert Laird Borden (1854–1937) was the Prime Minister of Canada from 1911 to 1920. Prior to entering politics, he worked as a teacher and a lawyer. After leaving politics, he served as Chancellor of Queen's University (1924 to 1930), and as the president of Crown Life Insurance (1928), Barclay's Bank—Canada (1929), and the Canadian Historical Association (1930).

Borden's accomplishments in office included leading the country through World War I (1914 to 1918), extending the vote to women (1918), and serving as the leader of the Canadian delegation to the Paris Peace Conference (1919). He is less fondly remembered for introducing the War Measures Act (1914), the Income War Tax Act (1917), and the Military Service Act (1917).

The War Measures Act

Soon after the outbreak of war, the Canadian government passed the War Measures Act (1914). The Act gave the government extraordinary powers, including the right to pass regulations (called orders-in-council) without obtaining the approval of Parliament.

The government used its expanded powers under the Act to introduce a series of new customs and excise duties on coffee, sugar, liquor, and tobacco (1914); a series of special taxes on items such as railway and steamship tickets (1915); a business profits tax (1916); and income tax (1917). The revenue from these new taxes was to be used to help finance the war effort.

The Wartime Economy

Prior to the outbreak of war, Canada had been experiencing a recession fuelled by both reduced investments from abroad and a decline in wheat prices. In 1913–14, farm incomes dropped significantly, construction activity declined, and urban employment fell by 25 per cent.

Voice from the Past

"There has arisen a very natural and, in my view a very just, sentiment that those who are in the enjoyment of substantial incomes should substantially and directly contribute to the growing war expenditure...."

—Borden's Minister of Finance, speaking about the need to introduce a progressive income tax to help pay for the war.

Stats

Canada's exports dropped from $443 million in 1913 to $399 million in 1914.

As would be the case with World War II a generation later, the beginning of the war led to a rapid expansion of the Canadian economy. The value of base metal exports, wood pulp, and newsprint rose significantly, and wheat acreage expanded by 80 per cent. Meat exports rose from $6 million to $85 million, and livestock exports rose from $10 million to $25 million. British orders for munitions and other war supplies created a $1 billion manufacturing boom, with the Canadian aircraft industry producing 3000 planes and Canadian shipyards building 103 ships. All in all, war contracts created an estimated 300,000 jobs.

To fuel the expansion of its economy, Canada was forced to look to new sources of revenue. Rather than turning to Britain, whose financial resources were being used to support its own war efforts, Canada obtained loans from the United States and raised $2.1 billion through the sale of Victory Bonds to Canadians.

The Homefront

During the early part of World War I, Canadians threw themselves firmly behind the war effort. Men volunteered to serve overseas, and women did whatever they could to support the war effort from home. In some cases, that meant assisting with the harvest; in others, it meant working in munitions factories to ensure that the Allies had the supplies they needed to win the war.

By 1915, the realities of the war had begun to set in. Nearly 25 per cent of the 100,000 Canadian men who had eagerly rallied behind the British flag a year earlier had been killed or injured. Rather than deterring Canadians from supporting the war effort, these early losses only strengthened their resolve to make the necessary sacrifices. When Borden announced his decision to increase the number of Canadian troops to 500,000, there was hardly a murmur of protest—except from Quebec.

French-Canadian Views of the War

In the early months of the war, French-speaking Canadians had been every bit as supportive of the war effort as their English-speaking counter-

Voice from the Past

"All persons in ordering their food ought to consider the needs of Great Britain and her Allies, and their armies, for wheat, beef, bacon, and fats, and the Canadian Food Board desires the public to do everything in their power to make these commodities available for export by eating as little as possible of them, and by making use of substitutes, and avoiding waste."

—A message printed on restaurant menus during World War I.

Voice from the Past

"How will you like to think that the man you love has allowed other men to do his duty for him while he sheltered himself behind the sacrifice of other men? How will you like to feel as the mother of sons when other mothers have sacrificed their sons for you and your sons? It is the duty of women to remind men that they are not fully awake to the war and their need of service."

—Emmeline Pankhurst, founder of the British-based Women's Social and Political Union, speaking in Vancouver in 1916 on the important role that women had to play in the war effort.

parts. Even ardent Quebec nationalist Henri Bourassa stressed that it was Canada's duty "to contribute, within the bounds of her strength and by the means which are proper to herself, to the triumph, and especially to the endurance, of the combined efforts of France and England."

Unfortunately, the federal government grossly mishandled the war effort in Quebec. A Protestant clergyman was put in charge of recruiting, and the government continued to deny requests for a French-speaking unit.

As a result, the number of French-Canadian enlistees began to drop off during 1916, and French Canada began to question the extent to which Canada had involved itself in "Britain's war."

The Conscription Crisis

By 1917, the government wasn't just having difficulty enlisting volunteers from Quebec. It was also having difficulty attracting recruits from other parts of the country. The initial enthusiasm for the war was waning, the main sources of recruits (unemployed city dwellers and recent British recruits) had long since been depleted, and the men who remained in Canada were much in demand for agricultural and manufacturing work. As a result, Borden was faced with the choice of either reducing the number of troops that he had promised to commit to the war effort or introducing conscription.

Word for the Day

Conscription means compulsory enlistment in the armed forces.

Unfortunately for Borden, a good part of the problem was of his own making. Early in the war, feeling frustrated that Canada was not being taken seriously by the British, Borden had rashly promised to supply the Allies with 500,000 troops. While his commitment impressed the British, he failed to consider the implications of his offer. At the time, Canada had a total population of 8 million, of which just 1.5 million were men between the ages of 17 and 40. Given the high number of casualties, he would need to come up with 300,000 additional recruits each year to keep his promise to the British.

To make matters worse, the need for recruits was having a divisive effect on the country. There was much finger-pointing at the so-called "enemy aliens" (recent immigrants to Canada who didn't feel obligated to defend the British Crown) and at French-speaking Quebecers (who showed a similar reluctance to become involved in the war).

Voice from the Past

"...The reinforcement now available will last for only a few months, the precise number of which, for military reasons, I am not at liberty to state. We all are proud that Canada has played a splendid and notable part in this war. The achievements of her troops have placed her in the very forefront of the nations, and the question before the House and the country to-day [sic] is this: Is Canada content to relax her efforts in the most critical period of a war which concerns her heritage, her status, and her liberty? I am confident that the answer of the House and the country will be the same, namely that Canada cannot and must not relax her effort."

—Sir Robert Borden speaking during the lengthy debate on the conscription bill in the House of Commons.

In June 1917, the government introduced the Military Service Bill, leading to riots in Montreal. Borden tried to make conscription more acceptable to Quebecers by attempting to form a union government with Laurier's Liberals, but Laurier, who believed that conscription was wrong for Canada, refused to have anything to do with Borden.

Realizing that he needed to shift the odds in his favour if he were to win the election that fall, Borden engaged in an electoral sleight of hand. He introduced the Military Voters Act, which allowed both men and women serving overseas to vote in the election. Rather than voting for a particular candidate, however, they were merely entitled to vote "yes" or "no" to indicate their support of the existing government. What's more, while those voters who specified their home riding on their ballot would have their votes applied in that riding, all other votes would be applied at the electoral officer's discretion. This crafty loophole allowed the government to manipulate approximately 25 per cent of the overseas vote!

To boost the Conservative's chances even further, Borden also introduced the Wartime Elections Act, which gave voting privileges to wives, mothers, sisters, and widows of military personnel and stripped voting privileges from those Canadians who had taken the oath of allegiance after 1902 and who had been born in one of the countries fighting on the other side of the war. (In 1918, the Act was expanded to give all women the right to vote in federal elections.)

Members of the opposition were quick to attack the government's tactics. "It would have been more direct and at the same time more honest if the bill simply stated that all who did not pledge themselves to vote Conservative would be disenfranchised," said one critic at the time.

In the end, however, many members of the Liberal opposition decided to jump ship, agreeing to form a union government with the Conservatives after the election. Laurier, however, was not among them.

Much as the new government might have liked it to, the Conscription Crisis didn't disappear after the election. If anything, it heated up. Although the government had promised during the election that farmers' sons would be exempt from conscription, by 1918 it was forced to go back on its word. To make matters worse, 40 per cent of the men conscripted in Quebec refused to show up for military duty. While conscription managed to raise some 60,000 troops for the war effort, it damaged relations between French- and English-speaking Canadians for generations to come.

Ypres and Vimy Ridge

While Canada's involvement in the war was being debated at home, Canadian troops played a significant role in the Allied victories at Ypres, Belgium, and Vimy Ridge, France.

Voice from the Past

"We went up Vimy Ridge as Albertans and Nova Scotians. We came down as Canadians."

—A Canadian veteran recalling the experience at Vimy Ridge.

On April 22, 1915, Canadian troops halted a German advance at Ypres, Belgium, even in the face of deadly chlorine gas. The French colonial troops who had been fighting alongside the Canadians broke rank and fled, but the Canadians managed to hold the German troops off until Allied reinforcements arrived.

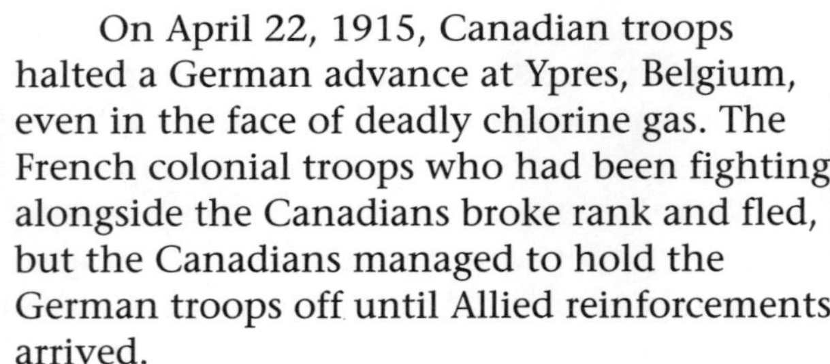

On April 19, 1917, Canadian commander Arthur Currie and his forces captured Vimy Ridge after two hours of intense fighting with the German troops. The victory was particularly noteworthy because the Germans had the better position (at the top of the ridge, overlooking the British army units below) and they were better fortified (they had dug an underground railway to supply their bigger guns). Despite the German advantage, more men, guns, and ground were captured at Vimy Ridge than at any other British offensive.

After these two victories, the Canadian troops earned a reputation for being excellent shock troops. The Germans learned to expect major Allied offensives whenever Canadian troops were moved into position.

Canada's Role in the Making of the Peace

While Canada played a major role on the Allied side of the war, it very nearly was excluded from the making of the peace!

Real Life

Before the war, Major-General Sir Arthur Currie worked as a school teacher and then as a real-estate agent. A "Saturday soldier," he was involved with the military on only a part-time basis prior to 1914. During the war, he became commander of the Canadian corps and earned a reputation as one of the most outstanding military leaders on the Allied side.

Voice from the Past

"How I hate this country. Hundreds of men work all night to do a piece of trench, and the next day the Germans throw a thousand shells or so at it and flatten it out. [The mud] is so deep that it is not possible to walk in it. Men lie on their bellies and wallow and wiggle through it...they are exhausted before the real attack starts."

—A young captain, writing home in the fall of 1916.

Main Event

While the Canadian troops were busy distinguishing themselves overseas, the government found itself embroiled in a scandal that threatened to destroy its credibility.

Militia Minister Sam Hughes—who might more aptly have been called the Minister of Patronage!—appointed his friends as "special purchasing agents" for the government. These "agents" supplied the government with substandard clothing and arms, including the notorious Ross rifle, which had a tendency to jam or misfire in battle. (The Ross rifle was such a poor weapon that Canadian soldiers made a habit of tossing them aside in favour of superior Lee-Enfields rifles acquired from their dead British comrades.)

A Royal Commission investigation in 1916 revealed that Hughes's friends had made millions in profits on uncovered shell and fuse contracts at the expense of the Canadian public. When the scandal became public, Borden demanded Hughes's resignation.

Despite the fact that Canada had pooled its resources with the Americans after the United States entered the war in 1917, the United States attempted to bar Canada (and the other dominions) from the peace negotiations. It argued that allowing the dominions to participate in the negotiations would have given Britain an additional six seats.

Stats

600,000 Canadians served during World War I; 60,661 were killed in action and another 172,000 were wounded.

To make matters worse, the Americans were equally opposed to Canada's membership in the League of Nations (the forerunner to the United Nations). They preferred to deal with Britain when it came to Canadian interests because Britain had proven more willing to sacrifice Canada's interests than the Canadians were likely to be! Borden pointed out that Canada had made tremendous sacrifices during the war, and that it didn't make sense to exclude the seventh-largest industrial power from the table if smaller states like Cuba and Liberia were going to be invited to participate.

In the end, the Americans withdrew their objections, and Canada won the right both to sign the peace treaty as a separate state and to join the League of Nations and the International Labour Organization as an individual nation.

The Least You Need to Know

- The War Measures Act (1914) gave the federal government the authority to pass orders-in-council without parliamentary approval.
- The war stimulated the Canadian economy and pulled Canada out of the recession that had set in during 1913–14.
- To deliver on his promise to supply the Allies with 500,000 troops, Borden was forced to introduce a Military Service Bill (1917) that provided for conscription. The resulting Conscription Crisis damaged relations between French- and English-speaking Canadians for generations to come.
- Canadian troops distinguished themselves during the Allied victories at Ypres and Vimy Ridge.
- While the Americans attempted to prevent Canada from participating in peacemaking activities, in the end Canada won the right to sign the peace treaty as a separate state and to join the League of Nations and the International Labour Organization as an individual nation.

Chapter 25

The Morning After (1918 to 1929)

In this chapter

- The post-war economy
- The Winnipeg General Strike
- Agrarian discontent
- Political highs and lows

In the months following the end of World War I on November 11, 1918, Canadians found themselves in for a rough economic ride.

Just as the war years had been a boom period for the Canadian economy, the years following the war were a time of economic readjustment and—for many Canadians—out-and-out hardship. Wages had failed to keep pace with inflation during the war years, so the average family's purchasing power was considerably less than what it had been at the beginning of the war.

To make matters worse, there was increased unemployment as the 500,000 veterans returned from overseas and sought to reenter the work force. As a result, the Dominion and the provinces cooperatively established employment services for veterans, offering them discharge gratuities, interim unemployment relief, and loans for vocational and university training.

Prosperity eventually returned in the mid-1920s—but not for everyone. Working-class people were trapped in jobs that paid poor wages, while farmers were burdened with debt. As a result, more than half of Canadians found themselves living in poverty.

Stats

The rate of inflation between 1916 and 1919 was twice that of wage increases, drastically reducing the purchasing power of the typical Canadian family. Prices increased by 8 per cent in 1916, 18 per cent in 1917, and 13.5 per cent in 1918.

The Winnipeg General Strike

The period after the war was also a time of labour unrest. The situation reached crisis proportions with the outbreak of the Winnipeg General Strike.

The strike began as a dispute over wages and collective bargaining rights in the building and metal trades. Members of the two trades took their grievances to the Winnipeg Trades and Labour Council, which called for a vote on a general strike. On May 15, 1919, 35,000 workers belonging to 50 different unions left their jobs, bringing the city to its knees. Stores closed and telephone and telegraph services were halted. Even toilets stopped flushing because the pressure was kept too low to raise the water above the first floor of most buildings! About the same time, a series of sympathy strikes broke out in Toronto, Vancouver, Edmonton, and Calgary.

Believing that Winnipeg was in the midst of a revolution, business and government leaders established the Committee of One Thousand (a.k.a. the Citizens Committee) whose sole mandate was to break the strike. The committee even established a force of "special police" to replace the unionized regular police officers who were at the beck and call of the strike leaders.

The strike reached its climax on June 21 ("Bloody Sunday") when a clash between the committee's special police and the strikers resulted in the deaths of 2 marchers, the injury of 34 others, and the arrest of yet another 80.

By the time the strike officially ended six days later, seven of the strike's leaders had been charged with "seditious conspiracy" and business leaders were more committed than ever to resisting union efforts to secure recognition and the right to collective bargaining.

While the strike leaders were almost uniformly Anglo-Saxon Protestants, many Canadians were quick to pin the blame for the strike on "enemy aliens" and "the German agents who are financing them." Even the Canadian government got in on the act, passing an amendment to the Immigration Act that provided for summary deportation without trial for any non-citizen suspected of revolutionary activity.

Agrarian Discontent

Union members weren't the only ones unhappy with the status quo in post-World War I Canada. Farmers also had their share of grievances. They were concerned about rural depopulation, anxious to see the federal government do something about the tariffs that kept the prices of manufactured goods artificially high and yet limited the markets for their grains, and angry about the federal government's refusal to honour its promise to exempt farmers' sons from conscription.

Deciding that the time had come to launch their own political party, farmers in Ontario banded together to form the United Farmers of Ontario (UFO). Much to the surprise of the established parties, the UFO swept the October 1919 provincial election. The party walked away with 43 seats, leaving just 28 for the Liberals, 26 for the Conservatives, 12 for members of the Labour party, and 2 for independent members of Parliament.

Stats

The Ku Klux Klan, infamous for the terror tactics it used against blacks in the American South, had between 10,000 and 15,000 members in Saskatchewan during the 1920s and 1930s. The Klan directed its hatred at Catholics and French-speaking Canadians, pressuring the Saskatchewan government to end French-language instruction in the early grades and to dismiss nuns teaching in the public school system.

The success of the UFO encouraged farmers in other parts of the country to organize. In the following session of the federal Parliament, several western members of the union government joined forces with a group of Liberals and decided to sit as farmers' representatives under the leadership of Thomas A. Crerar. At about the same time, United Farmers parties sprang up in all the Prairie provinces, forming a government in Alberta in 1921 and becoming the official opposition in the others.

When agricultural prices collapsed in 1920, the various groups and political parties representing the farmers' interests decided to hold a convention in Winnipeg to discuss their next steps. As a result of the convention, the National Progressive Party was formed under Crerar's leadership.

Voice from the Past

"We as farmers are downtrodden by every other class. We have grovelled and been ground into the dirt; we are determined that this shall not be. We will organize for our protection; we will nourish ourselves and gain strength, and then we shall strike out in our might and overthrow our enemies."

—Henry Wise Wood, speaking at the annual convention of the United Farmers of Alberta in 1917.

The Progressive party's platform was simple: reciprocity with the United States, free trade with Britain, lower tariffs, public ownership of railways and utilities, higher taxes on business profits, the establishment of government agencies that would assist farmers in marketing their products, and a more American-style form of government that would give the individual voter a greater say in the day-to-day operation of Parliament. (They were particularly interested in the recall, which allowed American voters to force an election at any time if they lost confidence in their local representative, and the referendum, which enabled voters to voice their opinions about a particular piece of legislation.)

A New Cast in Ottawa

While the farmers were busy organizing political parties, the federal government was making some changes of its own.

The union government began to collapse as growing numbers of ex-Liberals crossed the floor of the House of Commons to rejoin their old party or to sit as farmer independents. By the time Borden resigned as prime minister in 1920 due to ill health and handed the reigns of power over to his successor, Arthur Meighen, the government was—for all intents and purposes—Conservative once again.

But not for long.

The Liberals were also busy making some changes. Following Laurier's death in 1919, the party had found itself floundering, looking for a new leader. The man they ultimately settled on, William Lyon Mackenzie King, was chosen more by default than on the basis of his political skills. To be blunt, he was the best of a bad bunch.

Despite King's shortcomings, he managed to leave the Conservatives in the dust in the election of 1921. The Liberals took 117 seats, while the Progressives took 65, the Conservatives took 50, and independent members of Parliament picked up the remaining 3 seats. Because the Progressives agreed to support the Liberal minority government, King found himself governing from a position of relative strength.

Real Life

Arthur Meighen (1874–1960) was the Prime Minister of Canada for two brief periods: from 1920 to 1921 (after assuming control of the government from Borden, who was forced to retire due to ill health), and from June 26 to September 25, 1926 (when the Liberal government was temporarily defeated). He served as leader of the Conservative party from 1920 to 1926 and from 1941 to 1942, and as a senator from 1932 to 1941.

Prior to being elected to Parliament in 1908, Meighen practised law in Manitoba. He became the country's Solicitor General in 1913 and its Secretary of State in 1915.

Meighen is remembered for his role in the creation of the Canadian National Railways (1919) and in ending the Winnipeg General Strike (1919). A brilliant debater and parliamentarian, Meighen's tendency to antagonize western farmers, urban workers, Quebecers, and even his fellow Conservatives made him a less than successful leader.

Real Life

William Lyon Mackenzie King (1874–1950) was Canada's longest-serving prime minister, heading the federal Liberal government from 1921 to 1930 (other than during a three-month period in 1926, when the Conservatives temporarily gained control of the government) and from 1935 to 1948. He also served as leader of the Liberal party from 1919 to 1948.

The grandson of William Lyon Mackenzie of Rebellion-of-1837 fame, King enjoyed a successful career in both politics and private life before becoming prime minister. He served as the Minister of Labour in the Laurier government, and then worked as a labour consultant with the U.S.-based Rockefeller Foundation.

His accomplishments in office included introducing the Old Age Pension (1926), unemployment insurance (1940), and the family allowance (1944); appointing Carine Wilson, Canada's first woman senator (1930); and leading Canada through World War II.

Despite the fact that King was an exceptionally well-educated man who held a Ph.D. from Harvard, he tended to be a bit of a flake. Throughout his life, he conducted séances in which he attempted to establish contact with his mother, his grandfather, Laurier, Saints Luke and John, and others—all of whom advised him on his political undertakings! Fortunately, few Canadians at the time were aware of King's odd habits. They simply assumed he was the dull and stuffy bachelor that he appeared to be while in the House of Commons.

Happy Days Are Here Again! (For Some Folks At Least)

Prosperity returned to Canada in 1923. Unemployment began to decline, commodity prices began to rise, and immigration began to increase once again, with over 100,000 new arrivals stepping foot on Canadian soil each year during the 1920s.

The economy began to expand in new and exciting directions. There was a massive increase in mining, with most of the products of the mining sector being exported to the industrial markets of the

Stats

In the years after the war, the number of automobiles on the road tripled. As a result, the government increased its expenditures on highways by 350 per cent. Still, the car was out of the price range of most Canadian families: a 1926 model T Ford sold for $385.

Stats

By 1930, 70 per cent of Canadians had electricity and Canadians had distinguished themselves as the largest per capita users of electrical power in the world!

United States. Automotive production soared, and the pulp and paper industry expanded by leaps and bounds. Iron and steel output doubled to meet the needs of manufacturers. Saw mills, flour mills, breweries, food processing plants, and light engineering firms in British Columbia grew to meet both local and export demand. And the availability of cheap hydroelectric power created a countrywide market for a smorgasbord of electrically powered consumer appliances: refrigerators, stoves, washing machines, irons, radios, and more.

However, the agricultural sector did not share in the newfound prosperity to the same degree. Wheat prices dropped after 1924, leading to a 30 per cent decline in farm income between 1926 and 1928.

Neither did the Maritime provinces feel the boom in the economy. Nova Scotia and Prince Edward Island both experienced a decline in population, while New Brunswick experienced only a small population growth. Growing unemployment in the region meant that there was little to attract newcomers to the three provinces, and even less to keep them there. Canada was becoming a country of "haves" and "have nots."

The Elections of 1925...

In the election of 1925, the Conservatives managed to pick up 116 seats, leaving the Liberals with 101 and the Progressives with 24. What made the results even more embarrassing for the Liberals was the fact that King and the majority of his English-speaking Cabinet members were not re-elected! King managed to regain his seat in a hastily organized by-election, and then regained control of the government by acquiring the support of the Progressives and the Labour members in exchange for a promise to make changes to the tariff and introduce an old age pension.

King barely had time to hang his nameplate back on his door before it was time to take it down again. A major liquor-smuggling scandal that involved even the Minister of Customs rocked the government. (As much as the prohibition forces south of the border hated to admit it, there was a healthy market in the "dry" U.S. for contraband booze!) In the aftermath of the scandal, King and his government resigned, and Governor General Viscount Byng of Vimy asked Conservative Arthur Meighen to form the next government.

> **Stats**
>
> Slightly over 50 per cent of Canada's manufacturing output came from Ontario and another 30 per cent came from Quebec. The manufacturing boom in the two provinces encouraged a massive movement of people from rural areas to the cities of central Canada.

Meighen was so anxious to hold on to power (and who can blame him, given his experiences during the last two elections!) that he attempted to dodge a government regulation that required all ministers taking office more than 30 days after a general election to resign and seek re-election. He tried to get around the rule by appointing "acting ministers," but King wasn't about to let him get away with this particular maneuver. He attacked the Cabinet as being highly illegal because the acting ministers had failed to take an oath of office. In the end, Meighen had to ask Byng to dissolve Parliament for another election.

...and 1926

Clearly, the voters were every bit as appalled with the Conservatives' shenanigans as the Liberals had been. In the election of 1926, the Conservatives lost 25 seats and the Liberals gained 15. The balance of power was once again held by the Progressives, the United Farmers, the Labour party, and independents.

To make matters worse for the Conservatives, Meighen was defeated in his own riding. Clearly, he'd had enough of federal politics. He resigned as leader of the Conservative party the following year, passing the job on to a wealthy bachelor named Richard Bedford Bennett. When the Conservatives ultimately regained power four years later, Bennett would be the new prime minister.

Real Life

R.B. Bennett (1870–1947) was the Prime Minister of Canada from 1930 to 1935 and the leader of the Conservative party from 1927 to 1938.

Prior to entering federal politics, he served at the municipal and provincial levels. He also enjoyed successful careers in teaching, the law, and business.

He is remembered for creating the Canadian Radio Broadcasting Commission (the forerunner to the Canadian Broadcasting Corporation) in 1932 and the Bank of Canada in 1935, and for the progressive legislation (modelled on Franklin D. Roosevelt's "New Deal") that he attempted to introduce prior to his defeat to William Lyon Mackenzie King in the election of 1935.

Bennett, who is buried in Surrey, England, is the only prime minister buried outside of Canada.

The Least You Need to Know

- The Canadian economy went through a difficult time after the war, but—for most Canadians at least—prosperity returned by the mid-1920s.
- The Winnipeg General Strike reached its climax on June 21, 1919 ("Bloody Sunday"), when a clash between pro- and anti-union forces resulted in arrests, injuries, and two deaths.
- Farmers across Canada were so dissatisfied with their situation that they began to play an active role in provincial and federal politics.
- The Liberals held on to power throughout the 1920s, other than during a three-month period in 1926 when the government temporarily fell into the hands of the Conservatives.

Chapter 26

The Woman Problem (1914 to 1929)

In this chapter

- The suffrage movement
- The Mock Parliament
- The Person's Case
- The changing role of women

While society tried to convince women that they had an important role to play in the world around them by virtue of their moral superiority, some—like Nellie McClung—were not satisfied with the options presented to them.

During a speech in 1914, she scoffed at the notion that women should be content to play a behind-the-scenes role in public life. "The hand that rocks the cradle does not rule the world, or many things would be different. How long would the liquor traffic or the white slave traffic last if it did?"

Real Life

Nellie McClung (1873–1951) was a writer, a prominent campaigner for prohibition and women's suffrage, and a strong supporter of the war effort, working on behalf of both the Red Cross and the Canadian Patriotic Fund.

McClung belonged to the Women's Christian Temperance Union and was active in the drive for women's suffrage in both Manitoba and Alberta. She served as a member of the Legislative Assembly of Alberta (1921–26) and as a Canadian delegate to the League of Nations (1938).

She also opened a number of important doors for women: she was the only woman representative at the Canadian War Conference of 1918 and was the first woman member of the Canadian Broadcasting Corporation's Board of Governors.

McClung is perhaps best remembered for the roles she played in the Mock Parliament (1914) and the Person's Case (1929).

The Mock Parliament

McClung was not alone in agitating for a greater role for women. Thousands of other women rallied behind the cause of women's suffrage and began demanding the right to vote.

One of the most memorable tactics used by the suffragettes was the staging of a play written by Nellie McClung called "How the Vote Was Not Won" at the Regina Walker Theatre in Winnipeg in 1914. The play was presented the day after Manitoba Premier Rodmond Roblin denied the suffrage petition that had been presented to his government in the Legislative Assembly, and cleverly exposed the self-serving and sanctimonious arguments that had been made by many of the politicians.

Pretending to be the premier, Nellie McClung delivered an eloquent speech arguing why men should not be given the right to vote: "In this agricultural province, the man's place is the farm. Shall I call man away from the useful plow and harrow to talk loud on street corners about things which do not concern him? Politics unsettle men....

When you ask for the vote, you are asking me to break up peaceful, happy homes—to wreck innocent lives.... It may be that I am old-fashioned. I may be wrong. After all, men may be human. Perhaps the time will come when men may vote with women."

The play was a tremendous hit with both the men and the women in attendance, and newspapers of the day devoted considerable copy to the so-called Mock Parliament.

The Right to Vote

Victories at the provincial level came in dribs and drabs, with women winning the right to vote in Manitoba, Alberta, Saskatchewan, and British Columbia in 1916; in Ontario in 1917; in Nova Scotia in 1918; in New Brunswick in 1919; and in Prince Edward Island in 1922. Women in Quebec had to wait until 1940 before they won the right to vote.

Women won the right to vote in federal elections in 1918 and the right to serve as members of Parliament in 1920.

The More Things Change...

The role of women expanded tremendously during the war years, when women worked in munitions factories and tended to family farms while the men were away, and supported the war through volunteer work with such organizations as the Canadian Patriotic Fund.

When the war ended, many people wanted to turn the clock back to the way things were in 1914. For the most part, women were not prepared to do this. Many chose to hang on to their jobs, and those who were forced to leave the work force to create jobs for the veterans did so with great reluctance, vowing to return to paid employment as soon as the opportunity presented itself.

While society no longer had difficulty with the idea of single women working, it still hadn't reconciled itself to the idea of married women being in the work force. Now that the wartime emergency was over, it seemed best if women returned to their primary roles as homemakers and mothers. The pressure to conform came from all quarters: article after article in magazines such as *Canadian Home Journal* and *Maclean's* focused on how women who tried to juggle work and family ultimately discovered true happiness when they decided to leave their jobs behind!

Real Life

Agnes Macphail (1890–1954) was the first woman to be elected to the House of Commons.

After winning the United Farmers of Ontario federal nomination over 10 men at the South-East Grey (Ontario) convention in September of 1920, Macphail learned just how difficult her political career was likely to be. She was asked to resign from the party so that a man could be elected in her place. She refused.

During the election that followed, she was attacked on the basis of her gender, her "mannish" behaviour, and her religion (she belonged to the Church of Jesus Christ of the Latter Day Saints)—but she was elected nonetheless.

Shortly after being elected to office, Macphail received a number of offers of marriage. While she declined them all, she went to great pains to make these offers public. She was reluctant to be labelled a "spinster" in an era when marriage was highly valued.

Macphail sat as the member for South-East Grey from 1921 to 1940, initially representing the United Farmers of Ontario and later the Progressive party. Throughout her time in office, she saw herself as the representative of the women of Canada. She supported the struggle for women's suffrage in Quebec, prison reform, unemployment insurance, family allowances, and pensions for the elderly and the disabled.

In 1929, she served as a member of the Canadian delegation to the League of Nations, where she became the first woman to sit on the Disarmament Committee. (Other delegates tried to shuffle her off to the committee that dealt with issues such as welfare, women, and children, but Macphail had other plans!) She also represented Canada at the International Congress of the Women's International League for Peace and Freedom in Prague, Czechoslovakia, in 1929.

Following her defeat in the 1940 federal election (a defeat that resulted in large part from her views on pacifism), Macphail became one of the first two women to sit in the Ontario legislature.

Main Event

In 1919, the first conference of the Federated Women's Institutes of Canada passed a resolution stating that the prime minister should appoint a female senator. The resolution was subsequently supported by both the National Council of Women and the Montreal Women's Club.

Arguing that the terms of the British North America Act prevented women from being eligible for a seat in the Senate, both the Conservative Meighen and Liberal King governments managed to dodge the issue for some time. Eventually, however, a group of prominent women used an obscure section of the Supreme Court Act to petition the government for an order-in-council directing the Supreme Court to rule on the constitutional question of whether the term "qualified persons" in section 24 of the British North America Act included women. The ruling seemed unlikely to go in their favour: in 1876, a British court had ruled that "Women are persons in matters of pains and penalties, but are not persons in matters of rights and privileges."

The women behind the so-called Person's Case were Emily Murphy (who in 1916 had become the first woman magistrate in the British Empire), Nellie McClung (a writer, reformer, and former politician), Irene Parlby (an Alberta Cabinet minister), Louise McKinney (a former member of the Legislative Assembly of Alberta), and Henrietta Muir Edwards (one of the founders of the National Council of Women and the Victorian Order of Nurses).

The Supreme Court issued its decision in April of 1928, ruling that the term "qualified persons" did not include women. The group of five women then asked the government to allow an appeal to the Judicial Committee of the Privy Council of Canada in England. In the end, they were victorious. On October 19, 1929, the Judicial Committee overturned the Supreme Court's judgment and ruled that the term "persons" as it appeared in the British North America Act did, in fact, include women as well as men.

Stats

The number of women in the work force rose by nearly 40 per cent between 1921 and 1931.

Domestic Bliss?

Despite the new labour-saving appliances that had made their way into many Canadian households during the early decades of the new century, housework continued to be a time-consuming task for most Canadian women. Rising standards of cleanliness meant that many women found themselves with little—if any—free time as they worked to achieve a state of domestic order that would put even Martha Stewart to shame.

As if that weren't enough, society also decided to "professionalize" the business of raising a family. Women were given detailed information on all aspects of childrearing—when to feed an infant, how to toilet train a toddler, and so on—and were told that abiding by this scientific, informed approach to motherhood would enable them to reduce the time spent caring for young children and result in healthier offspring!

Dr. Helen MacMurchy—a doctor, writer, lecturer, and government official who specialized in maternal and infant health—expressed the prevailing attitude of the time: "Being a mother is the highest of all professions and the most extensive of all undertakings. Nothing that she can know is useless to a mother. She can use it all. The mother reports for special duty about 250 days before the baby is born and she is never demobilized until she meets the bearer of the Great Invitation. Mother, at ninety years, is still Mother."

Real Life

In 1936, Dorothea Palmer was charged with the criminal offence of distributing birth control information to women in Eastview, a working class, French-Canadian suburb of Ottawa. While Palmer was ultimately acquitted of the crime in 1937, the Canadian government allowed the law prohibiting the distribution of information about birth control to remain on the books for decades to come.

Given the new standards being demanded of mothers, it's no wonder that the birthrate dropped steadily from the beginning of World War I to 1939. (It's also no small miracle, given that it was against the law to distribute information about birth control during this period!) While Canadian women had come a long way in their battle for basic rights, they still had a long way to go.

The Least You Need to Know

- Women achieved the right to vote in federal elections in 1918. Most achieved the right to vote in provincial elections sometime between 1916 and 1922, but women in Quebec had to wait until 1940 before they were given this right.
- The Person's Case (1929) confirmed that women were "persons" as defined in the British North America Act, thereby giving them the right to serve in the Senate.
- The role of women changed significantly both during and after World War I.

Chapter 27

Boom, Bust, No Echo (1929 to 1941)

In this chapter

- The stock market crash of 1929
- The Great Depression
- Bennett's New Deal
- "King or Chaos"
- The Rowell-Sirois Report
- The emergence of the Co-operative Commonwealth Federation (CCF), Social Credit, and the Union Nationale

The New York stock market crashed on October 29, 1929, knocking the bottom out of what had been a dizzying period of economic expansion. Many investors were ruined on Black Tuesday—particularly those who had bought on margin (that is, those who borrowed money by using the stock they were buying as security). But that wasn't the worst of it. Because the rest of the world had become highly dependent on the U.S. currency, the stock market crash led to widespread economic problems that went far beyond America's borders.

No Wonder They Called It the Great Depression

> **Stats**
>
> On Black Tuesday—October 29, 1929—stocks fell an average of 40 points, wiping out many investors in an instant.

Canada was hit particularly badly by the worldwide depression that followed the stock market crash. Because 30 per cent of its national income came from exports, it was especially vulnerable to fluctuations in the world economy.

While industries such as lumber, mining, and pulp and paper took quite a beating, the biggest devastation was in the agricultural sector. The price of wheat dropped dramatically, falling from $1.60 per bushel for Number One Northern in 1929 to $0.54 per bushel in 1932. To make matters worse, international markets for Canadian wheat collapsed thanks to stiff competition from the Australians and Argentineans and hefty tariffs from many European countries.

When It Rains, It Pours (and When It Doesn't, It Doesn't!)

As if the economic crash weren't enough for Prairie farmers to contend with, Mother Nature decided to throw them an additional twist. The southern portions of Alberta and Saskatchewan were hit with a devastating drought that led to widespread crop failures. Farm incomes fell by as much as 75 per cent, and an estimated 214,000 people abandoned their farms during the 1930s.

The woes of the Prairie farmers were also felt by the railways (which began losing money again) and eastern manufacturers (who found the demand for their goods drastically curtailed by the decline in farm purchasing power).

The Best of a Bad Situation

For once, the Maritime provinces were not the worst-hit region in the country. While the situation wasn't pretty, the majority of Maritimers were able to hold on to their homes and hang tight while they waited for brighter times.

The situation was also relatively tolerable in Ontario and Quebec. Industry continued to chug along, although at a significantly reduced level.

The Human Costs

There's no doubt about it: the Great Depression was hard on Canadians.

During the 1930s, approximately one in ten Canadian families was forced to rely on the welfare relief offered by the municipal and provincial governments. The welfare burden was so great that some municipalities were unable to pay their own employees for weeks at a time.

The situation was equally grim when it came to health care. By 1937, doctors were routinely reporting cases of malnutrition, particularly among young children.

Married women who attempted to enter the work force to earn additional money to support their families were turned away, and those who already had jobs were asked to resign to create greater employment opportunities for men. (There was still a widespread misconception that women worked for pin money, while men worked to support their families!)

Voice from the Past

"Some [children] used to come at opening time and just stand there looking at those pink-cheeked, golden-haired lovely Shirley Temples. Little faces, they needed food. You could see alot [sic] who needed a pint of milk a day a thousand times more than they needed a Shirley doll. They'd stare for hours. We tried to shush them away, but it didn't do any good.... This, mind you, went on day after day, day after day, until some of the [sales]girls thought they would go crazy. One girl had a crying fit over just that, those hundreds of poor kids who would never own a Shirley Temple in a hundred years. They were lucky if they had breakfast that morning, or soup and bread that night."

—A saleswoman at Eaton's recalling Christmas during the Depression.

Real Life

One of the few bright spots for the Canadian public during the Depression years was the birth of the Dionne quintuplets on May 28, 1934. Unfortunately, the lives of the five little girls—Annette, Émilie, Yvonne, Cécile, and Marie—were turned into a sideshow. The Ontario government removed the infants from the care of their poor, rural, francophone parents and put them under the control of a board of guardians. The girls obtained over $1 million in endorsements, were the subject of Hollywood films, and became a major tourist attraction, attracting a total of 3 million visitors. While their parents eventually regained custody of the quints, by then the damage had been done. The girls carried the scars of their traumatic early experiences for the rest of their lives.

To make matters worse, the Depression dragged on—and on—and on. The economic situation didn't begin to turn around until the beginning of World War II.

A New Government

Remember how your mother told you that some things were better left unsaid? It was a lesson that William Lyon Mackenzie King either missed or chose to ignore.

When the provinces turned to King for financial assistance to help them meet their growing welfare costs, he made a snippy remark about not being willing to "give five cents" to those provinces with Conservative governments.

His flippancy and political one-upmanship didn't score very many points with the voters. King and his government were roundly defeated in the election of 1930, and Richard Bedford Bennett became Canada's next prime minister.

Bennett was an accomplished politician who had served in both Borden's and Meighen's Cabinets. He was also a very successful lawyer who had made his fortune through his Calgary-based law practice.

Unfortunately, while Bennett himself had a lot to offer, his Cabinet was weak.

That didn't stop him from trying to make his mark, however. Immediately after the election, he called a special session of Parliament in which tariffs were raised by up to 50 per cent. (Needless to say, he wasn't unduly popular among Prairie farmers!)

Then Bennett decided to tackle Canada's economic problems head-on. He invited Britain and other Commonwealth governments to attend a special Imperial Economic Conference in Ottawa in 1932. The purpose of the conference was to discuss the possibility of extending preferential tariffs to one another. Initially, it looked like the conference was going to be a bust. Each country was reluctant to expose its own domestic markets to competition. In the end, however, those in attendance agreed to extend preferences on a few specific commodities. Canada, for example, received preferential treatment in the British market for her foodstuffs, lumber, and metals in exchange for her willingness to extend preferential rates to certain British manufacturing sectors.

Stats

By 1933, the national unemployment rate had climbed to 22 per cent.

Nowhere to Go But Up

The worst years of the Depression were 1932 and 1933. In an effort to reduce the widespread misery, the federal government announced a major public works program aimed at creating jobs. It also gave the provinces a series of direct grants equal to approximately 50 per cent of their welfare costs. The Prairie provinces, which were buckling under the burden of rising relief costs, were given additional special subsidies.

The Caring Conservative

No one could accuse Bennett of not caring about the plight in which all too many Canadians found themselves. He put in long days, personally answering correspondence from Depression-weary Canadians who were about to lose their homes. In addition to expressing his sincere sympathy about their predicament, more often than not he tucked a little something extra into each envelope: a $5 bill.

While Bennett had accumulated a considerable fortune during his years in the legal profession, even his pockets weren't deep enough to cure all that ailed the country. He needed some fresh ideas to turn Canada's economic situation around.

When Bennett got wind of the innovative "New Deal" programs being implemented by U.S. President Franklin D. Roosevelt, he decided to come up with a New Deal of his own. In 1935, he introduced a smorgasbord of new legislation aimed at improving the quality of life of Canadians. The Trade and Industry Commission Act was designed to create a government watchdog over prices, unfair business practices, and anti-competitive behaviour. The Minimum Wages Act was to guarantee each working Canadian a decent standard of living. The Limitation of Hours of Work Act and the Weekly Rest in Industrial Undertakings Act were aimed at ensuring that workers could not be unduly exploited by their employers. The Unemployment Insurance Act sought to provide workers who were temporarily unemployed with enough cash to keep food on the table. The Natural Products Marketing Act established a federal marketing board with control over the export of farm, forest, and sea products, and gave the board the right to regulate interprovincial trade in these products. Finally, the Prairie Farm Rehabilitation Act sought to address the soil and wheat problems being faced by drought-ridden farmers and to establish a Wheat Marketing Board. All of the programs in Bennett's New Deal were based on the assumption that the federal government needed to play a more active role in the management of the country's economy.

Stats

Total relief costs soared from $18 million in 1930 to $173 million in 1935, with the Dominion government assuming responsibility for 40 per cent of these costs (through a combination of direct expenditures, grants, and loans to the provinces).

Main Event

Canadians played an active role in The Spanish Civil War, which broke out in 1935. While the war was not officially supported by the Canadian government, more than 1200 Canadians volunteered to fight in the war. Others—like Dr. Norman Bethune—tended to those injured in the fighting.

"King or Chaos"

It didn't take the Liberal opposition long to pounce on Bennett's "New Deal." King declared that the program was unconstitutional because it tread on the toes of the provinces. He also told Canadian voters that their choice in the upcoming election was "King or Chaos."

Rather than coming up with a concrete program of their own with which to fight the election of 1935, King's Liberals chose to use a tried and true campaign technique: waffling. It was a strategy that clearly paid off in the end, as the Liberals walked away with 179 seats, leaving just 40 for the Conservatives, 17 for the Social Credit party, and 7 for the Co-operative Commonwealth Federation. (The only other seat up for grabs was taken by the leader of the so-called Reconstruction party, a short-lived political body that disappeared shortly after the election.)

Immediately after the election, King negotiated a series of tariff reductions on imports from the United States. The deal gave approximately 200 different Canadian products (mainly natural products) easier access to the lucrative U.S. market.

King followed up his success south of the border by negotiating a similar deal with Britain in 1937. He lowered the Canadian duties on a series of consumer articles in return for minor tariff adjustments from Britain and a promise that Canada's principal staples would continue to be admitted to Britain duty-free.

King also served as an intermediary in a series of trade negotiations between Britain and the United States—and was handsomely rewarded for his efforts. The Americans agreed to grant Canada some additional trade concessions to thank King for his role in this crucial round of negotiations.

All in all, these various agreements managed to reduce the duties on over half of Canada's imports from the United States, as well as on more than 80 per cent of her exports to that country.

The Rowell-Sirois Report

Immediately after the election of 1935, King did what any savvy politician would have done with Bennett's New Deal legislation: he referred it to the Judicial Committee and waited for a ruling on its legality.

It was 1937 before the Judicial Committee issued a decision, and—

when it did—it was exactly what King had been hoping for. The committee ruled that the bulk of Bennett's legislation stepped outside the jurisdiction of the federal government. As a result, only the Natural Products Marketing Act was upheld.

King responded to the Judicial Committee decision by appointing a commission, headed by N.W. Rowell and Joseph Sirois, to examine "the economic and financial basis of confederation and the distribution of legislative powers in light of the economic and social developments of the last seventy years."

The commission's report—imaginatively called the Rowell-Sirois Report!—came up with a fairly comprehensive game plan for the government, but one that King was not particularly anxious to implement.

The report recommended a number of fairly radical measures: that the Dominion assume full responsibility for unemployment relief; that provincial debts be taken over by the federal government; that the provinces surrender to the Dominion the sole right to income and corporation taxes and succession duties; and that the existing system of provincial subsidies be replaced with a new system of adjustment grants that would enable the provinces to maintain satisfactory and uniform standards for administration and social services.

The reaction from the provinces was immediate. Quebec didn't like the increased centralization the report recommended, and the wealthier provinces—namely Ontario—didn't like the idea of having their powers curtailed and their resources used to help the poorer provinces. (Clearly, the Golden Rule wasn't all that popular among the provincial premiers of the time!)

King called a federal–provincial conference in 1941 to discuss the report. Ontario, Alberta, and British Columbia were so upset by the report's contents that they refused to discuss it at all. For a while, it looked like the conference was going to be a total washout but, in the end, King did manage to get the provinces to come to two important agreements—one concerning the establishment of a national unemployment insurance system and the second spelling out how the Dominion and the provinces would work together to meet the financial demands of wartime. The rest of the issues in the report were conveniently left on the back burner by King, who excused his inaction by pointing out that the country was now in the midst of another war.

It's My Party...

The 1930s weren't just a time of economic unrest. They were also a time of profound political change. It was during this decade that the two-party system found itself seriously challenged by a series of "third parties." Two of these parties—the Co-operative Commonwealth Federation and Social Credit—made their presence felt on the national stage. The third of these parties—the Union Nationale—confined its activities to Quebec.

The Co-operative Commonwealth Federation

The Co-operative Commonwealth Federation (CCF) was launched at a convention in Calgary in 1932. It drew its support from farm organizations and middle class intellectuals as well as the ranks of the Progressive and Independent Labour parties, and was formed on the assumption that greater government intervention was necessary to prevent the abuses of big business and to ensure the welfare of the people. The CCF's leader was James Shaver Woodsworth, a former Methodist minister who had led the small labour group in Parliament during the 1920s.

In 1933, the CCF drew up its program at a convention in Winnipeg. In addition to recommending slum clearance, rural electrification, public works projects, the socialization of financial and public utilities, and a guaranteed minimum standard of living, convention delegates issued a clear statement of the party's philosophy. The so-called Regina Manifesto declared that "We aim to replace the present capitalist system with its inherent injustice and inhumanity by a social order from which the domination and exploitation of one class by another will be eliminated, in which economic planning will supersede unregulated private enterprise and competition, and in which genuine democratic self-government, based upon economic equality, will be possible."

Following its initial success in the federal election of 1935 (when it took seven seats), the CCF made little progress. It was accused of being a Communist front full of dangerous radicals, and received little support from labour.

Social Credit Movement

The Social Credit party, which sprang up in Alberta in the early 1930s, was based on the idea that the government should pay "social dividends" to its citizens. According to Scottish engineer Major C.H. Douglas, the man who created the social credit concept, these social dividends would allow citizens to exercise a certain amount of purchasing power, therefore upholding the value of goods. According to the theory, the economic woes that the world was experiencing should be blamed on banks and financiers, who maintained unreasonably tight control over the money supply.

The party was led by William S. "Bible Bill" Aberhart, a high school principal and radio evangelist who had attracted an enormous following in Alberta.

In December of 1934, Aberhart announced that "reliable, honourable, bribe-proof businessmen who have definitely laid aside their party politic affiliations will be asked to represent Social Credit in every constituency" in the upcoming provincial and federal elections. After promising his constituents a $25 monthly dividend and repeatedly slamming the banks (a popular pastime in the West!), Aberhart swept to power in Alberta, taking 56 of the 63 seats. While the results in the federal election weren't quite so dramatic, they were noteworthy just the same, with the party picking up 17 seats in the election of 1935.

Real Life

William S. "Bible Bill" Aberhart (1878–1943) was born in Egmondville, Ontario. In the early 1920s, he organized the Calgary Prophetic Bible Conference. Large crowds came out to hear his two-hour interpretations of Christian fundamentalism and Bible prophesy. In 1924, Aberhart launched his own radio show, which subsequently attracted an estimated 200,000 to 300,000 followers. In the fall of 1932, he began to introduce Social Credit ideas into his Sunday afternoon religious broadcasts, and published a series of materials describing his ideas. Aberhart became Premier of Alberta after winning a decisive victory in the election of 1935. When he was unable to deliver the $25 per month "social dividend" he had promised his followers, however, many became deeply disillusioned with the Social Credit party.

After coming to power in Alberta in 1935, Aberhart introduced legislation making significant changes to the banking, finance, and credit systems, but much of this legislation was subsequently rejected by the federal government because it went beyond the limits of provincial control.

The Union Nationale

The Union Nationale emerged during the 1935 provincial election in Quebec. It represented a coalition of sorts between a group of provincial Liberals and the province's Conservative party who were dissatisfied with the two traditional parties' positions on economics and cultural preservation. Led by Maurice Duplessis (a.k.a. *Le chef*), the party managed to take 42 of 90 seats, thereby becoming the official opposition. After uncovering a scandal that showed that the Liberal government was involved in corruption, payoffs, and nepotism, and that it had been squandering public funds, the Union Nationale was able to force a new election, in which the party managed to boost its number of seats to 76.

The party continued to dominate Quebec politics until Duplessis's death in 1959, except for a period during World War II when the Liberals managed to regain control of the government. Throughout the 1930s, 1940s, and 1950s, Duplessis earned a reputation for arguing tirelessly on behalf of French and Quebec rights, the retention of Quebec's natural resources for the benefit of its population rather than the so-called "alien capitalists," and closer ties between church and state.

The Least You Need to Know

- The New York Stock Exchange crashed on October 29, 1929 (Black Tuesday), causing countless investors to lose their fortunes.
- Prime Minister Richard Bedford Bennett's attempt to introduce legislation modelled on U.S. President Roosevelt's "New Deal" was unsuccessful.
- The Rowell-Sirois Report recommended a greater role for the federal government.
- A series of "third parties" emerged during the 1930s, the most noteworthy being the Co-operative Commonwealth Federation (CCF), Social Credit, and the Union Nationale.

Chapter 28

For God and Country (1939 to 1945)

In this chapter

- ➤ Canada's role in World War II
- ➤ The economics of war
- ➤ Women and the war effort
- ➤ The internment of Japanese Canadians

On September 1, 1939, German armies invaded Poland. Two days later, both Great Britain and France declared war on Germany.

On September 10, Canada entered the war: "We do hereby Declare and Proclaim that a State of War with the German Reich exists and has existed in Our Dominion of Canada as and from the tenth day of September, 1939."

Despite its bold declaration, Canada was grossly unprepared for war. During the 1920s and 1930s, Canada's armed forces had been put on the back burner, deliberately neglected by a nation that was quite simply sick of war. As a result, when Canada entered World War II, it found itself with outdated weapons, aging aircraft, and just four destroyers in its navy, two of which were obsolete.

Materials, Not Men

From the outset of the war, Canada repeatedly stressed to Britain that this time her primary contribution would be materials, not men. The Dominion hoped to avoid another conscription crisis by offering to share her food and industrial resources rather than her people. In the end, Canada ended up offering both.

During the early months of the war, most Canadians expected the conflict to be short and successful. However, the Allied disaster at Dunkirk in May of 1940 and the fall of France in the following month soon convinced Canadians that the war would be anything but brief. Suddenly, Britain and the Commonwealth were on their own in the conflict with Germany and Italy.

The Incredible War Machine

As had been the case a generation earlier, the war acted as a tremendous stimulus to the Canadian economy, with the country's gross national product more than doubling between 1939 and 1945.

Stats

Despite his promise not to bring in conscription, King was forced to resort to compulsory military service in late 1944. In the end, only 13,000 conscripts were actually sent to war.

Stats

French-Canadian enlistment in World War II was significantly higher than it had been in World War I. Nineteen per cent of the overseas forces during World War II were French Canadian, as compared to 12 per cent of World War I forces.

Agricultural output increased by 30 per cent due to improved methods and mechanization. Other primary industries expanded as well, including the pulp and paper, timber, nickel, copper, lead, zinc, and uranium sectors. (Some of the uranium being mined would ultimately make its way to the Manhattan Project, the joint British-Canadian-American research project that produced the first atomic bomb.)

Stats

There were 900,000 unemployed Canadians at the beginning of the war. By 1942, most had found work in either industry or the armed forces.

Secondary industry grew even more quickly than primary industry because Canada was suddenly forced to produce items that she had previously imported, including electronic equipment, optical glass, roller bearings, and diesel engines. Canadians also began to work with synthetic rubber, petrochemicals, and plastics for the very first time.

Stats

Canadian industrial workers earned twice as much in 1941 as they did in 1939.

Government Intervention in the Economy

Having learned the hard way what wartime inflation could do to the post-war economy, the federal government was determined to keep a tighter reign on economic matters during World War II than it had in World War I.

In an effort to control inflation, the federal government established a Wartime Prices and Trade Board to establish production quotas and set maximum prices for consumer goods. The Board also introduced a forced savings plan that sought to control inflation by limiting the amount of money people had to spend. Because of the efforts of the Wartime Prices and Trade Board, the cost of goods increased by just 19 per cent during the war (as opposed to the 54 per cent increase the country had experienced during World War I).

The federal government entered into a "tax-rental agreement" with the provinces that allowed the federal government to collect personal and corporate income taxes (a provincial right) in exchange for increased subsidies to the provinces. This agreement was to remain in effect until a year after the end of the war.

The government also got average Canadians involved in the business of managing the economy. Canadians were encouraged to buy Victory Bonds to help underwrite the costs of the war. They were also asked to make personal sacrifices in support of the war effort: private cars were limited to just three gallons of gas per week, and items such as meat, sugar, and butter were rationed to ensure adequate supplies for the troops.

Word for the Day

Victory gardens were small vegetable gardens that provided some food to replace those items rationed by the government. In addition to providing food, they boosted morale by demonstrating civilian support of the war effort.

Women and the War

While Canadian women had made a significant contribution during World War I, they played an even greater role during World War II.

From the beginning, the Department of National War Services was anxious to get Canadian homemakers involved in the war effort. For example, it conducted a campaign designed to encourage women to collect fats, paper, glass, metals, rubber, rags, and bones for reuse in war production. "From the frying pan to the firing line," the campaign posters read. "Work at munitions production in your own kitchen."

Women were also asked to cooperate with the government's rationing and wartime savings programs, to plant victory gardens, to knit and sew clothing for the troops, and to organize blood banks. Rural women were also expected to assume extra responsibilities on the farm as men joined the armed forces or headed to urban areas to seek industrial work.

In March 1942, the federal government founded the National Selective Service agency to oversee the recruitment and allocation of labour. Later that year, the National Selective Service agency launched a Women's Division, which undertook a national registration of women between the ages of 22 and 24. The purpose of this registration was to identify a pool of women who could be recruited into war industries.

Initially, single women were the focus of the drive. The government initiated programs designed to relocate single women from the Prairies and the Maritimes to central Canada, where they could find war-related work. By the summer of 1943, however, the government was forced to recruit married women as well. They were initially recruited for part-time work, but eventually their labour was needed on a full-time basis.

Stats

By July 1, 1944, there were 42,000 women in Quebec and Ontario working in munitions factories. The hours were long and the work was often dangerous.

To enable women with young children to enter the work force, 28 government-funded day care centres were opened in Ontario and 6 were opened in Quebec. These centres provided care to children between the ages of two and six. In Ontario, child care was also provided for children under the age of two and for school-aged children. While women working in the war industries got priority when it came to the allocation of these day care spots, children of other working mothers were also considered for spaces.

Women were also trained for new types of work during the war years. The joint federal-provincial War Emergency Training Program trained women in such trades as welding, aircraft assembly, shipbuilding, electronics, drafting, and industrial chemistry. While the aim of the program was admirable—to enable increasing numbers of women to enter non-traditional fields of employment—women only received two

Voice from the Past

"Well, girls, you have done a nice job; you looked very cute in your overalls and we appreciate what you have done for us; but just run along; go home; we can get along without you very easily."

—Saskatchewan CCF member Dorise Nielsen, expressing the prevailing attitude towards women at the end of the war.

to six weeks of instruction, considerably less than their male counterparts received. Consequently, they had little opportunity to gain the specialized training that would have enabled them to obtain long-term employment once the war ended or to access higher-paying positions within the trades.

Stats

A 1944 Gallup poll revealed that 75 per cent of Canadian men and 68 per cent of Canadian women believed that post-war jobs should go to men rather than women.

They're in the Army Now!

The women serving on the homefront were not the only Canadian women involved in the war. Approximately 43,000 women served overseas as nurses, doctors, drivers, stretcher bearers, cooks, secretaries, and machine operators. These women—who belonged to the Canadian Women's Army Corps, the Women's Royal Navy Service, and the Women's Division of the Royal Canadian Air Force—played a critical role in the success of the Allies.

Women who served in the armed forces encountered a great deal of sexism. They were paid less than their male counterparts; initially, they received only 66 per cent of the pay received by men doing equivalent work, but in response to an outcry from the women, the armed forces raised this amount to 80 per cent.

Voice from the Past

"I remember seeing a flash [a shoulder patch] on one jacket lying across the foot of the bed and I knew that flash because it was the regiment which came from my home town.... I had to look at the face and he was unconscious and it was Billy C__ and I nearly dropped what I was carrying. I'd gone on skating parties with him, hayrides. I think I had a crush on him once. I don't think I ever knew what war and battle was until then."

—A female Red Cross Corps worker recalling her experiences of attending to the wounded in overseas field hospitals.

Main Event

One of the darkest moments in Canadian history took place during World War II, when the Canadian government forcibly relocated thousands of Japanese Canadians, believing that they would collaborate with the enemy in the event of a Japanese invasion. In fact, no Japanese Canadians were convicted of treason during the war.

The situation came to a head in late 1941. On December 7, Japanese bombers attacked Pearl Harbor in Hawaii. The next day, they struck Hong Kong (a British colony at the time). Within hours, the Canadian government declared war on Japan. In February of 1942, Prime Minister William Lyon Mackenzie King issued an order-in-council requiring the evacuation of all Japanese living within 62 km of the British Columbia coast.

Twenty-three thousand Japanese were relocated, 13,000 of whom were naturalized Canadian citizens or native-born Canadians. Their property was seized and their families were broken up; men were sent to work on labour gangs and women and children were shipped to abandoned ghost towns or settlements.

After the war ended, the persecution continued. The Canadian government refused to allow the Japanese to return to their former homes. Instead, they were given the choice of moving to eastern Canada or emigrating to Japan. While some compensation was ultimately given to the victims of this misguided policy, it was slow in coming and not particularly generous.

They were confined to support positions such as clerks, cooks, telephone operators, drivers, mess waiters, and canteen helpers. And they were gossiped about mercilessly. (Rumours of the day accused women in the armed forces of being former prostitutes, sexually promiscuous, and/or carriers of sexually transmitted diseases!)

On the Front Lines

Despite the government's initial reluctance to commit troops to the war, Canadians played a significant role in World War II. Large numbers of Canadians were captured or lost their lives during two particularly difficult battles: Hong Kong (1941) and Dieppe (1942). In continental Europe, Canadians were given the task of helping to defend the British Isles and preparing for the final assault on Europe. Squadrons of the Royal Canadian Air Force took part in bombing raids, and the Canadian navy escorted vital supplies in convoys across the Atlantic. Canadians were also on hand for the Allied victory on the beaches of Normandy on D-Day, June 6, 1944.

The End of the War

On September 2, 1945, World War II officially came to a close.

While Canada had made a noteworthy contribution to the war effort, like many other small countries, it was left out of the making of the peace. This was something that bothered King tremendously.

Main Event

On August 6, 1945, the Allies dropped Little Boy, the world's first atomic bomb, on Hiroshima, a Japanese city of 300,000. Seventy-eight thousand people were killed instantly, 70,000 were injured, and 10,000 others were never found.

Five days later, the Allies dropped Fat Man on Nagasaki, killing 40,000 people instantly and wounding another 40,000 in the city of 250,000.

The following day, Japan surrendered.

Stats

In total, 1,086,343 Canadian men and women served in the armed forces during World War II. Of these, 96,456 were killed, wounded, or died in service.

Stats

Canada spent approximately $20 billion on war and demobilization expenditures. As a result, the federal debt reached $13 billion by the end of the war, more than four times what it had been in 1939.

However, Canada was invited to the Dumbarton Oaks Conference in Washington in 1944, where plans were laid for the United Nations—an organization of 50 nations whose mandate was to prevent World War III from ever happening.

The Least You Need to Know

- While Canada had hoped to be able to supply materials rather than people to the war effort, it soon became apparent that both would be needed.
- World War II created a boom in the Canadian economy as factories worked overtime to produce munitions and other materials to ship overseas.
- Women played a major role in supporting the war effort. Some worked in munitions factories while others served overseas.
- The Canadian government ordered Japanese Canadians living within 62 km of the British Columbia coast to relocate to internment camps. Thousands of families were uprooted and separated, yet no Japanese Canadians were ever convicted of treason during the war.

Part 6
Happily Ever After?

The 50 years following World War II were a time of tremendous economic, political, and social change for Canada. Increasing numbers of Canadians put down their lunch pails and pursued white collar jobs in the rapidly expanding service sector. The provinces sought a more equal relationship with the federal government. The country assumed an increasingly important role on the international stage. Women, natives, and ethnic groups began to demand fair treatment from the rest of society. And Quebecers began to question whether they wanted to be a part of Canada after all....

Chapter 29

Bungalows and Babies (1945 to 1993)

In this chapter

- The post-war economy and the baby boom
- Economic change
- Foreign investment in Canada
- Economic nationalism
- Free trade
- Deficit reduction

While the 1950s and 1960s were boom times for Canadians, by the early 1970s, the Canadian economy was in considerable trouble—and none of the governments of the day seemed to know how to fix what was broken.

The Post-War Economy

The period from 1945 to 1970 was a golden age for Canadians. The economy was booming, jobs were plentiful, and the standard of living was on the rise.

The good times didn't just happen by accident, however. Anxious to avoid the economic chaos that had occurred following World War I, the Canadian government devoted considerable energies to ensuring that returning veterans were reintegrated into the Canadian work force as smoothly as possible. The government passed legislation that gave veterans first crack at the jobs they had left behind when they enlisted and provided them with educational allowances and low-interest loans.

Stats

By 1956, the average income was $3250 per year, and the average consumer's purchasing power had doubled since the Great Depression.

The government also played an active role in managing the economy. The Wartime Prices and Trade Board continued to implement policies designed to prevent the increased demand for goods from causing inflation to go spiralling out of control. As a result, the post-war recession that many had been dreading never materialized.

Home Is Where the Mortgage Is

The post-war years were boom times for homebuilders. During the 1950s alone, $60 million of new housing was constructed—more than twice as much as had been constructed during the previous 25 years. As a result, the number of Canadians who owned homes jumped from one in three in 1948 to two in three by 1961.

The homebuilding bonanza was stimulated by tremendous population growth. The population jumped from 11.5 million in 1941 to 16.5 million in 1957 to 20.5 million in 1968. While high levels of immigration throughout the 1950s contributed to the rise (when an estimated 150,000 people entered the country each year), much of the population increase was due to a massive post-war baby boom.

Stats

By 1961, there was one automobile for every four Canadians.

The Have Nots

However, the good times were not shared by all. One in four Canadians continued to live in poverty. Those most likely to be living in poverty included natives, African Canadians, francophones, recent immigrants, families led by women, and those living in the Atlantic provinces or the North. Average weekly wages in 1961 ranged from a low of $57.03 in Prince Edward Island to a high of $85.20 in Ontario.

A Changing Economy

The 1950s were a time of spectacular growth in the construction, consumer durable, staple, and service industries. As a result, the country's gross national product doubled between 1950 and 1960, growing from $18 billion to $36 billion. A brief economic slump in 1957 made everyone nervous and spurred considerable debate about the best way to manage the economy, but fortunately it was just a blip.

At the heart of all this post-war productivity was technological innovation. Synthetic fibres, plastics, pesticides, television sets, computers, and high-tech pharmaceutical products were just a few of the exciting new products that rolled off assembly lines in the years following the war. These products soon became so essential to Canadians that future generations would scratch their heads trying to envision life without them.

The country also experienced a significant economic shift as it began to move from a resource-based economy to a service-based economy. By 1955, service industries accounted for 50 per cent of the country's income, with the remaining 50 per cent coming from manufacturing and construction, and the extraction and processing of primary products.

Agriculture

Just as the economy as a whole was changing, so was the agricultural sector.

For one thing, fewer Canadians were making their living from farming. While 34 per cent had been involved in agriculture in 1911, that number had dipped to 10 per cent by the 1950s.

Those who decided to stick with farming began to treat their farms as commercial operations. They relied on marketing boards that established quotas, set prices, and defined market boundaries, and took advantage of federal subsidies designed to encourage them to plant lucrative new crops such as oats, barley, and flax. What's more, they began to sell their produce to giant canning and freezing companies that used them to create a smorgasbord of processed foods—everything from potato chips to TV dinners!

Fishing

There were equally dramatic developments in the fishing industry. While there was a 40 per cent decline in the number of people employed in the Atlantic fisheries between 1951 and 1961, high-tech trawlers enabled large conglomerates to harvest as much as 180,000 kilograms of fish in a two-week period. Unfortunately, this led to a rapid depletion of Atlantic fish stocks.

During this period, the vast majority of people working in the fishing industry abandoned self-employment and joined the payroll of such fishing industry giants as National Sea Products, Atlantic Fish Producers, and B.C. Packers.

Mining

The mining industry also underwent significant changes.

The development of the atomic bomb and nuclear reactors led to the rapid growth of the Canadian nuclear industry. In 1952, Atomic Energy of Canada was created to find peacetime uses for atomic energy (a natural role for a Canadian Crown corporation, because the country was supplying one third of the world's uranium).

There were equally significant developments in the oil and gas industry. The discovery of oil at Imperial Oil's Leduc No. 1 well near Edmonton on February 3, 1947, led to massive investment from around the world. By 1956, there were over 1200 companies exploring for oil in the Canadian West.

Foreign Investment

The growing amount of foreign investment did not go unnoticed by Canadians. Many began to express concern about the increasing percentage of foreign (particularly American) ownership.

In 1955, the St. Laurent government appointed Walter Gordon, a partner in one of Toronto's largest accounting firms, to chair the Royal Commission on Canada's Economic Prospects. The so-called Gordon

Stats

By 1960, 75 per cent of foreign investment in Canada came from the United States. What's more, the United States was Canada's largest export customer, consuming roughly two-thirds of its goods. By this time, the British were only responsible for 15 per cent of Canada's foreign investments.

Report stressed the growing problems caused by the "Americanization" of the Canadian economy, and urged the government to exercise tighter control over foreign investment. It recommended that foreign corporations be required to employ more Canadians in senior management positions, to invite more Canadians to sit on their boards, and to sell an "appreciable interest" in their equity stocks to Canadians.

Not everyone was opposed to the high level of American investment, however. Speaking to the Hamilton Chamber of Commerce in April of 1956, Minister of Trade and Industry C.D. Howe cut to the chase: "Let us face facts. Had it not been for the enterprise and capital of the United States, which has been so freely at our disposal in postwar years, our development would have been slower, and some of the spectacular projects about which we are so proud and so rightly proud, since they are Canadian projects, would still be far in the future."

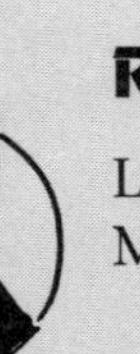

Real Life

Louis Stephen St. Laurent (1882–1973) was the Prime Minister of Canada from 1948 to 1957.

Prior to entering federal politics, he was a lawyer, a law professor at Laval University, and a counsel to the Rowell-Sirois Commission on Dominion-Provincial Relations. He entered politics at King's invitation, but initially only agreed to serve in King's Liberal government until the end of the war.

St. Laurent stuck with politics considerably longer than he had originally planned. He is remembered for his role in overseeing the entry of Newfoundland into Confederation (1949), establishing equalization payments to the provinces, improving social welfare programs, and encouraging Canada to play a larger role in international peacekeeping missions.

Economic Policy During the 1960s

When John Diefenbaker's Conservative government came to power in 1957, it decided to pursue the British market more aggressively, offer tax incentives to Canadian-based companies, and enter into trade agreements with communist countries such as Cuba and the Soviet Union. (The latter course of action earned Diefenbaker the wrath of the U.S. government, which shamelessly worked to see him defeated in the following election.)

The Americans were understandably less than thrilled to discover that Lester B. Pearson—Diefenbaker's successor—was

Main Event

In 1954, Canada and the United States agreed to jointly finance the development of the St. Lawrence Seaway. This massive undertaking involved enlarging canals and developing the power potential of the 3800-km inland waterway. The project was completed in 1959.

Real Life

John George Diefenbaker (1895–1979) was the Prime Minister of Canada from 1957 to 1963. He served as the leader of the Progressive Conservatives from 1956 to 1967.

Prior to entering politics, Diefenbaker had a successful career as a criminal lawyer and enjoyed a brief stint as the leader of the Saskatchewan Conservative Party (1936 to 1938).

He is remembered for his role in helping to create a Canadian Bill of Rights (1958); appointing Canada's first aboriginal senator, James Gladstone (1958); and his ongoing efforts on behalf of the country's minority groups.

Diefenbaker once said: "I am the first prime minister of this country of neither altogether English or French origin. So I'm determined to bring about a Canadian citizenship that knew no hyphenated consideration....I'm very happy to be able to say that in the House of Commons today in my party we have members of Italian, Dutch, German, Scandinavian, Chinese, and Ukrainian origin—and they are all Canadians."

equally committed to minimizing foreign investment. Not only did he appoint Walter Gordon as Minister of Finance, he introduced a 30 per cent takeover tax that applied to foreign takeovers of Canadian companies and introduced legislation designed both to protect Canadian banks, insurance companies, and other financial services from foreign control and to reduce American dominance of the Canadian media. (For a detailed discussion of the "Americanization" of Canadian culture, see Chapter 32.)

Economic Nationalism

On August 15, 1971, U.S. President Richard Nixon took the U.S. currency off the gold standard and introduced a series of protective measures designed to jump-start the American economy.

Canadians were shocked by the suddenness of Nixon's actions; in the past, they had always been alerted of significant shifts in American economic policy before such announcements were made.

Real Life

Lester Bowles Pearson (1897–1972) was the Prime Minister of Canada from 1963 to 1968. He was also the leader of the Liberal party from 1958 to 1968.

Prior to entering federal politics, Pearson had a distinguished career in the foreign service. He served as the Canadian ambassador to the United Nations (1945 to 1946), the chairman of the NATO Council (1951 to 1952), and the president of the United Nations General Assembly (1952 to 1953). He won a Nobel Peace Prize in 1957 for his efforts in resolving the Suez Crisis the year before.

Pearson's accomplishments in office included appointing the Royal Commission on Bilingualism and Biculturalism (1963), establishing the Canada Pension Plan (1965) and universal medicare (1966), and introducing a new national flag (1965).

Pearson was also an accomplished athlete who served on both Oxford University's hockey team and the British Olympic hockey team in 1922. Rumour has it that he had a television installed in his office while he was prime minister so he wouldn't have to miss a single game of the World Series!

Prime Minister Pierre Elliott Trudeau (whose government had swept to power in 1968) decided to fight fire with fire and introduce his own program of economic nationalism. He created the Canada Development Corporation (to encourage Canadian ownership and management of vital areas of the Canadian economy), the Foreign Investment Review Agency (to screen proposals for takeovers of Canadian businesses), and Petro-Canada (a Crown corporation whose mandate was to develop a Canadian presence in the American-dominated oil industry). A much later program—the National Energy Program (1980)—was intended to promote Canadian self-sufficiency in oil.

The Oil Crisis

In 1973, the Oil and Petroleum Exporting Countries (OPEC) declared an embargo on oil exports. Their actions were motivated by anger at Western support of Israel during the Yom Kippur War.

The oil embargo had a devastating impact on Western industrial economies. By the time the embargo was lifted in 1975, the price of oil had increased from $3 to $12 a barrel and the Canadian economy was

Real Life

Pierre Elliott Trudeau (1919–present) was the Prime Minister of Canada from 1968 to 1979 and from 1980 to 1984. He also served as the leader of the Liberal party throughout that period.

Trudeau is a highly educated man who studied at Harvard University and the London School of Economics prior to pursuing a career in law and academics.

While Trudeau is remembered for introducing the Official Languages Act (1969) and Wage and Price Controls (1975) and for his decision to implement the War Measures Act during the October Crisis (1970), his legacy to Canada was the introduction of the Canadian Charter of Rights and Freedoms (1982) and the Constitution Act (1982).

During his early years in politics, Trudeau enjoyed extraordinary personal appeal. An outbreak of "Trudeaumania" during the election of 1968 swept him into office with a majority government.

experiencing "stagflation" (a particularly nasty economic ailment that involves both high inflation and high unemployment).

The 1980s

The economic problems triggered by the oil embargo, the U.S. program of economic nationalism, and the growing economic power exercised by Pacific Rim countries plagued the Trudeau government throughout the remainder of the decade and into the 1980s. (Prime Minister Joe Clark—who managed to wrestle power away from the Liberals from June 4, 1979, to March 3, 1980—was also saddled with these problems temporarily.)

By 1981, the global economy was facing the worst economic slump since the Great Depression.

At a loss at what to do about Canada's sluggish economy, in 1982 Trudeau appointed the Royal Commission on Canada's Economic Union and Development Prospects (a.k.a. the Royal Commission on Canada's Future). The Commission's report, tabled in 1985, concluded

Real Life

(Charles) Joseph Clark (1939–present) was the Prime Minister of Canada from 1979 to 1980. He served as the leader of the Conservative party from 1976 to 1983.

Because he seemed to appear out of nowhere to assume leadership of the party, the press nicknamed him "Joe Who." The fact of the matter, however, was that Clark had worked behind the scenes in the Conservative party for a number of years and went on to play an active role in the Mulroney government, serving as Minister of External Affairs (1984 to 1991) and Minister of Constitutional Affairs (1991 to 1993).

Clark is remembered for his role in ensuring that American embassy personnel were sheltered in the Canadian embassy in Iran during the hostage crisis (1979 to 1980) and for appointing Canada's first black Cabinet minister, Lincoln Alexander (1979).

that Canada's economy needed to adapt to global economic change and rapidly evolving technologies. It argued that free trade with the United States was Canada's only hope for continued economic prosperity.

Word for the Day

The *New Democratic party* (NDP) was formed in 1961 as the result of a union of the Co-operative Commonwealth Federation, the Canadian Labour Congress, and the so-called "New Party."

Free Trade

The idea of free trade was frightening to many Canadians, who feared that it would lead to job losses and wage cuts and threaten Canada's cultural industries and social programs. It encountered significant resistance from labour unions, feminists, church groups, nationalists, and members of both the New Democratic party and the Liberal party. One of the most outspoken critics of free trade was Trudeau himself.

Trudeau didn't stick around to fight the issue in an election, however. He took a long walk one chilly February day in 1984, and decided to announce his retirement. His successor John Turner was unable to lead the Liberals to victory in the election of 1984.

Real Life

John Napier Turner (1929–present) was the Prime Minister of Canada for a brief period during 1984, following Trudeau's resignation.

Prior to becoming prime minister, Turner worked as a lawyer and assumed a series of increasingly responsible portfolios in the Pearson and Trudeau governments.

His major political accomplishments occurred before he became prime minister. He played a role in the introduction of a Criminal Code amendment concerning hate propaganda (1970) and in the establishment of the Law Reform Commission (1971). He is also remembered for the strong anti–free trade stand he took during the election of 1984.

While Conservative Brian Mulroney didn't say much about free trade during the election of 1984, it didn't take him long to start pursuing the Americans once he assumed control of government.

The Americans were characteristically forthright about what they wanted: freedom to invest in Canada, access to Canadian energy and water supplies and other resources, and guaranteed access to the Canadian market for America's service industries. The Canadians were equally sure of what they wanted: elimination of duties and access to the mammoth market to the south.

By the fall of 1987, Canadian and American negotiators had managed to hammer out the details of the treaty. A year of heated debate followed in the House of Commons. When it became clear that the Liberal-dominated Senate was unwilling to ratify the Free Trade Agreement unless the Conservatives received an electoral mandate to pursue such a course of action, Mulroney called Canadians to the polls. The Conservatives returned to power in November of 1988—even though the majority of Canadians voted against them!

The Free Trade Agreement came into effect on January 1, 1989. Under its terms, Canada and the United States agreed to eliminate tariffs on primary and manufactured goods over a 10-year period, and to allow for free trade in services as well.

Real Life

(Martin) Brian Mulroney (1939–present) was the Prime Minister of Canada from 1984 to 1993.

Prior to becoming prime minister, Mulroney enjoyed successful careers in law and in business. He was the president of the Iron Ore Company from 1977 to 1983.

Mulroney is remembered for his role in the Meech Lake Accord (1987), the Canada–U.S. Free Trade Agreement (1988), Canada's participation in the Gulf War (1991), the Goods and Services Tax (1991), the North American Free Trade Agreement (1992), the Constitutional Accord (a.k.a. the Charlottetown Accord, 1992), and the Nunavut Settlement Agreement (1993).

Almost overnight, the Americans announced that they were negotiating a similar deal with Mexico. Fearing that such a deal would nullify the effects of the Free Trade Agreement, the Mulroney government asked to be included in the negotiations with Mexico.

Despite massive public outcry (many Canadians argued that Canada should only enter into free trade agreements with countries that had social programs, pollution standards, and collective-bargaining legislation similar to that in effect in Canada), the North American Free Trade Agreement (NAFTA) came into effect on January 1, 1994.

Till Debt Do Us Part

Throughout the 1980s, Mulroney attempted to fight Canada's growing deficit by reducing spending on social programs, privatizing government activities, and cutting back on the size of the civil service. Despite his efforts, the deficit continued to rise and a new global recession set in during mid-1990. While things certainly got worse before they got better, the country eventually began to experience economic growth once again.

The Least You Need to Know

- The years following World War II were extremely prosperous ones for Canadians.
- The Canadian economy has undergone tremendous change since World War II, shifting from a resource-based economy to a service-based economy.
- The high level of foreign investment has been a cause of ongoing concern to Canadians. During the 1960s, a series of policies were put into place to discourage foreign investment.
- The U.S.–Canada Free Trade Agreement came into effect on January 1, 1989, and the North American Free Trade Agreement (NAFTA) came into effect on January 1, 1994.
- Recent governments have cut social spending and the size of the civil service in an effort to reduce the country's deficit.

Chapter 30

Weaving the Social Safety Net (1945 to 1990)

In this chapter

- Canada's social programs
- Cooperative federalism

From the beginning, Canada's social problems were intended as a means of preventing destitution in the event of job loss or illness. They were also designed to keep income in the hands of consumers, regardless of what the economy was doing at the time.

Between 1960 and 1981, Canada's social expenditures rose from 12.1 per cent to 21.7 per cent of the gross domestic product. (While this amount sounds like a lot, it was nowhere near what was being spent by countries such as Belgium (38 per cent), and it was just a fraction above what the U.S. was spending at the time (21 per cent).)

By the mid-1980s, however, the tide had turned. The cash-strapped Mulroney government was desperately seeking ways to trim fat from its budget in order to attain its deficit management goals, and social expenditures were an all-too-easy target.

Aid to Rural Canadians

The Agricultural Rehabilitation and Development Act (ARDA), introduced by the Diefenbaker government in June of 1961, was specifically designed to improve living standards and provide greater employment opportunities for Canadians living in rural Canada. The program became the prototype for a series of other federally funded programs designed to encourage private industry to locate in underdeveloped areas.

Canada Pension Plan

The Canada Pension Plan (CPP) was introduced by the Pearson government in 1965. Its rates were deliberately kept low to appease private insurance companies.

Medicare

Canada's first medicare system appeared in Saskatchewan in 1962. The brainchild of T.C. "Tommy" Douglas's Co-operative Commonwealth Federation government, medicare initially met with considerable resistance from the medical community, who went on strike for three weeks to protest its introduction. In the end, the program became the inspiration for other provincially funded medicare programs.

Stats

In 1980, Statistics Canada reported that 27 per cent of seniors were living on "limited incomes," and that the percentage of women living at or below the poverty line was even higher. In 1985, following the Trudeau government's decision to increase the amount of the Guaranteed Income Supplement, the rate of poverty among the elderly dropped to 19 per cent. Seniors were outraged, therefore, when the Mulroney government threatened to stop indexing pension payments to inflation. In the end, the tremendous public outcry forced Mulroney to retreat on the issue.

Word for the Day

From the mid-1950s onward, the provinces and the federal government met regularly to negotiate mutually acceptable agreements concerning pensions, medicare, and federal aid to education. Pearson described the new relationship as *cooperative federalism*, a system in which the two levels of government worked together to find solutions.

During this period, Pearson showed a great willingness to allow the provinces to opt out of federal programs, design their own equivalents, and receive federal support as if they were participating in the original program. Quebec took advantage of this situation, forming its own pension program (the Quebec Pension Plan) rather than participating in the Canada Pension Plan.

Most Canadians disapproved of the opting-out provision, feeling that Quebec was exercising undue influence over the federal government. When Trudeau came to power in 1968, he put the provinces on notice that the era of cooperative federalism was over; from that point forward, provinces that opted out of federal programs would not receive funding for their own programs.

Stats

Surveys conducted in 1944 and 1949 indicated that 80 per cent of Canadians wanted a federal health plan that covered complete medical and hospital care for a flat monthly rate.

In 1964, the Pearson government received the report of the Royal Commission on Health Services. The Commission recommended a universal medicare system. Following their victory in the election of 1965 (in which medicare was a central issue), the Liberals announced a national shared-cost health insurance program. The program was based on four basic principles: universal coverage, coverage of most types of medical treatment, portability of benefits, and provincial administration. By 1970, every province had established a medicare program.

Canada Assistance Plan

While Canadians were quick to rally behind medicare and the Canada Pension Plan, they were less eager to support income security programs such as the Canada Assistance Plan (CAP) of 1966. As a result, the Plan remained woefully underfunded, and many families ran out of money long before their next CAP cheque was due.

Cuts to Social Spending

Anxious to cut costs in order to meet its deficit-reduction targets, in 1986 the Mulroney government announced that federal cash grants for medicare and post-secondary education would be reduced by 2 per cent annually.

While Canadians reacted strongly to this announcement, this first round of cuts was only the beginning. Others followed in quick succession: child benefits were partially de-indexed from inflation, federal supplements for hiring and training workers were eliminated, a program designed to help municipalities maintain low-cost rental units was put on the chopping block, family allowance and old age security payments were limited to only the most needy Canadians, future increases to pension plan funding were capped, and unemployment insurance benefits were reduced.

Many Canadians feared that these cuts signalled the beginning of the end for the country's social programs.

> **Stats**
>
> By 1992, 150,000 people were being served each month by Toronto's Daily Bread Food Bank. That same year, an estimated 2 million Canadians turned to food banks across the country.

The Least You Need to Know

- A wide range of social programs were introduced during the 1960s.
- While Pearson was willing to allow certain provinces to opt out of federally funded programs and receive full funding for their own equivalent programs, Trudeau was not.
- The Mulroney government cut funding to social programs in the 1980s in an effort to meet its deficit-reduction targets.

Chapter 31

Keeping the Peace (1945 to 1997)

In this chapter

- The United Nations and NATO
- The Korean War
- The Suez Crisis
- The Cuban Missile Crisis
- The Vietnam War
- The Gulf War
- The Somalia Affair

At the beginning of World War II, Britain and Germany were the world's two major superpowers. By the end of the War, the Soviets and the Americans had assumed that role.

While Canadians clearly didn't attract nearly as much attention on the world stage as the two muscle-flexing superpowers, they had an important role to play nonetheless in the post–World War II era.

The Big Chill

The term "Cold War" aptly describes the outright chilly relationships between the United States and the Soviet Union in the years following World War II. First coined by American journalist Herbert Bayard Swope, the term refers to the post-war strategic and political struggle between the U.S. and its allies and the Soviet Union and other communist countries.

Much of the Cold War was fought in the United Nations (UN), which came into existence on October 24, 1945, and included representatives from 50 different nations.

Stats

A Gallup poll conducted in 1948 revealed that 51 per cent of Canadians felt that World War III was inevitable.

The North Atlantic Treaty Organization (NATO)

While Canada was extremely supportive of the United Nations, it was acutely aware of the organization's one weakness: it couldn't prevent member nations from suffering aggression.

Given the realities of geography, Canada was more than a little concerned about what the fallout of the aggression between the United States and the Soviet Union might mean for its own security. (After all, there's nothing like being sandwiched between two restless giants!)

Voice from the Past

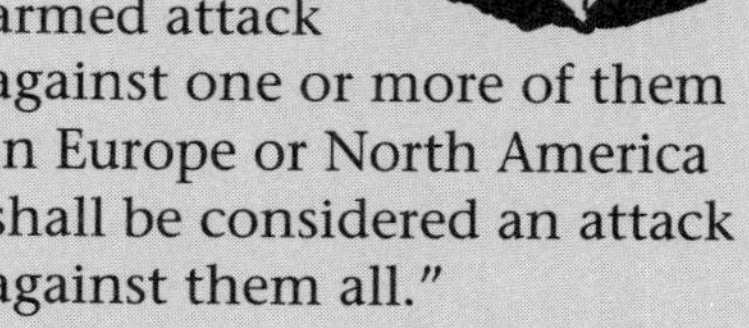

"The parties agree that an armed attack against one or more of them in Europe or North America shall be considered an attack against them all."

—Article 5 of the North Atlantic Treaty.

In April of 1948, Prime Minister Louis St. Laurent proposed a solution. He called for "the creation and preservation by the nations of the Free World under the leadership of Great Britain, the United States, and France of an overwhelming preponderance of force over any adversary or possible combination of adversaries." This long-winded utterance ultimately led to the signing of the North Atlantic Treaty of April 4, 1949, and the formation of the North Atlantic Treaty Organization (NATO).

The Korean War

One of first challenges facing the newly created United Nations was the outbreak of the Korean War.

Voice from the Past

"If Southeast and South Asia are not to be conquered by communism, we of the free democratic world must demonstrate it is we and not the Russians who stand for national liberation and economic and social progress."

—Lester B. Pearson, 1950

Before World War II, Korea was occupied by Japan. After the War, it was divided along the 38th Parallel into two separate zones, with the Soviet Union controlling the North and the Americans controlling the South.

In November 1947, the United Nations sought to create a unified, independent Korea, but the communist forces in the North refused to allow free elections to take place. The South decided to proceed with the elections nonetheless, and on August 15, 1948, the Republic of Korea was born. (North Korea subsequently became known as the Democratic People's Republic of Korea.)

Tensions between the two countries intensified until war broke out on June 25, 1950, when communist-backed forces from the North attacked South Korea. The United Nations issued sanctions against the invasion and provided troops to repel it. Canada was one of 16 countries to supply troops. Eventually the UN forces succeeded in pushing back the North Koreans.

Other International Involvements

The Korean War had no sooner concluded than Canada found itself being asked to participate in other UN missions around the world. In 1954, it agreed to serve on the commission supervising the drafting of cease-fire agreements in Indochina. It also participated in subsequent UN military engagements in the Congo (1960 to 1964), Cyprus (1964), Lebanon (1953), West New Guinea (1962), Yemen (1963), and Pakistan (1965). By the mid-1960s, it was apparent that Canada's international responsibilities were likely to continue to draw it into conflicts in far-off parts of the world.

Suez Crisis

In 1956, Egyptian President Gamal Abdel Nasser nationalized the Suez Canal, a key transportation corridor in the Middle East. What Nasser neglected to acknowledge was that the canal had been owned by a private firm backed by British and French investors. When negotiations failed to resolve the issue, Britain and France invaded the canal zone.

Canadian External Affairs Minister Lester B. Pearson took on the task of finding a solution to the problem. He was the ideal person for the job, having developed a network of international connections through his work at the UN. Pearson managed to convince Nasser to accept the presence of a United Nations Emergency Force (UNEF), which would patrol the Suez Canal and supervise the cessation of hostilities. Pearson was ultimately awarded a Nobel Peace Prize for his exceptionally skillful handling of the conflict.

Canada–U.S. Relations

While Canada and the United States remained allies during the post-war period, there were numerous sources of friction between the two countries. One of the most noteworthy instances of conflict occurred when the infamous U.S. Senator Joseph McCarthy of Wisconsin started recklessly accusing high-profile Canadians of being communists. (In the end, one high-placed Canadian diplomat committed suicide as a result of the attacks.)

Despite the friction, however, Canada and the United States maintained the close cooperation in world affairs that had begun with the formation of the Permanent Joint Board on Defence in 1940. They co-operated in the area of air defence, standardizing both training methods and equipment and providing reciprocal access to one another's defence facilities. They also jointly developed a series of radar systems designed to prevent the two countries from a long-range bomber attack. The Pinetree Line, which followed the border, was jointly financed; the McGill Fence, which followed the 55th Parallel, was paid for by Canada; and the Distant Early Warning System, which rang in at a hefty $600 million, was paid for by the Americans.

Cuban Missile Crisis

One of the scariest moments in post-war history occurred in October 1962, when U.S. President John F. Kennedy demanded that the Soviet Union remove its missiles from Cuba. The situation came so close to exploding that Kennedy called on Canada to put its North Atlantic Air Defence (NORAD) forces on alert in the event that the Soviet Union refused to back down. (While Diefenbaker secretly put the troops on alert right away, he didn't announce that he had done so for three days because he was concerned that Kennedy was being overly belligerent with the Soviets. This delay annoyed Kennedy to no end and led the U.S. government, which was already infuriated by Diefenbaker's economic policies, to work to ensure his defeat in the following year's federal election!) In the end, the Soviets agreed to withdraw the offending missiles and the crisis was averted.

Stats

Thirty thousand Canadians volunteered to serve in the Vietnam War. Roughly the same number of American "draft dodgers" fled to Canada to avoid being sent to Vietnam.

The Vietnam War

In 1965, Lester B. Pearson gave a speech at Temple University in Philadelphia in which he encouraged the American government to temporarily cease bombing North Vietnam in an effort to bring about peace.

U.S. President Lyndon Johnson didn't exactly welcome Pearson's advice. In fact, he was outraged that the Canadian prime minister had dared to criticize American foreign policy. (Johnson momentarily forgot that Canada had compromised its role on the International Control Commission to defend America's views of the conflict, and that it had agreed to spy on North Vietnam on behalf of the U.S!) The next time the two men were together, the giant Texan grabbed the smaller Canadian by the collar and shouted an obscenity at him. Pearson was quite simply too stunned to reply.

A New Game Plan

When Pierre Elliott Trudeau was elected in 1968, he immediately began examining Canada's foreign policy. He concluded that the country needed to play a less active role in international affairs, and cut the number of forces the country had committed to NATO in half.

At the same time, however, Trudeau launched a comprehensive program of foreign aid. In 1968, the Canadian International Development Agency (CIDA) was launched to assist Third World countries to develop their own industries in the hope that they would gradually become self-sufficient. Ironically, CIDA was launched at the very time when the U.S.

and other countries were cutting their own foreign aid budgets.

The Cold War Begins to Thaw

When Ronald Reagan became the U.S. president in early 1980, protests and marches broke out across North America. Peace activists across the continent were convinced that Reagan's election would chill American–Soviet relations further and intensify the arms race.

In 1984, events on the other side of the world led to an easing of Cold War tensions. Mikhail Gorbachev, the new chairman of the Communist party in the Soviet Union, began calling for "new political thinking" and proposed radical reductions in both nuclear and conventional armaments. Three successful summits between 1985 and 1987 led to more cordial relations between the two superpowers, as well as to an important series of arms limitation talks.

Voice from the Past

"In the long run the overwhelming threat to Canada will not come from foreign investments, or foreign ideologies, or even...foreign nuclear weapons. It will come instead from the two thirds of the people of the world who are steadily falling farther and farther behind in their search for a decent standard of living."

—Pierre Elliott Trudeau, 1968

The Gulf War

On August 1, 1990, Iraq invaded Kuwait. The following day, UN resolution 600 demanded the immediate and unconditional withdrawal of Iraqi troops. When Iraq failed to budge, a series of economic embargoes

Main Event

In 1982, the Trudeau government agreed to allow the U.S. to test the cruise missile over Canada. Trudeau told peace activists across the country who urged the Liberals to "refuse the cruise" that agreeing to allow cruise missile testing was simply part of Canada's NATO commitments.

were imposed. On November 29, the UN Security Council gave Iraq until January 15, 1991, to comply with the UN resolution. It failed to do so. On January 16, UN coalition forces led by the United States began the first of thousands of bombing raids on Iraq as preparation for a ground offensive. By the time the ground offensive began on February 23, Iraq was on the verge of surrender. The war formally came to a close on February 28. Canada had been involved in the war from the very beginning, supplying both equipment and troops.

The Somalia Affair

While Canadian peacekeepers had earned a reputation over the years for conducting themselves with honour and integrity during their missions overseas, the conduct of the Canadian Airborne Regiment in Somalia in 1993 tarnished Canada's reputation on the world stage.

On the night of March 4, 1993, two Somalia citizens were shot outside the Canadian forces' compound. Ahmed Afrahow Aruush died from his wounds. Then, on the night of March 16, Shidane Abukhar Arone was tortured and killed by Canadian Airborne soldiers.

The Report of the Somalia Commission of Inquiry, delivered to the Canadian government in June of 1997, concluded that the Canadian Airborne Regiment was unfit for duty in Somalia, that Parliament should set clear guidelines for future peacekeeping missions, and that the military justice system should be reformed.

While the Somalia Affair was clearly an isolated incident, it was a source of considerable embarrassment to Canadians who—up until that point—had taken great pride in Canada's role as a peacekeeping nation.

The Least You Need to Know

- The United Nations was founded on October 24, 1945, and the North Atlantic Treaty Organization (NATO) was founded on April 4, 1949.
- Canada played an active role in international affairs throughout the 1950s and 1960s.
- The Americans were less than pleased with the Canadian government's responses to the Cuban Missile Crisis and the Vietnam War.
- The Somalia Affair tarnished the reputation of Canadian peacekeepers.

Chapter 32

The Times They Were A-Changin' (1960 to 1996)

In this chapter

- Social change after 1960
- The "Americanization" of Canadian culture
- The Canadian civil rights movement

The years after World War II were a time of rapid social change. The "second wave" of feminism emerged, ethnic groups demanded an end to discrimination, and native Canadians began to demand that the federal government pay serious attention to their long-standing grievances.

Reinventing the Family

Motivated by a desire to improve their families' standard of living after years of depression and war, many women entered the work force in the years after 1945. By the early 1960s, nearly half of the women employed in the work force were married. (Most of them, however, were women who had not yet started their families or who had school-aged children.)

At the very same time that married women were entering the work force in record numbers, media images looked to the past. In English Canada, the print and broadcast media portrayed women as committed wives and mothers who were pleased to make use of modern products that would contribute to their families' health and well-being. (Think *Leave It to Beaver*!) In French Canada, the images being promoted were of devoted wives and mothers who were attached to the rural way of life and the teachings of the Catholic Church.

During the 1960s, women began to make a conscious effort to limit the size of their families. Initially, birth control was only available to married women in large, urban centres, however, and the penalties for displaying and selling contraceptives remained in effect until 1969.

The post-war years were also a time of increasing numbers of divorces. While many men and women celebrated the end of the war by marching to the altar, significant numbers decided to go their separate ways. Divorce rates almost tripled at the end of World War II. When divorce laws were liberalized in 1969, the number of divorces increased significantly once again. By 1982, one in three marriages were ending in divorce.

Stats

The Canadian birthrate fell steadily after 1957. By 1970, less than one in three of all live births were third or later children.

By 1970, Quebec had the lowest birthrate of any of the provinces. Demographers predicted that Quebec's influence within Confederation would decrease as a result of its slower growth rate.

The Second Wave of Feminism

In 1966, Laura Sabia, president of the Canadian Federation of University Women, called together representatives of 30 national women's organizations to discuss their common concerns. The group, which began calling itself the Committee on Equality for Women, called for a Royal Commission on the Status of Women. When Pearson appeared to be dragging his feet on the issue, Sabia threatened to march 2 million women to Ottawa to ensure that the group's demands were taken seriously.

The Royal Commission on the Status of Women was formally established in February of 1967. Its mandate was "to inquire and

Main Event

A key concern during the 1950s and 1960s was the so-called "Americanization" of Canadian culture.

In 1949, the St. Laurent government appointed the Royal Commission on National Development in the Arts, Letters, and Sciences to examine the state of culture in Canada. In 1951, the Commission pointed out a series of weaknesses in Canadian culture. There was no national art gallery, library, or archive for the systematic preservation of public records; there was no national support for universities, museums, theatres, or libraries; and almost all popular entertainment was American in content, theme, and origin.

The report stated that "Canadian achievement in every field depends mainly on the quality of the Canadian mind and spirit. This quality is determined by what Canadians think, and think about; by the books they read, the pictures they see and the programmes they hear. These things, whether we call them arts and letters or use other words to describe them, we believe to lie at the roots of our life as a nation."

One of the Commission's key recommendations—that the Canadian government establish the Canada Council to give modest funds to writers, painters, musicians, and scholars—was initially scoffed at by many Canadians, including the prime minister himself. (St. Laurent publicly stated that the federal government had no business "subsidizing ballet dancing"!) Despite this initial scepticism, the Canada Council was established after all.

Unfortunately, American culture continued to flood into Canada. Given the scarcity of Canadian programming during the early years of TV, much of what came through the "boob tube" originated in the United States. In 1953, nearly 75 per cent of the 1289 feature films distributed in Canada were made in the United States. (Just one Canadian film made its way into the theatres that year.) In 1954, 80 per cent of the magazines purchased on Canadian newsstands were American. And throughout this period, much of the wire copy printed by Canadian newspapers was supplied by American news services.

Main Event

In 1968, the marriage of Alberta farm woman Irene Murdoch broke down due to domestic violence. The Supreme Court denied her claim to her share of the family ranch, even though her work had included "haying, raking, swathing, mowing, driving trucks and tractors and teams, quietening horses, taking cattle back and forth to the reserve, dehorning, vaccinating, and branding" and she had been responsible for running the ranch for four months out of every year. Outrage over the handling of her case led to family law reform across the country.

report upon the status of women in Canada, and to recommend what steps might be taken by the Federal Government to ensure for women equal opportunities with men in all aspects of Canadian society...."

The Commission reported in 1970. It stated that women should be free to choose to seek employment outside the home; that caring for children was a responsibility to be shared equally between mothers, fathers, and society as a whole; that special treatment related to maternity would always be necessary; and that women would need special treatment for an interim period to overcome the adverse effects of discriminatory practices. The report—which *Toronto Star* reporter Anthony Westell described as "a bomb already primed and ticking...packed with more explosive potential than any device manufactured by terrorists...a call to revolution...."—represented the agenda for Canadian feminism's second wave.

Main Event

On December 6, 1989, Marc Lepine killed 14 young female engineering students at the École Polytechnique at the Université de Montréal. After declaring, "You're all a bunch of feminists," the deranged Lepine turned the gun on himself. The Montreal Massacre became a symbol of violence against women.

The Women's Movement in the 1980s

When the Trudeau government announced that Canada's new Constitution was to

Real Life

(Avril) Kim Campbell (1947–present) was Canada's first female prime minister, serving for a brief period during 1993 following the resignation of Brian Mulroney.

Prior to entering federal politics, Campbell taught political science courses at the University of British Columbia and Vancouver Community College. She also served as a member of the Legislative Assembly of British Columbia during the mid-1980s.

She then went on to assume a series of Cabinet positions within the Mulroney government, serving as Minister of State—Indian Affairs and Northern Development (1989 to 1990), Minister of Justice and Attorney General (1990 to 1993), and Minister of National Defence and Veterans Affairs (1993). She was responsible for introducing Criminal Code amendments concerning firearms control (1991) and sexual assault (1992).

Bearing the brunt of voter dissatisfaction concerning free trade, the Goods and Services Tax, constitutional troubles, and the economic recession, the Conservatives under Campbell suffered an extraordinary defeat in the election of 1993. The Conservative party was reduced to just two seats in the House of Commons.

include a Charter of Rights and Freedoms, women's groups campaigned to have women's rights enshrined in the Charter. In the end, they achieved a degree of success that made them the envy of their sisters to the south, who had campaigned unsuccessfully to have an Equal Rights Amendment included in the American Bill of Rights. Article 15 of the Charter reads: "Every individual is equal before and under the law and has the right to equal protection of the law and equal benefit of the law," and Article 28 reads: "Notwithstanding anything in this Charter, the rights and freedoms referred to in it are guaranteed equally to male and female persons."

Including this language in the Charter made a difference in the lives of many Canadian women. In 1985, Bill C-31 removed the sections of the Indian Act that deprived native women of their status upon marriage to non-status men. (Men had not been stripped of their status upon marriage to non-status women.) In 1987, women were given the right to participate in combat roles within the Canadian Armed Forces. And in 1988, the federal law on abortion was overturned.

Fighting Racism

Women weren't the only ones demanding a more even playing field during the decades after World War II. Members of Canada's ethnic groups also began demanding fairer treatment.

In 1946—in an incident that bears a striking resemblance to Rosa Parks's 1955 refusal to give up her seat on a Montgomery, Alabama, city bus to a white passenger—Viola Desmond was arrested in a movie theatre in New Glasgow, Nova Scotia, for sitting downstairs rather than in the balcony seats that were reserved for African Canadian patrons. Desmond was thrown in jail and fined for attempting to defraud the provincial government of one cent in amusement tax! The Nova Scotia Association for the Advancement of Coloured People raised money to help Desmond pay her $20 fine.

Encouraged by the Black Power movement in the United States, groups of African Canadians become even more assertive about protesting discrimination during the 1960s. In 1969, following a student protest at Sir George William University (now Concordia University) in which the university's computer system was destroyed, the federal government began to fund the Black United Front (BUF) and other similar organizations in an effort to defuse the Canadian Black Power movement's growing militancy.

In 1971, the Trudeau government created the position of Secretary of State for Multiculturalism to look into ways to resolve the grievances of Canadians of various cultures.

Native Unrest

In 1969, the Trudeau government issued a White Paper on Indian Policy. The Paper stated the government's plans to relinquish native lands while at the same time removing the special status that had been given to Canada's First Nations, and its intention to dismantle the Department of Indian Affairs and have the provinces assume responsibility for providing services to native people.

The National Indian Brotherhood (known as the Assembly of First

Nations after 1982) were quick to criticize the document, claiming that natives wanted self-government, not assimilation. The Trudeau government withdrew the White Paper, but didn't offer to begin negotiating native demands for self-government.

Land Claims

In the 1980s and 1990s, a series of native land settlement claims were negotiated. In 1984, the Inuit of the Mackenzie Delta received a settlement of 242,000 square kilometres of land. And in 1992, the Inuit of the eastern Arctic received 350,000 square kilometres of surface and 36,000 square kilometres of subsurface mineral rights. At the same time, they voted to partition the Northwest Territories, with the eastern Arctic portion becoming a separately administered territory called Nunavut (which means "the people's land" in Inuktitut).

Elsewhere, land claims proceeded much more slowly. While there were over 500 claims outstanding by 1990, only three or four were being settled each year. (Until this point, the federal government had stuck to its policy of negotiating no more than six land claims at a time.)

Frustration with the painfully slow land claims process led to growing militancy among native groups, who frequently clashed with government and private industry concerning the uses of land they considered to be rightfully theirs. The standoffs between the Lubicon Cree of northern Alberta and the oil companies, the Temagami of Ontario and the logging companies, and the Cree of northern Quebec and Hydro-Québec were typical of the conflicts that arose during this period.

Oka

One of the ugliest confrontations happened in the early morning of July 11, 1990, at Oka, Quebec. Following a four-month standoff with area Mohawk, officers of the Quebec provincial police put the natives on notice that they had four hours to dismantle their roadblock and withdraw. When the deadline passed, 100 police officers stormed the roadblock. Instead of retreating, as the police had anticipated, the Mohawk fought back. In the end, one police officer, Corporal Marcel Lemay, was killed as the result of a gunshot wound.

The issue at stake in the dispute was the Town of Oka's decision to construct a golf course on lands that the Mohawk regarded as sacred.

Voice from the Past

"When we have AK-47s, you see, they listen. It's the only way."

—Herby Nicholls, one of the Mohawk involved in the standoff at Oka, quoted in *Maclean's*, July 23, 1990.

On March 11, 1990, the Mohawk barricaded the main road leading to the golf course. Oka's municipal council obtained an injunction from the Superior Court of Quebec that ordered the natives to remove their barricade by June 30. The Mohawk ignored the court order, demanding the right to negotiate "nation to nation" with the federal government.

Nine days after the outbreak of violence in mid-July, Thomas Siddon, Minister of Indian Affairs, announced that Ottawa had bought part of the land that was in dispute, and that it would negotiate to buy the remainder. The Mohawk would receive the land after the barricades came down. On August 17, at the request of Quebec Premier Robert Bourassa, the Canadian army was sent in to maintain the peace while a surrender was worked out. On October 3, 1990—78 days after it began—the standoff ended.

Stating that "Canada's aboriginal peoples deserve a special place in this country as our first citizens," Prime Minister Brian Mulroney promised that Ottawa would deal with native grievances, improve conditions on reserves, and accelerate the land claims settlement process.

The Royal Commission on Aboriginal Peoples

In 1991, The Mulroney government appointed the Royal Commission on Aboriginal Peoples to examine the grievances of Canada's native peoples. Five years later, the Commission released its report.

Stats

In 1990, only 43 per cent of aboriginal people over the age of 15 had jobs, compared to 61 per cent of the rest of Canadians.

The Commission pointed to four areas where action was needed: to aid in the healing of individuals, families, communities, and nations; to promote economic development; to assist in the development of human resources; and to strengthen native communities through the establishment of new aboriginal institutions.

The Commission concluded its report by looking forward to a brighter future for native

Canadians: "The relationship between Aboriginal and non-Aboriginal people in Canada has long been troubled and recently has shown signs of slipping into more serious trouble. The relationship can most certainly be mended—indeed, turned from a problem into an asset and one of the country's greatest strengths."

Stats

In 1991, aboriginal people in the work force earned an average of $21,270 per year, just 76 per cent of the Canadian average of $27,880.

The Least You Need to Know

- After 1960, Canadian society went through a period of rapid social change. The birthrate declined, the divorce rate rose, and increasing numbers of married women entered the work force.
- The Royal Commission on National Development in the Arts, Letters, and Sciences pointed to the harmful affects of the "Americanization" of Canadian culture.
- Women and members of ethnic minorities began demanding an end to discrimination.
- Native Canadians began to insist that the federal government take their long-standing grievances, particularly the need for land claim settlements, more seriously.

Chapter 33

A Country in Peril (1945 to 1995)

In this chapter

- Western alienation
- Atlantic discontent
- Quebec and Canada

In the years since World War II, Canada has experienced an ongoing series of threats to national unity. The discontent has come from three main sources: western Canada, the Atlantic provinces, and Quebec.

Western Alienation

By the early 1970s, westerners had accumulated a lengthy list of grievances with Ottawa. They were unhappy about the country's new official bilingualism policy, its decision to switch to the metric system, overly high freight rates, and what they perceived as federal indifference to the plight of farmers.

Westerners began to conclude that if the federal government wasn't about to help them out, they had to start taking care of themselves. Following the outbreak of the 1973 oil crisis, Peter Lougheed, the Conservative premier of Alberta, decided to establish the Heritage Trust Fund to prepare for the day when the province's resources would be depleted. The Fund, which was financed by a portion of oil royalties, was to be used to diversify the economy.

Discontent in the West also led to the emergence of two new political parties in the 1980s. Western Canadian Concept, a separatist party, rejected the welfare state, official bilingualism, and what it perceived as ongoing federal attempts to satisfy Quebec at the expense of the West. The Reform Party, which was anti–big business, anti–big government, and anti–big labour, gained enough popular support outside of the West to became the country's official opposition in the 1997 federal election.

Atlantic Woes

Westerners weren't the only ones who were feeling less than charitable towards the politicians in Ottawa. The Atlantic provinces had their share of grievances as well.

During the late 1970s, the large Hibernia oil field was discovered off of Newfoundland. Newfoundland Premier Brian Peckford felt that his province should have every bit as much say in its development as Ottawa. After all, it had a much greater interest in balancing the benefits to be derived from oil development with the need to protect the province's vital fishing industry. When the Supreme Court ruled in 1984 that the federal government was not obligated to share control of Hibernia with the Peckford government, the province was outraged. A crisis was averted, however, with the election of Brian Mulroney in 1984. Mulroney, who had spoken about the importance of cooperative federalism during the election campaign, agreed to allow the Peckford government to co-manage the development with Ottawa.

At the same time that the Trudeau and Mulroney governments were grappling with the Hibernia issue, the Atlantic fishing industry—which had been producing record fish harvests since the 1960s—was fast becoming a victim of its own success. By the early 1980s, the Atlantic fisheries were quite simply running out of fish. Quotas were cut, fish processing plants were shut down, and community after community was faced with extinction. When the federal government announced a two-year moratorium on northern cod fishing in July of 1992, more than 19,000 fishing industry workers lost their jobs.

Main Event

In the spring of 1964, Prime Minister Lester B. Pearson suggested that the time had come for Canada to have its own flag: one that would be devoid of any symbols that might imply the superiority of one ethnic group over another. There would be no stars, no crosses, no fleurs-de-lis, and—above all—no Union Jacks!

On May 17, 1964, he unveiled the flag he preferred: three red maple leaves set in the middle of a white field with a blue bar at each end.

Unfortunately, Pearson didn't pick the most sympathetic audience for the great unveiling. He was mercilessly jeered by a crowd of war veterans (not all of whom were completely sober!) at the Canadian Legion in Winnipeg.

He got a similarly negative response when he took his flag to Parliament. Opposition MPs took great delight in scorning the so-called "Pearson pennant."

Because the Conservative opposition wanted the country to stick with the status quo (the Canadian Red Ensign—the flag of the British marine with Canada's coat of arms incorporated on one side), they came up with a deliberately ludicrous design of their own: a single red maple leaf set in the middle of a white field with a red bar at each end.

Much to the Conservatives' horror, the Liberals and independent members of Parliament loved the flag. The Conservatives found themselves in the rather awkward predicament of having to oppose their own idea.

Despite the fact that many Canadians were equally put off by the flag (respected historian Donald Creighton pointed out that it "bore a disturbingly close resemblance to the flag of a new 'instant' African nation"), the design stuck. Since February 15, 1965, Canadians have been flying the Maple Leaf.

The Quiet Revolution

As if the problems in the East and the West were not enough for the federal government to contend with, the post-war years led to an intensification of the long-standing distrust between Ottawa and Quebec.

In 1960, the Liberal party under Jean Lesage won the provincial election, ushering in what would become known as the Quiet Revolution. Over the subsequent six years, the Lesage government passed legislation altering virtually every aspect of Quebec society. The primary focuses of this program of modernization were education and economic development. The educational system was modernized and secularized, and a series of measures designed to discourage foreign management of the Quebec economy were introduced.

Just as important as the program of modernization was the cultural renaissance that occurred in Quebec during this period. Francophones in Quebec began to think of themselves as Québécois rather than as Canadians, and they became anxious to promote French-Canadian culture outside of Quebec and to establish contact with the French-speaking world beyond Canada's borders.

This sense of Quebec nationalism reached an all-time high during the visit of Charles de Gaulle, the president of France, during Expo '67 in Montreal. De Gaulle gave a rousing speech in which he stated, "Vive Montréal, vive Québec, vive le Québec libre, vive le Canada français, vive la France." It was hardly an appropriate sentiment for a visiting dignitary to utter during the country's centennial year. Not surprisingly, Pearson was quick to object to de Gaulle's comments, leading the French president to cut his visit short.

Canada's centennial year was a momentous year for Quebec for other reasons. René Lévesque, a prominent member of the Liberal party, decided to form a separatist party, the Parti Québécois. His party would ultimately lead the government of Quebec and hold the province's first referendum on sovereignty association. What's more, in 1967 the first volume of the report of the Royal Commission on Bilingualism and Biculturalism was released. The Commission recommended that French and English be formally declared official languages and that they be given equal status in government, administration, and the courts. This recommendation ultimately resulted in the passage of the Official Languages Act (1969).

Word for the Day

Sovereignty association refers to the creation of a separate Quebec state that would maintain close economic links with Canada.

Voice from the Past

Many English Canadians resented the Official Languages Act (1969) and the government's plans to promote official bilingualism. One Conservative member of the government earned the wrath of French-speaking Quebecers—to say nothing of the tactless-remark-of-the-decade award!—when he stated: "The cold hard fact is that Canadians of French origin should be learning English as fast as they can instead of the English learning French." (It didn't help that he expressed his opinion that English was "the easier and more reasonable language to learn"!) The backlash against bilingualism lasted throughout the 1970s.

Stats

While the Front de Libération du Québec (FLQ) was not a household name for most Canadians until the October Crisis of 1970, the group had been around since the early 1960s. Between 1963 and 1970, the FLQ claimed responsibility for 200 bombings. Their targets included McGill University, the home of Montreal mayor Jean Drapeau, and the Montreal Stock Exchange.

The October Crisis

On October 5, 1970, the Front de Libération du Québec (FLQ) kidnapped British trade commissioner James Cross. Five days later, a second cell of the FLQ abducted Pierre Laporte, Quebec's Minister of Labour and Immigration. The FLQ, a radical separatist group, was upset by the recent victory of Liberal Robert Bourassa in the Quebec provincial election, believing that the Liberal victory had been engineered by the anglophone business community and federalists.

In exchange for an agreement to release the hostages, the FLQ demanded publicity for its manifesto, free passage to Cuba or Algeria for a number of terrorists ("political prisoners") who were then in detention, and $500,000 in gold bullion.

The federal government sent in soldiers to protect potential targets of terrorist action—a move that made many Canadians nervous. Trudeau had cutting words for those who dared to criticize his actions: "I think the society must take every means at its disposal to defend itself against the emergence of a parallel power which defies the elected power in this country and I think that goes to any distance....It's only...weak-kneed bleeding hearts who are afraid to take these measures."

On October 16, the Trudeau government proclaimed the War Measures Act, banned the FLQ, suspended civil rights, and imposed martial law on the nation. Four hundred and sixty-eight people were arrested because they were suspected of belonging to the now-outlawed FLQ. (By the end of the year, all but 41 of them had been released.) The night after the War Measures Act was proclaimed, Laporte's body was found in the trunk of an abandoned car. Cross was ultimately freed by his captors, who were given free passage to Cuba in exchange for his life.

The October Crisis neither weakened separatism nor ended the violence in Quebec. Over time, many FLQ members found another way to channel their pro-separatist sentiments: by supporting the Parti Québécois.

Stats

Eighty-eight per cent of all Canadians and 86 per cent of Quebecers approved of the Trudeau government's decision to invoke the War Measures Act.

Main Event

Shortly after its first provincial election victory in 1976, the Parti Québécois introduced Bill 101 (also known as the Charter of the French Language). One of the more controversial aspects of the Bill was its stipulation that all commercial and road signs in Quebec be written in French only.

The Emergence of the Parti Québécois

The Parti Québécois, with its platform of sovereignty association, gathered strength throughout the 1970s. Its support increased from 24 per cent in the provincial election of 1970 to 30 per cent in 1973 (when it became the official opposition) to 42 per cent in 1976 (when it won a legislative majority).

In 1980, Parti Québécois leader René Lévesque asked Quebecers for a mandate to negotiate sovereignty association with the federal government. Despite his high hopes for a separate Quebec, he only managed to attract the support of 40 per cent of the Quebecers who voted in the referendum held on the issue.

The referendum represented a significant setback for separatist forces in the province. By 1985, the Liberal government, led by Robert Bourassa, was back in power.

The Constitution

During the 1960s and 1970s, several attempts were made to patriate the Canadian Constitution. On a number of different occasions, the federal and provincial governments came close to reaching an agreement regarding the formula that would be used to decide future amendments to the Constitution. On each occasion, however, the situation turned into a stalemate when Quebec insisted on greater constitutional powers than the other provinces were prepared to grant it.

Over time, Trudeau grew impatient with the delays. Following the defeat of Quebec separatist forces in the 1980 referendum, Trudeau announced that he planned to ask the British government to place the Constitution in Canada's hands—with or without Quebec's approval. The patriated Constitution was to include both a Charter of Rights and Freedoms and an amending formula. The amending formula would allow Ottawa to call a referendum and take constitutional amendments directly to the people in the event that the governments of Ontario, Quebec, or a majority of western and Atlantic provinces objected to a particular amendment.

Word for the Day

Patriate means to bring home. In this case, the Canadian government was anxious to make the Constitution a Canadian document, thereby removing the last bits of control—however symbolic—that Britain had over Canada.

The majority of the provinces saw Trudeau's initiative as an attempt to weaken provincial rights. Ontario and New Brunswick were the only two provinces to speak out in favour of the initiative. The rest decided to challenge Trudeau's actions in the courts.

The Supreme Court reached a judgment on the issue in September of 1981, ruling that the "substantial consent" of the provinces (but not full unanimity) was all that was required for the federal government to proceed with its plans for patriation. At this point, nine of the ten premiers decided that if they couldn't beat Trudeau, it certainly made sense to join him. Lévesque—the sole holdout in the group—claimed that he had been betrayed.

The deal that the nine premiers struck with Trudeau resulted in the creation of the Constitution Act. The Constitution Act consisted of the renamed British North America Act, an amending formula, and the Charter of Rights and Freedoms.

The amending formula allowed the federal government to change the Constitution provided it had the approval of both Parliament and two-thirds of the provinces. (The provinces had to, in turn, represent at least 50 per cent of Canadians.) However, the unanimous consent of all provinces plus both houses of Parliament would be required for changes affecting representation in the House of Commons, the Senate, and the Supreme Court; and for changes regarding the country's designated official languages.

The Constitution Act also offered the provinces a few other bells and whistles. If a province felt that its legislative or proprietary rights were attacked by a particular amendment, it had the right to declare that amendment null and void within its boundaries. The provinces could opt out with full financial compensation from any program established by an amendment that affected educational or cultural matters. As a special concession to Atlantic Canada, one section of the Constitution committed the government to the principle of equalization to "ensure that provincial governments have sufficient revenue to provide reasonably comparable levels of public services at reasonably comparable levels of taxation."

The Charter guaranteed Canadians the right to freedom of speech, association, conscience, and religion, and prohibited discrimination on the basis of colour, sex, or creed. It also enshrined such basic human rights as the right to vote, the right to seek legal counsel, and the right to be protected against arbitrary arrest.

While the Constitution failed to specifically acknowledge the right to self-determination, native Canadians won acknowledgment of aboriginal concerns by securing a guarantee that nothing in the document would affect existing treaty rights or prejudice unsettled land claims. They also obtained a promise from the federal government that a constitutional conference on native rights would be called within one year of the proclamation of the Constitution.

The Meech Lake Accord

The Constitutional Act was proclaimed on April 17, 1982.

While Quebec's approval was technically unnecessary, Prime Minister Brian Mulroney—who came to power in September of 1984—was anxious to gain the province's support.

Quebec Premier Robert Bourassa was characteristically frank about what Quebec wanted: recognition as a distinct society, a veto for constitutional amendments, a greater share in immigration policy, the ability to opt out of any new cost-sharing programs without financial penalty, and the ability to require the federal government to choose new Supreme Court judges from a list provided by the province.

Mulroney invited the premiers to a First Ministers' Conference at Meech Lake in April of 1987. The premiers tentatively approved a package that met Quebec's key demands and incorporated the concerns of the other provinces. The final agreement was then hammered out during an all-night session in Ottawa on June 3, 1987.

The Meech Lake Accord had to be ratified by both Parliament and the 10 provincial legislatures by June 30, 1990, or else the deal would expire. The controversy started almost immediately. Separatists complained that the distinct society clause didn't go far enough; federalists—including Trudeau—thought it went too far. There were fears that the unanimity requirement for constitutional amendments would prevent reforms from being implemented. There were also concerns that the clause about cost-sharing programs made no mention of national standards.

Stats

Public opinion polls conducted in 1990 indicated that the majority of Canadians opposed the Meech Lake Accord—even though 70 per cent claimed to know little or nothing about it!

During the three-year ratification period, the New Brunswick, Newfoundland, and Manitoba governments changed hands. The newly elected governments of Frank McKenna (New Brunswick), Clyde Wells (Newfoundland), and Gary Filmon (Manitoba) were less committed to ensuring that the Meech Lake Accord be passed than their predecessors had been. When Elijah Harper (the sole native member of the Manitoba legislature) used procedural meth-

Main Event

Opposition to the Meech Lake Accord in English Canada increased dramatically when Quebec Premier Robert Bourassa invoked the notwithstanding clause in the Constitution to nullify a Supreme Court decision regarding the province's new sign law, Bill 178. (The notwithstanding clause allows a province that feels that its legislative or proprietary rights have been attacked by a particular amendment to declare that amendment null and void within its boundaries.) The Supreme Court had ruled that Bill 178 violated the guarantee of freedom of expression provided in the Charter of Rights and Freedoms.

ods to prevent the Accord from passing in Manitoba before the deadline, Filmon decided not to interfere.

Bourassa was furious about the failure of the Meech Lake Accord. He said that Quebec had been humiliated, and insisted that his province would never again attend a constitutional conference with the other premiers. His government then passed legislation demanding either a referendum on sovereignty or an offer of constitutional renewal from the rest of Canada.

But that wasn't the only fallout from the failure of the Meech Lake Accord. The Bloc Québécois, a federal party that sought an independent Quebec, was formed under the leadership of Lucien Bouchard, a former Conservative Cabinet minister.

The Charlottetown Accord

The premiers—including Bourassa—headed back to the bargaining table in the summer of 1992 to make one last effort at reaching a consensus. This time they were joined by representatives of Canada's native community.

The Charlottetown Accord of August 28, 1992, made concessions to all concerned. Quebec received a guarantee that its representation in the Senate wouldn't fall below 25 per cent, and the other provinces were granted representation on a per-province rather than per-region basis. Native leaders secured recognition of aboriginal rights to self-government.

The Mulroney government decided to hold a national referendum on the terms of the Charlottetown Accord. The referendum question stated: "Do you agree that the Constitution of Canada should be renewed on the basis of the agreement reached on August 28, 1992?" Fifty-four per cent of Canadians said no.

Main Event

Shortly before the Quebec referendum, 150,000 Canadians attended a massive unity rally in Montreal. Busloads of Canadians from all over the country poured into Montreal to support the "No" campaign.

The 1995 Quebec Referendum

On December 6, 1994, Jacques Parizeau released his Draft Bill on the Sovereignty of Quebec, which announced that his government intended to proclaim Quebec "a sovereign country" after obtaining the support of Quebecers in an upcoming referendum.

On October 30, 1995, Quebecers were asked to vote on the following question: "Do you agree that Quebec should become sovereign, after having made a formal offer to Canada for a new economic and political partnership, within the scope of the bill

Stats

In the 1995 Quebec referendum, 49.4 per cent of Quebecers voted "yes" to have Quebec declared sovereign and to seek a partnership with the rest of Canada, while 50.6 per cent voted "no." The vote was incredibly close, with just 53,498 of the nearly 4.7 million votes cast separating the two sides. What's more, an astounding 94 per cent of Quebecers turned out to cast their votes.

respecting the future of Quebec and of the agreement signed on June 12, 1995?"

The vote was hair-raisingly close: 49.4 per cent voted yes and 50.6 per cent voted no.

Prime Minister Jean Chrétien was gracious in his response to the outcome: "The people have spoken and it is time to accept that verdict."

Parizeau was less gracious. "The battle for a country is not over," he exclaimed. "And it will not be over until we have one."

The federalist forces had won the "battle"—but the final outcome of the "war" was anything but clear. One hundred and twenty-eight years after Confederation, the tug of war between Quebec and Ottawa appeared destined to continue.

Real Life

(Joseph Jacques) Jean Chrétien (1934–present) has been the Prime Minister of Canada since 1993. While he has only been heading the government for the past few years, he's been active in politics since the early 1960s. After a few years of service as the Member of Parliament for St.-Maurice-Lafleche, Quebec, Chrétien assumed a series of increasingly responsible Cabinet posts within the Pearson, Trudeau, and Turner governments. Prior to entering federal politics, Chrétien practised law.

Voice from the Past

Jacques Parizeau enraged English-speaking Canadians when he blamed the referendum defeat on "money and the ethnic vote."

Stats

A 1995 *Maclean's/* CBC news poll revealed that 23 per cent of Canadians felt that national unity was the most important issue facing Canada. A year later, just 9 per cent of Canadians saw national unity as the most important issue.

The Least You Need to Know

- Both the western and Atlantic provinces continued to experience a certain degree of dissatisfaction with Confederation.
- Quebec has gone through a period of extraordinary political, economic, and social change since the end of World War II.
- Since the late 1960s, separatists have been pursuing sovereignty association with Canada.
- The 1995 Quebec referendum resulted in a victory for federalism, but the vote was frighteningly close with 49.4 per cent of Quebecers voting for sovereignty association and 50.6 per cent voting against it.

Appendix A

Canadian Prime Ministers

Sir John A. Macdonald	Conservative	1867–1873
Alexander Mackenzie	Liberal	1873–1878
Sir John A. Macdonald	Conservative	1878–1891
Sir John J.C. Abbott	Conservative	1891–1892
Sir John S.D. Thompson	Conservative	1892–1894
Sir Mackenzie Bowell	Conservative	1894–1896
Sir Charles Tupper	Conservative	1896
Sir Wilfrid Laurier	Liberal	1896–1911
Sir Robert L. Borden	Conservative/Union	1911–1920
Arthur Meighen	Conservative/Union	1920–1921
William Lyon Mackenzie King	Liberal	1921–1926
Arthur Meighen	Conservative/Union	1926
William Lyon Mackenzie King	Liberal	1926–1930
R.B. Bennett	Conservative	1930–1935
William Lyon Mackenzie King	Liberal	1935–1948
Louis St. Laurent	Liberal	1948–1957
John G. Diefenbaker	Progressive Conservative	1957–1963
Lester B. Pearson	Liberal	1963–1968
Pierre Elliott Trudeau	Liberal	1968–1979
Joe Clark	Progressive Conservative	1979–1980
Pierre Elliott Trudeau	Liberal	1980–1984
John Turner	Liberal	1984
Brian Mulroney	Progressive Conservative	1984–1993
Kim Campbell	Progressive Conservative	1993
Jean Chrétien	Liberal	1993–present

Appendix B

When Each Province Joined Confederation

Ontario	July 1, 1867
Quebec	July 1, 1867
Nova Scotia	July 1, 1867
New Brunswick	July 1, 1867
Manitoba	July 15, 1870
British Columbia	July 20, 1871
Prince Edward Island	July 1, 1873
Alberta	September 1, 1905
Saskatchewan	September 1, 1905
Newfoundland	March 31, 1949

Appendix C

Further Reading

The following books will help you to round out your knowledge of Canada's past.

Brown, Robert Craig, and Ramsay Cook. *Canada 1896–1921: A Nation Transformed*. Toronto: McClelland and Stewart, 1974.

Creighton, Donald. *Canada: The Heroic Beginnings*. Toronto: Macmillan of Canada, 1974.

Finkel, Alvin, Margaret Conrad, and Veronica Strong-Boag. *History of the Canadian Peoples: 1867 to the Present*. Toronto: Copp Clark Pitman Ltd., 1993.

Finlay, J.L. and D.N. Sprague. *The Structure of Canadian History*. Scarborough: Prentice Hall, 1979.

Friesen, Gerald. *The Canadian Prairies: A History*. Toronto: University of Toronto Press, 1984.

McConnell, Barbara. *Sainte-Marie-Among-The-Hurons*. Toronto: Oxford University Press, 1980.

McInnis, Edgar. *Canada: A Political and Social History*. Fourth edition. Toronto: Holt, Rinehart and Winston, 1982.

McMillan, Alan D. *Native Peoples and Cultures of Canada*. Toronto: Douglas and McIntyre, 1988.

Prentice, Alison, *et al*. *Canadian Women: A History*. Toronto: Harcourt Brace Jovanovich Canada, 1988.

Index

Y

10,000 - 45,000 y ago Beiringia
5000 - 8000 y ago ice melted
2000 y ago Dorset extinct
986 AD. Viking Bjarni
1000 AD Lief the Lucky
1015 AD Vikings stopped going to N. America
1492 AD Columbus - (Caribbean)
1497 AD J. Cabot . Cape Breton
1534 AD J. Cartier { . Stadacona (Quebec City)
{ . Hochelaga
1576 AD Frobisher
1604 AD S. Champlain St Croix
1605 AD S. Champlain Port Royal (Nova Scotia)
1610 AD H. Hudson → co. est. 1670 (Radissen + Groseilliers)
1608 - 1650 S. Champlain Quebec City
1614* *Recollets Jesuits (1625) → Ste Marie @ Hurons (popln = 80 1628)
1635 Small pox epidemic
1648 Iroquois attack St Joseph, St Ignace, St Louis mission
1649 Burning of St Marie @ Huron
1663 Attempts to colonize : popln 3000